CW00766545

COLLECTED WORKS OF RENÉ GUÉNON

PERSPECTIVES ON INITIATION

RENÉ GUÉNON

PERSPECTIVES ON INITIATION

Translator
Henry D. Fohr

Editor
Samuel D. Fohr

SOPHIA PERENNIS

HILLSDALE NY

Originally published in French as
Aperçus sur l'Initiation
© Les Éditions Traditionnelles 1946
English translation © Sophia Perennis 2001
First English Edition 2001
Second Impression 2004
All rights reserved

Series editor: James R. Wetmore

No part of this book may be reproduced or transmitted,
in any form or by any means, without permission

For information, address:
Sophia Perennis, P.O. Box 611
Hillsdale NY 12529
sophiaperennis.com

Library of Congress Cataloging-in-Publication Data

Guénon, René
[Aperçus sur l'initiation. English]
Perspectives on initiation / René Guénon ; translated by
Henry D. Fohr ; edited by Samuel D. Fohr

p. cm. — (Collected works of René Guénon)
Includes bibliographical references and index.
ISBN 0 900588 32 2 (pbk: alk. paper)
ISBN 0 900588 41 1 (cloth: alk. paper)
1. Initiation rites—Religious aspects I. Fohr, S.D., 1943–
II. Title.
BL615.G7913 2001
291.3'8—dc21   2001000431

THE PUBLISHER
GIVES SPECIAL THANKS TO
HENRY D. AND JENNIE L. FOHR
FOR MAKING THIS EDITION POSSIBLE

CONTENTS

EDITORIAL NOTE

THE PAST CENTURY HAS WITNESSED an erosion of earlier cultural values as well as a blurring of the distinctive characteristics of the world's traditional civilizations, giving rise to philosophic and moral relativism, multiculturalism, and dangerous fundamentalist reactions. As early as the 1920s, the French metaphysician René Guénon (1886–1951) had diagnosed these tendencies and presented what he believed to be the only possible reconciliation of the legitimate, although apparently conflicting, demands of outward religious forms, 'exoterisms', with their essential core, 'esoterism'. His works are characterized by a foundational critique of the modern world coupled with a call for intellectual reform; a renewed examination of metaphysics, the traditional sciences, and symbolism, with special reference to the ultimate unanimity of all spiritual traditions; and finally, a call to the work of spiritual realization. Despite their wide influence, translation of Guénon's works into English has so far been piecemeal. The *Sophia Perennis* edition is intended to fill the urgent need to present them in a more authoritative and systematic form. A complete list of Guénon's works, given in the order of their original publication in French, follows this note.

Perspectives on Initiation, first published at the close of World War II, is based on a series of articles on initiation originally written between 1932 and 1938 for *Le Voile d'Isis* (later renamed *Études Traditionnelles*). Initiation is presented as essentially the transmission, by the appropriate rites of a given tradition, of a 'spiritual influence'. This transmission is, precisely, the 'beginning' (*initium*) of the spiritual journey, and is indispensable for the one who wishes to embark on a spiritual way. The work is unique in giving a comprehensive account both of the conditions of initiation and of the characteristics of organizations qualified to transmit it, and has led to some controversy regarding the distinction it draws between the initiatic and the mystical paths, which some believe to be one and the same.

Related articles were later published (1952) in the posthumous collection *Initiation and Spiritual Realization*.

Guénon often uses words or expressions set off in 'scare quotes'. To avoid clutter, single quotation marks have been used throughout. As for transliterations, Guénon was more concerned with phonetic fidelity than academic usage. The system adopted here reflects the views of scholars familiar both with the languages and Guénon's writings. Brackets indicate editorial insertions, or, within citations, Guénon's additions. Wherever possible, references have been updated, and English editions substituted.

The present translation is based on the work of Henry Fohr, edited by his son Samuel Fohr. The text was checked for accuracy and further revised by Patrick Moore and Marie Hansen. For help with selected chapters and proofreading thanks go to John Riess, John Champoux, and William Stoddart, and, for final reviews, to Brian Latham, Benjamin Hardman, and John Ahmed Herlihy. A special debt of thanks is owed to Cecil Bethell, who revised and proofread the text at several stages and provided the index. Cover design by Michael Buchino and Gray Henry, based on a drawing by Guénon's friend and collaborator Ananda K. Coomaraswamy.

THE WORKS
OF RENÉ GUÉNON

PREFACE

WE HAVE RECEIVED repeated requests to select from the pages of the journal *Études Traditionnelles* those of our articles that bear directly on the theme of initiation and to publish them together in one volume. It was not possible for us to satisfy these requests at once, for we are of the opinion that a book must be something more than a mere collection of articles, all the more so in this case as these particular articles were written at the inclination of the moment and often in answer to questions. We had therefore first to revise, complete, and arrange them differently, and that is what we have done here. We have not, however, wanted to make of this a more or less complete and, as it were, 'didactic' treatise; such a thing might be conceivable if it were strictly necessary and involved only the study of one particular form of initiation, but since on the contrary we are here dealing with initiation in general, it would amount to an altogether impossible task, for an indefinite number of questions could be raised—the very nature of the subject resisting any set limit—so that there could not be the slightest pretension of having treated them all. In the end, all that one can do is to examine certain aspects, to look at them from certain points of view which, even if their importance is immediately evident, still leave out many others equally worthy of consideration. This is why we thought that the word 'perspectives' would best characterize the content of the present work, the more so because, even with respect to the questions treated, it is no doubt impossible to completely 'exhaust' a single one of them. It also goes without saying that we could not repeat here what we have already said on the same subject in other books, but must rest content to refer the reader back to these books whenever necessary; moreover, in the order of ideas with which all our writings are concerned, everything is linked together in such a way that it would be impossible to proceed otherwise.

We have just said that our intention is essentially to treat questions which concern initiation in general; it must therefore be understood that when we refer to this or that specific initiatic form we are doing so as an example only, so as to specify and better explain what might remain vague without the help of these particular cases. It is important to stress this especially where Western forms are concerned, in order to avoid any kind of ambiguity or misunderstanding; if we refer to these forms so frequently, it is because the 'illustrations' we can derive from them often seem to be more easily accessible to the general reader than others, as these forms are already familiar to many; and it should be clear that this is entirely independent of what one may think of the present state of the organizations in which these initiatic forms are conserved and practiced. When we realize the degree of degeneration of the modern West, it is only too easy to understand that many things of a traditional order, and all the more so of the initiatic order, could scarcely subsist there except as vestiges largely misunderstood by the very people charged with their safekeeping; and it is just this that makes possible the appearance, alongside these authentic remnants, of the numerous 'counterfeits' upon which we have already had occasion to remark, for it is only in such conditions that they can deceive and be taken for what they are not. However that may be, the traditional forms in themselves always remain independent of these contingencies, and we would add further that when we come to consider these same contingencies, and speak, not of initiatic forms but of the state of initiatic and pseudo-initiatic organizations in the West today, we are stating facts with no other intention or concern than expressing the truth in this regard as disinterestedly as possible, just as we will treat everything else to be considered in the course of our study, from which each is free to draw the conclusions he finds appropriate. We do not take it upon ourselves to maneuver anyone either toward or away from any organization whatsoever; nor do we propose that anyone seek initiation either here or there, or refrain from doing so, for this in no way concerns us and could never be our role. Some will perhaps be surprised that we insist on this point so strongly, and in truth such an emphasis is called for only by the incomprehension of so many of our contemporaries, as well as the dishonesty of far too many of them; unfortunately, individuals, even coming from apparently quite opposite positions, have so often attributed to us all sorts of intentions we have never had that we must take all necessary precautions in this regard, though we dare not describe these as sufficient, for who can foresee everything that some people are capable of inventing?

It should occasion no surprise, then, that we often elaborate on commonly held errors and confusions regarding the subject of initiation, for, besides the clear benefit of dispelling them, it is precisely in noting them that we have frequently been led to see the necessity for a closer treatment of particular points that otherwise we would have thought self-evident or at most to require very little explanation. It is important to note that some of these errors are made not only by the profane or by pseudo-initiates, which would hardly be extraordinary, but also by members of authentically initiatic organizations who, in their respective circles, are counted among the 'illuminati'. This is perhaps one of the most striking proofs of the present state of degeneration to which we have referred. In this regard, we think that without too great a risk of its being interpreted in a distorted way we can express our wish that among the representatives of these organizations at least a few can be found for whom these present reflections will contribute to their knowledge of what initiation really is; however, we do not entertain any more exaggerated hopes in this regard than we do for the overall possibilities of restoration that the West may yet possess. Still, while there are clearly some who are more deficient in genuine knowledge than in good will, such good will alone is not sufficient, for the question is really just how far their intellectual horizons can be extended and whether they are qualified to pass from virtual to effective initiation; in any event, we can do no more than provide information from which those who are able may benefit to the extent that their dispositions and circumstances permit. Such people will certainly never be numerous, but as we have often said, it is not numbers that are important in things of this order, although a sufficient number must be present to properly constitute an initiatic organization.

Until now, the few experiments we know about that have been attempted along these lines have for various reasons not developed far enough to allow any judgment of their results, results that might have been different had the circumstances been more favorable.

It is quite clear that by its very nature the modern ambiance is and always will be one of the principal obstacles, in the initiatic domain as in every other, to any attempt at a traditional restoration in the West. While it is true in principle that the initiatic domain, because of its 'closed' character, should be safe from hostile external influences, the existing organizations have in fact long since permitted their entry, and certain 'breaches' are now too wide to be easily repaired. For example, in adopting the administrative forms of secular governments these organizations have opened themselves to hostile actions that otherwise would not have been effective and would simply have come to nothing; such an imitation of the profane world constitutes, moreover, one of those inversions of normal relationships characteristic of the modern disorder. Today one would have to be blind not to see the manifest consequences of this 'contamination', and yet we strongly doubt that many know their real cause; the mania for 'societies' is so entrenched that most of our contemporaries are unable to conceive of the simple possibility of getting along without purely external forms, but for this reason such tendencies are the very thing that must be resisted by anyone wishing to attempt an initiatic restoration on a truly secure foundation. But we will not go further with these preliminary reflections for—let us repeat—it is not for us to actively intervene in attempts of this nature, for our only intention is to point out a course to those willing and able to so engage themselves. Furthermore, our remarks are in no way limited in application to any particular initiatic form, for above all else they pertain to the fundamental principles common to all initiation, of both East and West. Indeed, the essence and aim of initiation is always and everywhere the same, only its modalities differing as a result of adaptation to different times and places; to which we hasten to add, in order to avoid misunderstanding, that adaptation is legitimate only when it shuns all 'innovation', that is, the product of a merely individual caprice;

instead, as with traditional forms in general, initiation must always and unequivocally proceed from a 'non-human' origin, lacking which it is in truth neither tradition nor initiation but only one of those 'parodies' so often encountered in the modern world that come from nothing and lead to nothing, and so do not really represent anything but a pure and simple nothingness, if one may so express it, unless they be perhaps the unconscious instruments of something far worse.

1

THE INITIATIC
AND MYSTICAL PATHS

TODAY THE ESOTERIC or INITIATIC DOMAIN and the mystical
domain—or, if one prefers, their respective points of view—are
often confused, and in a manner that does not always seem entirely
disinterested. Moreover, this represents a fairly new attitude, or at
least one that has become more widespread in recent years within
certain circles, which is why we thought it necessary to begin by
clarifying our position on this point. It is currently the fashion so to
speak among those with limited horizons to construe all Eastern
doctrines as 'mystical', including those that lack even a semblance of
the outward aspects that could justify such an attribution; naturally,
the origin of this false interpretation is to be traced to certain orientalists, whose conclusions indeed may not have derived originally
from any clearly defined ulterior motive but rather from their
incomprehension and their habitual and more or less unconscious
bias of relating everything to Western points of view.[1] Others, however, have subsequently seized upon this false assimilation and, seeing how they could exploit it for their own ends, have done their
utmost to propagate this idea outside the special and limited world

1. Thus it is that, especially since the English orientalist R. A. Nicholson took it
into his head to translate taṣawwuf by mysticism, it has been accepted by Westerners
that Islamic esoterism is something essentially 'mystical'; and even in this case they
do not speak of esoterism, but only of mysticism, which is to say that they have
ended by veritably substituting the one point of view for the other. And the worst of
it is that on questions of this kind the opinions of the orientalists, who know of
such things only through books, obviously count for more in the eyes of the great
majority in the West than do the opinions of those who have a direct and effective
knowledge of them!

of the orientalists and their clientele; and this is more serious, not only because the confusion in question becomes more widespread in this way but also because it is not difficult to discern here unmistakable signs of an attempt at 'annexation', against which we must be on our guard. Indeed, those to whom we refer can be considered to be the most 'serious' deniers of esoterism, namely the religious exoterists who refuse to admit anything whatsoever beyond their own domain, but who doubtless consider this assimilation or 'annexation' more clever than a crude negation. To see how some of them devote themselves to disguising as 'mysticism' the most obviously initiatic doctrines, it would truly seem that this task assumes for them a particularly urgent character.[2] Nevertheless, there may truly be something in this same religious domain to which mysticism belongs, something which in certain respects could better lend itself to an assimilation, or rather to an appearance of assimilation. This is what is called 'asceticism', for this at least is an 'active' method rather than the absence of method and 'passivity' that characterize mysticism, a subject to which we shall return.[3] But it goes without saying that these similarities are quite external; besides, for its part asceticism has perhaps only limited objectives, too limited to be used with benefit for initiatic purposes, whereas in the case of mysticism one never knows just where one is headed, and this very vagueness no doubt lends itself to confusion. Yet those who make attempts of this kind deliberately, as well as those who do so unconsciously, seem not to suspect that in everything pertaining to initiation there is really nothing vague or nebulous, for on the contrary it is as precise and 'positive' as can be, so that initiation by its very nature is in fact incompatible with mysticism.

2. Others attempt to disguise the Eastern doctrines as 'philosophy', but this false assimilation is perhaps less fundamentally dangerous than the other by reason of the narrow limitations of the philosophical point of view itself. In any case they hardly succeed in making their assimilations of any interest at all because of the peculiar way they present these doctrines, the results of all their efforts conveying nothing but a prodigious impression of *ennui*.

3. We can cite as an example of 'asceticism' the *Spiritual Exercises* of Saint Ignatius of Loyola, whose mind was incontestably as unmystical as can be, and which were probably inspired at least partially by certain initiatic methods of Islamic origin that he of course applied to an entirely different end.

This incompatibility does not, however, derive from what the word mysticism itself implied originally, for this meaning quite obviously refers to the ancient 'mysteries', that is, to something that on the contrary belongs to the initiatic order. Nonetheless, this is one of those words that can in no way be understood only from its etymology but must be considered strictly in light of the meaning imposed by usage, which is in fact the only one currently attached to it. Since the current meaning of 'mysticism' has been established for centuries it is not possible to use this term to designate anything else, and it is this current meaning that we say does not and cannot have anything in common with initiation, firstly because mysticism in this sense pertains exclusively to the religious or exoteric domain, and then also because the mystical path differs from the initiatic path in all its essential characteristics, which difference is such as to render the two truly incompatible. Let us make clear moreover that this incompatibility is one of fact rather than of principle, for we in no way deny the at least relative value of mysticism or its legitimate place in certain traditional forms; the initiatic and mystical paths can thus perfectly well coexist,[4] but we only wish to stress the impossibility of following both paths simultaneously, and this without prejudging the end to which each may lead, although because of the profound difference between the domains involved one knows in advance that these ends cannot actually coincide.

We have observed that the confusion leading some people to see mysticism where there is not the faintest trace of it results from the tendency to reduce everything to Western points of view, mysticism properly speaking being exclusively Western and, what is more, specifically Christian. In this connection we have noticed something curious enough to warrant our attention here. In a book that we have already mentioned elsewhere,[5] Henri Bergson, opposing what he calls 'static religion' to 'dynamic religion', sees the latter's highest expression in mysticism, which as a matter of fact he

4. It would be interesting in this connection to draw a comparison with the 'dry way' and the 'moist way' of the alchemists, but that would take us beyond the framework of the present study.

5. *The Two Sources of Morality and Religion.* On this subject see *The Reign of Quantity and the Signs of the Times* (hereafter cited as *Reign of Quantity*), chap. 33.

scarcely comprehends and which he admires especially for what we on the contrary find vague and in certain respects even defective. But what is truly strange, coming from a 'non-Christian', is that his 'complete mysticism', however unsatisfactory may be his conception of it, is nonetheless that of the Christian mystics. Because of his low regard for 'static religion', he is all too prone to forget that these mystics are Christians before they are mystics, or at least he improperly places mysticism at the very origin of Christianity in order to justify their being Christians; and, in order to establish a kind of continuity between Christianity and Judaism, he ends by transforming the Jewish prophets into 'mystics' as well, evidently having not the slightest idea of the character of the prophets' mission or of the nature of their inspiration.[6] Be that as it may, if Christian mysticism, however distorted or diminished its conception, is in his eyes the true model, the reason is easy to see, for strictly speaking scarcely any other mysticism exists, and even the mystics he calls 'independent' (whom we would sooner call 'aberrant') draw their real inspiration, albeit unknowingly, only from Christian ideas denatured and more or less entirely emptied of their original content. This fact too, like so many others, escapes our philosopher, who does his best to discover some 'outlines of the future mysticism' prior to Christianity even though something altogether different is involved here. He even supplies us with several pages on India that bear witness to an unbelievable lack of understanding. When he turns to the Greek mysteries, the comparison, based on the etymological relationship noted above, is reduced to a ridiculous play on words; for the rest, Bergson is himself forced to admit that 'most of the mysteries had nothing to do with mysticism'; but then why does he speak of them using that word? As to what those mysteries were, he represents them in the most 'profane' manner possible; ignorant of everything having to do with initiation, how could he understand that here as well as in India there was something that in no way belonged to religion, something that went incomparably further than his 'mysticism'; even, let us add, than authentic mysticism,

---

6. Jewish mysticism properly speaking is in fact e found only in Hassidism — that is, in very recent times.

which by the very fact that it exists within the purely exoteric domain also necessarily has its limitations?[7]

We do not propose to describe here all of the differences that in fact separate the initiatic and mystical points of view, for that would require an entire volume. Our intention is above all to insist that initiation has characteristics entirely different from, and indeed even contrary to, those of mysticism, which is enough to demonstrate that these two 'paths' are not only distinct but also incompatible in the sense that we have already explained. One often hears it said that mysticism is 'passive' whereas initiation is 'active'; this is certainly true, but only if one determines precisely what is meant by this. In the case of mysticism the individual simply limits himself to what is presented to him and to the manner in which it is presented, having himself no say in the matter; and let us immediately add that in this lies his principal danger, for he is thus 'open' to every kind of influence, and generally, with only rare exceptions, he will not have the doctrinal preparation necessary for any discrimination among them.[8] In the case of initiation, on the contrary, the individual is the source of the initiative toward 'realization', pursued methodically under rigorous and unremitting control, and normally reaching

7. Alfred Loisy wanted to reply to Bergson and argue against him that there is only one 'source' of morality and religion; in his capacity as specialist in the 'history of religions' he prefers the theories of Frazer and Durkheim, as well as the idea of continuous 'evolution' to one characterized by abrupt mutations. In our opinion all of this is equally worthless, but there is at least one point on which we must concede that he is right, and he no doubt owes this to his ecclesiastical education. Thanks to this he is more familiar with the mystics than Bergson is, and points out that they never put forth the least conjecture about anything bearing the slightest resemblance to an 'elan vital' (Bergson had evidently wanted to make of them 'pre-Bergsonian Bergsonians', which hardly accords with simple historical truth), and he is also justly astonished to see Joan of Arc placed among the mystics. Let us note in passing, as it really should be put on record, that Loisy begins his book with a rather amusing confession: 'The author of the present short treatise,' he declares, 'is not aware that he has any particular inclination for questions of a purely speculative order.' Now this at least is a laudable frankness; and since he has said it of his own accord we willingly take him at his word!

8. This character of 'passivity' also explains, though it in no way justifies, the modern errors that tend to confuse the mystics either with 'mediums' or with 'sensitives' (as this word is understood by the 'psychics'), or simply with the infirm.

beyond the very possibilities of the individual as such. We must not fail to add that this initiative alone does not suffice, for it is quite evident that the individual cannot surpass himself through his own efforts; but what should be emphasized here is that it is this initiative that necessarily provides the point of departure for any 'realization' on the part of the initiate, whereas the mystic lacks such an initiative even in the case of things that clearly do not in any way go beyond the domain of individual possibilities. This distinction may already seem quite clear, since it establishes without question that one cannot simultaneously follow the initiatic and mystical paths, but it is nevertheless insufficient, for it still addresses only the most 'exoteric' aspect of the matter, and in any case it is far from explaining all the necessary conditions for initiation. But before we undertake a study of these conditions a few more confusions must first be dispelled.

2

MAGIC
AND MYSTICISM

THE CONFUSION of initiation with mysticism is largely due to those
who for whatever reasons wish to deny expressly the reality of initiation by reducing it to something else; on the other hand, in such
circles as those of the occultists, replete with their unwarranted initiatic pretensions, there is a tendency to include as integral aspects,
if not as essential elements, of the initiatic domain numerous things
altogether foreign to it, among which magic is often the most prom-
inent. The factors behind this error also explain why magic presents
especially grave dangers for modern Westerners, the chief one being
the tendency to attribute excessive importance to 'phenomena', to
which their development of the experimental sciences bears witness.
If they are so easily seduced by magic and entertain such illusions as
to its real import, this is because it is indeed also an experimental science, although certainly quite different from those the academic
world designates by this term. We must not deceive ourselves on this
point: this is an order of things that contains absolutely nothing
'transcendent'; if such a science, like every other science, can be legit-
imized by its connection with those higher principles upon which
everything depends, in accordance with the general conception of
the traditional sciences, it can still only be situated in the last rank of
secondary and contingent applications, among those furthest from
these principles, which therefore must be regarded as the most inferior of all. This is how magic is considered in all the civilizations of
the East, and although it cannot be denied that magic exists there, it
is far from being held in esteem as Westerners very often imagine
because they are too easily disposed to project onto others their own
tendencies and ideas. Even in Tibet, as well as in India and China,

where the practice of magic is something of a 'specialty', it is left to those incapable of rising to anything higher. This of course does not imply that others cannot in exceptional circumstances and for limited purposes also occasionally produce phenomena outwardly similar to those of magic, but the objective and even the means employed are really altogether different. Besides, confining ourselves to what is known of these things in the West, we need only consider the stories surrounding both saints and sorcerers to see how similar are the facts in both cases; and this shows quite clearly, contrary to the belief of the modern 'man of science', that phenomena of whatever kind can never prove anything in themselves.[1]

Now it is obvious that illusions about the value and importance of these things considerably augment their danger, and what is particularly problematic for those Westerners who 'dabble in magic' is their complete ignorance, unavoidable in the current state of affairs and in the absence of any traditional teaching, of what is involved in such matters. Even leaving aside both the many mountebanks and charlatans who in short do nothing but exploit the credulous, and the simple-minded fantasists who would improvise a 'science' of their own design, those who would seriously study these phenomena lack both the necessary data to guide them and an organization to support and protect them and are thus reduced to a sort of crude empiricism, reminding one of children who, left to themselves, want to handle redoubtable forces without knowing anything about them; and if deplorable accidents too often result from such imprudence we should not be unduly surprised.

Speaking of accidents, we especially want to point out the risks of mental imbalance to which those who act in this way are exposed, such disequilibrium being an all too frequent consequence of communication with what some call the 'vital plane', which is nothing other than the domain of subtle manifestation envisaged particularly in those modalities nearest to the corporeal order and so most easily accessible to the average man. The explanation is simple enough, for it is exclusively a matter of the development of certain individual possibilities, often of a rather inferior order; and if this

1. Cf. *Reign of Quantity*, chap. 39.

development proceeds in an abnormal, that is, disordered and inharmonious way that precludes the development of higher possibilities, it is natural and even inevitable that such a result should follow, not to mention the reactions—in no way negligible and some-times even terrible—of all types of forces with which the individual unthinkingly puts himself in contact. We say 'forces' with no inclination to be more specific because the matter is of little importance to our present concerns; vague as it is, we prefer this word to 'entities', which, at least for those not sufficiently accustomed to certain symbolic ways of speaking, has the risk of too easily evoking more or less fantastical 'personifications'. As we have often had occasion to explain, this 'intermediary world' is much more complex and extensive than the corporeal world; still, the study of both worlds comes within the purview of the 'natural sciences' in the truest sense of the term, and to see in the former anything more is, we repeat, to delude oneself in a most peculiar way. There is absolutely nothing in this intermediary world that belongs to the 'initiatic' any more than to the 'religious' domain; indeed, we find herein many more obstacles than supports to reaching a genuinely transcendent knowledge, a knowledge completely different from that of the contingent sciences, a knowledge which contains no trace of any 'phenomenalism', depending only on pure intellectual intuition, which alone is pure spirituality.

After applying themselves for a considerable time to the search for extraordinary phenomena, or what passes for such, some people for various reasons eventually tire of it all or become disappointed by insignificant results that fall short of their hopes. It is worth noting that often these same people then turn to mysticism,[2] for astonishing as it may seem at first glance, this latter still satisfies similar needs and aspirations, although under another form. Certainly, we

2. It also sometimes happens that others, after having truly entered into the initiatic way, and not just into the illusions of the pseudo-initiation about which we have been speaking, abandon that way for mysticism; the motives are then naturally quite different and mainly of a sentimental order, but whatever they may be we must see above all in such cases the consequence of some defect in initiatic qualifications, at least as concerns the aptitude to realize effective initiation; as a typical example one could cite Louis-Claude de Saint-Martin.

are far from denying that mysticism in itself may have a character much more elevated than magic; nonetheless, if we look more deeply, we soon realize that at least from a certain point of view the difference is not as great as one might imagine, for here again it is in fact only a matter of 'phenomena', visions, or the other tangible and sentimental manifestations that characterize the domain of individual possibilities alone.[3] In mysticism, then, illusion and disequilibrium are far from being left behind, and although they may manifest themselves here in unaccustomed forms they are no less dangerous and are even aggravated in a sense by the passive attitude of the mystic who, as stated before, leaves the door open to every influence that may present itself, whereas the magician is granted at least a measure of protection by the active attitude he attempts to maintain with respect to these same influences, which certainly does not mean, however, that in the end he is not often overwhelmed by them. Moreover, it is also true that the mystic is almost always too easily the dupe of his own imagination, the productions of which, without his suspecting it, become almost inextricably mixed with his genuine 'experiences'. For this reason we must not exaggerate the importance of the 'revelations' of the mystics, or at least we should never accept them without verification.[4] The interest of certain visions consists only in their many points of agreement with traditional information clearly unknown to the mystic concerned;[5] but it would be a mistake, and even a reversal of normal relationships, to wish to find in this a 'confirmation' of this traditional information, which in no way requires it and which is on the contrary the only guarantee that the visions in question are something more than the mere product of individual imagination or fantasy.

---

3. Naturally, this is not to say that the phenomena in question pertain solely to the psychological order, as certain moderns claim.

4. This attitude of prudent caution, necessitated by the natural tendency of mystics to 'divagation' in the proper sense of the word, is in any case the one that Catholicism invariably observes with respect to them.

5. The visions of Anne Catherine Emmerich can be cited here as an example. [See *The King of the World*, chap. 8, n12. Ed.]

3

VARIOUS ERRORS
CONCERNING
INITIATION

IN ORDER TO PREPARE THE GROUND, we do not think it superfluous to recall here certain additional errors concerning the nature and aim of initiation, for everything we have had occasion to read on this subject over the years has brought almost daily proof of widespread misunderstanding. We cannot of course think of undertaking here a kind of 'survey' in which we would methodically examine every error in detail—a tedious and uninteresting exercise; better to confine ourselves to a consideration of certain 'typical' cases, which has the further advantage of sparing us from having to make direct references to particular authors or schools, for it should be understood that these remarks have an import altogether independent of any question of 'personalities' — or rather, to speak more precisely, of individualities.

We would first of all remind the reader, without wishing to stress the point unduly, of the all too prevalent notion that initiation belongs to a merely 'social' or 'moral' order,[1] which latter are much too limited and so to speak 'terrestrial', although, as we have often stated elsewhere, the crudest error is often not the most dangerous.

---

1. This is the point of view of most modern Masons, and it too is limited to the same exclusively 'social' terrain where those who combat them are arrayed, proving once again that initiatic organizations lend themselves to attack from without only within the limits of their own degeneration.

To cut short all confusion we will only say that such notions do not even apply to that preliminary aspect of initiation that antiquity designated by the expression 'lesser mysteries'; as we shall explain further on, these do indeed concern the human individuality, but have to do with the integral development of its possibilities and therefore go beyond the corporeal modality through which activity is exercised in the domain common to all men. We can hardly see the value or even the justification of a so-called initiation limited to repeating what is most banal in profane knowledge — what is 'within everyone's reach' — all the while disguising itself under a more or less enigmatic form. In saying this we do not deny that initiatic knowledge may have applications in the social order as well as in all other orders, but this is an altogether different question. First of all, such contingent applications in no way constitute the aim of initiation any more than the secondary traditional sciences constitute the essence of a tradition, and then they also have an intrinsic quality that sets them apart, for they are derived from principles having nothing to do with current precepts of 'morality', especially the celebrated 'lay morality' dear to many of our contemporaries; and in any case, the traditional applications proceed in ways that by the very nature of things cannot be comprehended by the profane and are therefore very far from what someone once called 'the preoccupation with living properly'. He who restricts himself to 'moralizing' about symbols, no matter how laudable his intentions, will certainly not produce any work of initiation; but we will return to this later when we treat the initiatic teachings more directly.

Errors more subtle, and so the more to be feared, sometimes arise when a 'communication' with superior states or 'spiritual worlds' is mentioned in connection with initiation, for this involves the all too frequent illusion that something is 'superior' simply because it appears to be in some way extraordinary or 'abnormal'. We will recall here what we have said elsewhere about the confusion of the psychic with the spiritual, which is the error most often committed in this regard,[2] for the psychic states in fact have nothing 'superior' or 'transcendent' about them, but are merely a part of the individual

2. See *Reign of Quantity*, chap. 35.

human state;[3] and when we speak of superior states of the being we mean, and without any abuse of language, exclusively the supra-individual states. Some worsen the confusion and make 'spiritual' almost synonymous with 'invisible' by indiscriminately taking as 'spiritual' all that is not accessible to the ordinary and 'normal' senses; in just this way for example we have seen the term 'etheric' applied to what is quite simply that part of the corporeal world of least density! In such a climate one greatly fears that the 'communication' in question will turn out to be nothing more than 'clairvoyance' or the exercise of some other psychic faculty of similar insignificance, even if it were genuine. This is what in fact always happens, for in the final analysis this is the orientation of all the modern Western pseudo-initiatic schools, some of which even expressly take as their aim 'the development of the latent psychic powers in man'. We will return later to this question of alleged 'psychic powers' and the illusions to which they lend themselves.

Yet there is more to this, for we must admit that with some individuals there really is communication with the superior states; however, this is still far from being adequate to characterize initiation. In fact, such a communication is also established by rites, particularly religious rites, of a purely exoteric order; and we should not forget that in such a case spiritual influences, and not only psychic ones, do indeed play a role, although for ends quite different from those of the initiatic domain. All that is authentically traditional may be generally defined as the intervention of a 'non-human' element, but the presence of this common feature is not sufficient reason to permit of our failing to make the necessary distinctions, and in particular of conflating the religious and initiatic domains, or of seeing at most a simple difference of degree when there is really a difference of nature, and indeed of a profound nature. This confusion is especially frequent among those who claim to study initiation 'from the outside', moreover with intentions that can differ greatly; therefore

---

3. Following the geometric symbolism explained in *The Symbolism of the Cross*, these modalities of a single state are simple extensions developing in the horizontal direction, that is on one and the same level, and not in the vertical direction that characterizes the hierarchy of the superior and inferior states of the being.

it is necessary to denounce such confusion formally: esoterism is not the 'interior' aspect of a religion but is essentially something other than religion, even when its base and support are found therein, as happens in certain traditional forms, in Islam for example;[4] and initiation is not some sort of special religion reserved for a minority, as those seem to imagine who speak of the ancient mysteries as 'religious'.[5] It is not feasible for us to develop here all the differences that separate the religious and initiatic domains, which task would certainly carry us even further afield than the mystical domain, itself only a part of the former. For our present purposes it must suffice to emphasize that religion considers the human being exclusively in his state of individuality and does not aim to bring him beyond it but rather to assure him of the most favorable conditions in this state,[6] whereas the essential aim of initiation is to go beyond the possibilities of this state and to effect a passage to the superior states, and even finally to lead the being beyond every conditioned state of whatever kind.

Concerning initiation, it follows that mere communication with the superior states cannot be regarded as an end but only as a point of departure. If this communication must be established at the very start by the action of a spiritual influence, it is only to permit the prospective initiate effectively to take possession of these states and not simply, as in the order of religion, to have 'grace' descend upon him, a 'grace' that does link him to these states in a certain way but does not grant him entry to them. To express this in a manner perhaps more easily understood we can say that if, for example, someone can communicate with angels without thereby ceasing to be himself, that is to say remaining enclosed in the conditions of human individuality, he will not be any the more advanced from the

---

4. It is to emphasize this and to avoid any ambiguity that we deem it proper to say 'Islamic esoterism' or 'Christian esoterism', and not, as some do, 'esoteric Islam' or 'esoteric Christianity'; it is easy to see that the point being made here is no mere nuance.

5. We are aware that the expression 'mystery religions' is one of those that recur constantly in the specialized terminology adopted by the 'historians of religions'.

6. Here, of course, it is a question of the human state envisaged in its integrality, including the indefinite extension of its extra-corporeal prolongations.

initiatic point of view,[7] for here it is not a matter of communicating with beings in an 'angelic' state but of realizing such a supra-individual state oneself; not of course as a human individual, which would obviously be absurd, but insofar as the being that manifests itself as a human individual in a certain state also contains the possibilities of all other states. All initiatic realization is therefore essentially and purely 'interior', just the opposite of that 'going out of oneself' that constitutes 'ecstasy' in the proper and etymological sense of the word;[8] this is certainly not the only difference but it is at least one of the major differences between the mystical states, which belong entirely to the religious domain, and the initiatic states. It is indeed this point to which we must always return eventually, since the confusion of the initiatic with the mystical point of view — the insidious character of which we have emphasized from the outset — is capable of deceiving minds that would not be caught by the more crude deformations of modern pseudo-initiations and that might, without too much difficulty, come to understand what initiation really is, if they did not encounter these subtle errors along the way, errors seemingly put there expressly to deflect them from such an understanding.

7. From this one can see how greatly those who wish, for example, to attribute an initiatic value to writings such as those of Swedenborg are deceived.

8. It goes without saying, moreover, that this 'going out of oneself' has absolutely nothing in common with the supposed 'astral journeys' that play so great a role in occultist fantasies.

4

CONDITIONS
FOR INITIATION

WE CAN NOW RETURN to the question of the conditions necessary for initiation. Although it seems self-evident, we should begin by saying that the first of these conditions is a certain natural aptitude or disposition without which all effort would be in vain, for the individual obviously can only develop those possibilities he possesses at the outset; this aptitude, forming what some call 'initiability', properly constitutes the requisite 'qualification' demanded by all initiatic traditions.[1] This condition is moreover the only one that is in a certain sense common to both initiation and mysticism, for it is clear that the mystic must likewise have a particular natural disposition, though one entirely different from, and even in certain ways opposed to, that of the 'initiable' person. But in addition to being necessary for the mystic, this condition is also sufficient; no other need be added, as circumstances will take care of the rest and facilitate the passage from 'potency' to 'act' of those possibilities contained in the disposition in question. This is the direct result of that 'passivity' we mentioned earlier: in such a case it could never be a question of any effort or personal exertion of whatever sort; the mystic will have nothing to effect, indeed he will even have to guard himself carefully against this, as something that might hinder his 'path',[2] whereas in the case of initiation, and its 'active' character,

---

1. From the special examination we will undertake later about other aspects of initiatic qualifications it will be seen that this question is really much more complex than one might at first gather from the very general notion we give of it here.

2. Thus theologians not without reason readily see a 'false mystic' in anyone who seeks by any means to obtain visions or other extraordinary states, even where this effort is limited to a mere desire.

this exertion constitutes a further condition no less necessary than the first, without which the passage from potency to act, or 'realization', could never be accomplished.[3]

More remains to be said, however, for we have developed this distinction between initiatic 'activity' and mystical 'passivity' in the first instance in order to make the point that initiation requires a condition that could never obtain in mysticism; but there is another condition no less necessary that we have not yet mentioned and that in a way falls between those alluded to above. This condition is in fact the most characteristic of all, that is to say that which allows us to define initiation in such a way as to preclude any possible misunderstanding and to avoid confusing it with anything else whatsoever, a point we must insist upon all the more as Westerners are often rather prone to ignore it or to minimize its importance. As a result, initiation is more clearly delimited than mysticism could ever be, and for which no such condition exists. Indeed it is often very difficult, if not altogether impossible, to distinguish false mysticism from true, for the mystic is by very definition isolated and 'irregular', and sometimes does not himself know just what he is. The fact that any genuine knowledge he possesses is not in its pure state but is always conditioned by a mixture of sentiment and imagination is far from simplifying the matter; in any case, there is something in mysticism that escapes all control, which we can express by saying that for the mystic there are no 'means of recognition'.[4] One could also say that the mystic has no 'genealogy', that he

3. One result of this among others is that while doctrinal knowledge is indispensable for the initiate—since a theoretical understanding of it is for him a preliminary condition to any 'realization'—it can be wholly lacking in the mystic; from this often comes a strange incapacity in the latter to express himself intelligibly, not to mention many possibilities for error and confusion. The knowledge in question has of course absolutely nothing to do with any outward instruction or profane 'knowledge', which is here of no value whatsoever—as we will later explain—and is even, given modern education, rather an obstacle than an aid in many cases. A man might very well not know how to read or write yet nonetheless reach the highest degrees of initiation, and such cases are not so rare in the East, whereas there are those who in the eyes of the profane are 'scholars' and even 'geniuses' who are not 'initiable' in any degree whatsoever.

4. By this we do not mean words or outward and conventional signs, but that of which such means are really only the symbolic representation.

is a mystic only by a kind of 'spontaneous generation', expressions easily enough understood and requiring no further explanation. How then can anyone venture to claim unequivocally that one person is authentically a mystic and another is not, when to all appearances they are the same? On the contrary, imitations of initiation can be detected without fail by the absence of that condition we have just alluded to, and which is nothing other than attachment to a regular, traditional organization.

There are ignorant persons who imagine that one 'initiates' oneself, which is a contradiction in terms; forgetting, if they ever knew it, that the word *initium* means 'entrance' or 'beginning', they confuse initiation understood in its strict etymological sense with the work that must be accomplished subsequently in order that this initiation, at first virtual, may become more or less fully effective. Understood in this way, initiation is what all traditions designate as the 'second birth'; and how could a being act by itself before being born?[5] We are well acquainted with the objection: if the human being is truly 'qualified', he already carries in himself the possibilities to be developed, and if this is the case, why could he not realize these through his own efforts, without any outside intervention? Now such a thing can indeed be entertained in theory provided that one see it as the case of a man 'twice-born' from the first moment of his individual existence; however, if that is not impossible in principle, it is nonetheless impossible in fact, in the sense that it contradicts the established order of our world, at least in its present conditions. We are not in that primordial epoch when all men naturally and spontaneously possessed a state that today is only attached to a high degree of initiation;[6] and even so, in such an epoch the very word 'initiation' could not have any meaning. We are instead in the *Kali-Yuga*, that is, in a time when spiritual knowledge has become hidden and only a few are able to attain it, provided they place themselves within the conditions required for obtaining

---

5. Let us recall the elementary scholastic adage, 'To act one first must be.'

6. This is what is indicated in the Hindu tradition by the word *Hamsa*, the name given to the sole caste that existed in the beginning and strictly speaking designating a state that is *ativarna*, that is to say above the distinction of present-day castes.

it. Now one of these conditions is precisely that which we are discussing, just as another is that effort of which men of the first ages had no need at all, since spiritual development was effected in them just as naturally as bodily development.

What is involved, therefore, is a necessary condition imposed in conformity with the laws governing our present world, something perhaps better understood by recourse to an analogy: all beings that will develop in the course of a cycle are from the very beginning contained as subtle embryos in the 'World Egg'; this being so, one might well ask why they are not born into the corporeal state by themselves rather than through parents; nor is this an absolute impossibility, and we can conceive of a world where things would happen in this way, although such a world is in fact not ours. We reserve, of course, the question of anomalies, for it may be that there are exceptional cases of 'spontaneous generation'; and in the spiritual order, we ourselves have just applied this expression to the case of the mystic. But we added that the mystic is 'irregular', whereas initiation is essentially 'regular', having nothing to do with anomalies. Besides, we would have to understand just how far such cases can extend, as they, too, must ultimately be under the rule of some law, for nothing can exist except as an element of the total and universal order. This alone, upon reflection, would be a sufficient cause for us to think that the states realized by the mystic are not precisely the same as those realized by the initiate, and that if their realization is not subject to the same laws as his, it is because something different is indeed involved; but since we have established enough for our present purposes, we can now leave aside the case of mysticism altogether and turn exclusively to that of initiation.

It remains now to clarify the role of attachment to a traditional organization, which could of course never exempt one from the necessary inner work that each must accomplish by himself; it is, rather, a preliminary condition for such work effectively to bear fruit. It must henceforth be understood that those who have been made depositaries of initiatic knowledge cannot communicate this knowledge in the same way that a secular teacher communicates to his pupils bookish formulas that they need only store in their memories, for what is involved here is something that is in its very essence 'incommunicable' since it concerns states that are realized inwardly. What can be taught are only the preparatory methods for obtaining these states; what can be furnished from the outside in this respect is only an aid, a support, that greatly facilitates the work to be accomplished, and also a control that dispels those obstacles and dangers that may present themselves. All this is far from negligible, and he who is deprived of it runs a high risk of failure, but this alone would still not entirely justify what we said about a necessary condition, for this was not really what we had in view, at least immediately. This is a secondary consideration (somewhat under the heading of consequences) coming after initiation understood in the strict sense we have explained, and involving an effective development of the virtuality that initiation establishes; but then again it is necessary before all else that this virtuality pre-exist. So we must understand the initiatic transmission proper in another way, and we could not characterize it better than by saying that it is essentially the transmission of a spiritual influence. We will return to this later for fuller treatment, limiting ourselves for the moment to determining more precisely the role played by that influence in mediating between the natural aptitude of the individual at the outset and the work of realization that he will accomplish later.

Elsewhere we have explained that the phases of initiation, as also those of the Hermetic 'Great Work'—which is one of its symbolic expressions—reproduce those of the cosmogonic process;[7] more than any other consideration, this analogy, based directly on the correspondence of 'microcosm' with 'macrocosm', allows us to clarify the questions that concern us here. We can say that the aptitudes or possibilities included in the individual nature are, in themselves, first of all only a *materia prima*, that is, a pure potentiality, where nothing is developed or differentiated.[8] Here is that dark, chaotic

---

7. See *The Esoterism of Dante,* chap. 8.

8. It goes without saying that strictly speaking this is a *materia prima* only in a relative sense, not in the absolute sense, but this distinction is not important from our present point of view. Moreover, it is the same with the *materia prima* of a world such as our own, which, being already determined in a certain way is, with respect to universal substance, really only a *materia secunda* (cf. *Reign of Quantity,* chap. 2), so that even in this respect the analogy with the development of our world from initial chaos is quite exact.

state that initiatic symbolism equates with the profane world and in which the being that has not yet attained the 'second birth' finds itself. For this chaos to begin taking form and organizing itself, an initial vibration must be communicated to it by the spiritual powers, which the Hebrew Genesis designates as *Elohim*; this vibration is the *Fiat Lux* that illuminates the chaos and is the necessary starting-point for all later developments. From the initiatic point of view this illumination consists precisely in the transmission of the spiritual influence we have just mentioned.[9] Thereafter, and by virtue of this influence, the spiritual possibilities of the being are no longer the simple potentiality they were before but have become a virtuality ready to be made actual within the various stages of initiatic realization.

We can summarize all our preceding remarks by saying that initiation implies three conditions that present themselves successively and correspond respectively to the terms 'potentiality', 'virtuality', and 'actuality': (i) 'qualification', consisting in certain possibilities inherent in the nature of the individual, which is the *materia prima* upon which the initiatic work is to be effected; (ii) transmission, by means of filiation with a traditional organization, of a spiritual influence giving to the individual the 'illumination' that will allow him to order and develop those possibilities that he carries within himself; and (iii) interior work by which, with the help of 'adjuvants' or exterior 'supports' (as needed, and especially in the first stages), this development will be gradually realized as the individual passes stage by stage through the different degrees of the initiatic hierarchy and is led to the final goal of 'Deliverance' or the 'Supreme Identity'.

9. Whence expressions like 'shedding light' and 'receiving light', used with respect to the initiator and the initiated, respectively, to designate initiation in the restricted sense, that is the transmission here in question. It will also be noted that the septenary number attributed to the *Elohim* relates to the form of initiatic organizations, which must be an image of the cosmic order.

5

INITIATIC
REGULARITY

WE HAVE SAID THAT AFFILIATION with a regular traditional organization is not only a necessary condition of initiation but even constitutes initiation itself in the strictest sense as defined by the etymology of the word, and which is everywhere represented as a 'second birth' or as a 'regeneration': a 'second birth' because it opens to the being a world other than that in which the activity of its corporeal modality is exercised, a world that will provide the field for the development of its higher possibilities; and a 'regeneration' because it re-establishes for this being the prerogatives that were natural and normal in the first ages of humanity, when man had not yet fallen away from his original spirituality, as he would do in later ages, to sink ever deeper into materiality, and because, as the first step in his realization, it will lead to the restoration in him of the 'primordial state', which is the fullness and perfection of human individuality lying at the unique and invariable center from which the being can thereafter rise to higher states.

We must now re-emphasize a key point: this affiliation must be real and effective, and a so-called 'ideal' affiliation, as is sometimes fancied today, is wholly vain and ineffectual.[1] This is easy to understand since it necessarily involves the transmission of a spiritual influence which must be effected according to definite laws. These

---

1. For examples of this so-called 'ideal' affiliation, by which some have gone so far as to claim to have revived traditional forms that have entirely disappeared, see *Reign of Quantity*, chap. 36. We shall return to this point later.

laws, while obviously different from those that govern the forces of the corporeal world, are no less rigorous, and despite profound differences there is a certain analogy between them in virtue of the continuity and the correspondence obtaining among all the states or degrees of universal Existence. It is this analogy that allows us to speak for example of a 'vibration' in regard to the *Fiat Lux*, by which the chaos of spiritual potentialities is illuminated and ordered, although this in no way involves vibrations of a perceptible kind like those studied by physicists, any more than the 'light' in question can be identified with that grasped by the visual faculty of the corporeal organism.[2] But while these ways of speaking are necessarily symbolic since they are founded on analogy or correspondence, they are nonetheless legitimate and strictly justified in that such analogy and correspondence does truly exist in the very nature of things, and in a certain sense even extends much further than might be supposed.[3] We shall have to return to these considerations more fully when we come to initiatic rites and their efficacy; for the moment it will suffice to recall that the laws in question must be taken into account, lacking which the end in view could no more be attained than could a physical effect be produced outside the conditions required by the laws governing its production. And as soon as it is a matter of an effective transmission there must obviously be a real

---

2. Expressions such as 'intelligible light' and 'spiritual light', or others equivalent to them, are well-known in all traditional doctrines, both Western and Eastern; we will note in particular here only the assimilation, in the Islamic tradition, of the Spirit (*ar-Rūḥ*) in its very essence to the Light (*an-Nūr*).

3. The incomprehension of this kind of analogy, mistakenly taken for an identity, together with the observation of a certain similarity in modes of action and exterior effects, has led some to a mistaken and rather crudely materialistic idea, not only of psychic or subtle influences, but of spiritual influences themselves, which they assimilate purely and simply to 'physical' forces in the narrowest sense of this word, such as electricity or magnetism; and from this same incomprehension has also come, at least in part, the all too widespread project of trying to forge a connection between traditional knowledge and the point of view of modern and profane science—an absolutely vain and illusory idea, since these are things that do not even belong to the same domain; and besides, the profane point of view itself is strictly speaking illegitimate. Cf. *Reign of Quantity*, chap. 18.

contact, whatever may be the modalities by which this contact is established—modalities that will naturally be determined by the laws governing the action of spiritual influences to which we have just alluded.

Several important consequences, both for the individual who aspires to initiation and for initiatic organizations themselves, result immediately from this necessity for an effective affiliation, and it is these consequences that we now propose to examine. We know that for some, and perhaps for many, these considerations will be quite unpleasant, either because they will disturb the too comfortable and overly 'simplistic' notion they have formed of initiation, or because they will destroy certain unjustified claims and more or less self-seeking assertions that lack any authority; but these are things we could not even in the least refrain from saying, since here as elsewhere we are, and could only be, concerned with the truth.

First of all, as to the individual, it is evident from what we have just said that even if he really has the intention of affiliating himself with a tradition of which he may have some 'exterior' knowledge, his intent to undergo initiation in no way suffices by itself for true initiation.[4] Initiation has nothing to do with 'erudition', which, as with everything that relates to profane knowledge, is without value here; neither has it anything to do with dreams or fantasies, any more than with sentimental aspirations of some kind. It would truly be all too easy if, in order to say one is initiated, it was enough to read books, even if they were the sacred scriptures of an orthodox tradition, accompanied if one likes by their most deeply esoteric commentaries; or vaguely to imagine some past or present organization to which one complacently attributes (and all the more easily the less well it is known) one's own 'ideal', a word used indiscriminately nowadays for anything and everything, and which really means nothing at all. This would also do away entirely with the preliminary question of 'qualification', for each person, being naturally

---

4. We mean by this not only a fully effective initiation but even only one that is merely virtual, following the distinction required here and which we shall consider more precisely.

inclined to consider himself 'well and duly qualified', and standing thus as both judge and jury in his own case, would without difficulty surely find excellent reasons (excellent at least in his own eyes and according to his own particular fancies) for considering himself initiated without further formalities; and we see no reason why he should stop while things are going so well and not claim for himself at one fell blow the most transcendent degrees as well. Have those who imagine that they can 'initiate themselves' really reflected on these rather awkward consequences that their position implies? Under these conditions there would be no more selection or control, no more 'means of recognition' in the sense in which we have already used this expression, no more hierarchy, and, of course, no more transmission of anything at all; in a word, no remnant of what essentially characterizes initiation and of what in fact makes it what it is; and yet this is what some people, with an astonishing ignorance, dare to put forward as a 'modern' conception of initiation (very modern indeed, and most worthy of secular, democratic, and egalitarian 'ideals'), without even suspecting that, instead of having to do with at least 'virtual' initiates—which, after all, is still something—one would thereby be reduced to the merely profane wrongfully posing as initiates.

But let us end these digressions which can appear trifling. If we feel obliged to speak of them briefly, it is because the incomprehension and intellectual disorder that unhappily characterize our time permit their propagation with a deplorable ease. What must be clearly understood is that initiation has to do exclusively with serious matters and 'positive' realities ('positive' being a word we would willingly use had profane 'scientists' not so abused it). Either one accepts things as they are or one no longer speaks of initiation, for there is no possible middle ground between these two attitudes, and it is better to frankly renounce initiation altogether than to give its name to what is only a vain parody of it, one without even the outward appearances that certain other counterfeits, of which we shall have to speak shortly, at least make an effort to retain.

To return to the starting-point of this digression, we will say that the individual must not only have the intention of being initiated but he must be 'accepted' by a regular traditional organization that is qualified to confer initiation on him,[5] that is, to transmit the spiritual influence without the help of which he could never, despite all his efforts, free himself from the limitations and impediments of the profane world. It may happen that, by reason of a lack of 'qualifications', his intention, however sincere, may meet with no response, for it is not a question of sincerity, nor of 'morality', but it is solely a matter of 'technical' rules relating to 'positive' laws (a word we employ again for want of one more adequate) that impose themselves with as ineluctable a necessity as do, in another order, the physical and mental conditions indispensable to the exercise of certain professions. Such a person can never consider himself initiated, whatever may be the theoretical knowledge he otherwise acquires; and one must in any case presume that even in this respect he will never go very far (naturally we are speaking of a true though still exterior knowledge and not of mere erudition, that is, of an accumulation of notions requiring the memory alone, as in profane teaching); for beyond a certain degree theoretical knowledge itself normally presupposes the requisite 'qualification' for initiation that will enable him to transform theory, by interior 'realization', into an effective knowledge. Thus no one can be prevented from developing the possibilities he truly bears within himself; in short, only those are turned away who deceive themselves about their own qualifications and believe they can receive something that is really incompatible with their individual nature.

Passing now to the other side of the question, that concerning initiatic organizations themselves, we will say this: it is all too evident that one can only transmit what one possesses; it is necessary, then, that an organization truly be the repository of a spiritual influence if it is to be able to communicate this influence to those attached to it;

---

5. By this we do not mean only that it must be a strictly initiatic organization, to the exclusion of any other kind of traditional organization, which is after all only too obvious, but further that this organization must not belong to a traditional form outwardly foreign to the individual in question. There are even cases where what one could call the 'jurisdiction' of an initiatic organization is yet more limited, such as that of an initiation based on a craft, which can only be conferred on those belonging to this craft or at least having certain very definite ties to it.

and this immediately excludes all the pseudo-initiatic groups, so common in our time, that lack any authentically traditional character. Under these conditions an initiatic organization could hardly be the product of an individual fantasy; unlike a profane association it cannot be established by the initiative of a few people who decide to meet after adopting certain forms. Even if these forms are not wholly invented but are borrowed from truly traditional rites of which the founders have some acquaintance through their 'erudition', this will not make them any the more valid, for without a regular filiation the transmission of the spiritual influence is impossible and non-existent, so much so that in such cases there can only be a common counterfeit of initiation. With all the more reason is this so for the purely hypothetical, not to say imaginary, reconstitutions of traditional forms long since disappeared, like those of ancient Egypt or Chaldea for example; even if these forms were seriously meant to establish a link to the tradition to which they belonged they would be no more efficacious, for in reality one can only attach oneself to something that actually exists, and even then it is necessary, as we said in regard to individuals, to be 'accepted' by the authorized representatives of the tradition in question, so that an apparently new organization will only be legitimate if it is as it were a prolongation of a pre-existing organization, maintaining without interruption the continuity of the initiatic 'chain'.

In all of this we are after all only expressing in other words and more explicitly what we have already said above about the necessity for an effective and direct affiliation, and the vanity of an 'ideal' one; and no one should be duped in this regard by the names certain organizations adopt without warrant, hoping thereby to lend themselves an air of authenticity. Thus, to take an example that we have already cited elsewhere, there exist a multitude of groups of recent origin who call themselves 'Rosicrucian' without having even indirect and roundabout contact with the true Brotherhood of the Rose-Cross, and without even knowing what this really was since they almost invariably imagine it as a 'society', which is a gross and indeed a specifically modern error. For the most part one should see nothing more here than the desire to put on an imposing title, or to impress the gullible; but even in the most favorable case, that is to say when it is conceded that some of these groups arise from a sincere desire to attach themselves 'ideally' to the Brotherhood of the Rose-Cross, this would still essentially amount to nothing from the initiatic point of view. What we are saying about this particular example applies equally to all the organizations invented by occultists and 'neo-spiritualists' of every sort, who, whatever their claims, can truly be classified only as 'pseudo-initiatic' because they have absolutely nothing real to transmit, for what they offer is nothing but a counterfeit and all too often even a parody or a caricature of initiation.[6]

6. Investigations we were obliged to undertake long ago on this subject led us to the formal and indubitable conclusion that we must clearly state here without concern for the passions it risks exciting in various quarters: if one leaves aside the case of possible survivals of certain rare groups of medieval Christian Hermeticists— which were in any case very restricted—it is a fact that among all the organizations with initiatic claims that exist in the Western world today, there are only two that can claim an authentically traditional origin and a real initiatic transmission, however degenerate they both may be through the ignorance and incomprehension of the vast majority of their members. These two organizations, which to tell the truth were originally only one, although with multiple branches, are the Compagnonnage and Masonry. All the rest is only fantasy or charlatanism, when it does not conceal something worse, and in this order of ideas there is no invention so absurd or so extravagant that in our time it has no chance of succeeding and being taken seriously, from occultist dreams about 'astral initiations' to the commercially motivated American system of 'initiations by mail'!

[The Compagnonnage is closely related to Freemasonry, but is largely restricted to France, where it is still an active presence. In the Middle Ages various craft organizations, such as Guénon describes, were especially to be found in proximity to the great cathedrals, giving rise in England to the Masonic Lodges, in France to the Compagnonnage, and in Germany to the Bauhütte, according to some sources. The origins of these organizations, as Guénon intimates, are undoubtedly somewhat more complex than this, and some people prefer to regard them as vestiges from earlier times that, during the period of the Crusades, assumed a significance in their own order analogous in a certain way to that of the Knights Templars and the Orders of Chivalry in theirs. What does seem clear is that unlike Masonry, the Compagnonnage was originally grouped around four ancient crafts: the Stonemasons, the Carpenters, the Joiners, and the Locksmiths (ironworkers). The word 'Compagnonnage' itself, of course, derives from the Latin *cum panis*, 'sharers of the bread', as does its English cognate 'companion'. For an excellent summary of this subject see Bro. Peter Fischel, 'Le Compagnonnage and its Survival in France Today', *Ars Quatuar Coronatorum* 79 (1966): pp 203–215. ED.]

As another consequence of the foregoing let us add that even where an initiatic organization is in fact involved, the members have no power to change its forms at whim or to alter them in their essentials. This does not exclude certain possibilities of adaptation to circumstances, but these are much rather imposed on individuals than willed by them, and they are circumscribed by the need not to injure the means that ensure the conservation and transmission of the spiritual influence of which the organization in question is the repository. If this condition is not met, the result will be a veritable rupture with the tradition and the organization will thereby lose its 'regularity'. Besides, an initiatic organization cannot validly incorporate in its own rites elements borrowed from traditional forms other than that in which it is itself established;[7] such elements could only be adopted in a wholly artificial way and would represent nothing more than superfluous fantasies without any initiatic efficacy; they would consequently add absolutely nothing real, although, because of their heterogeneity, their presence could occasion trouble and disharmony. Moreover, the danger of such mingling is far from being limited to the initiatic domain, and this is a point important enough to merit separate treatment. The laws that direct the handling of spiritual influences are too complex and delicate for those without sufficient knowledge of them to modify ritual forms arbitrarily and with impunity, where everything has its purpose, the exact import of which is very likely to escape them.

The clear result of all this is the nullity of individual initiatives with respect to the establishment of initiatic organizations, whether it be a question of their origin or of the forms they adopt, and it can be noted here that in fact there exist no traditional ritual forms to which any specific individual authors can be assigned. It is easy to understand why this must be so if one considers that the essential and final goal of initiation transcends the domain of the individuality and its particular possibilities, something impossible were one

---

7. Thus some have recently tried to introduce into Masonry, a Western initiatic form, elements borrowed from Eastern doctrines, about which they have only a very superficial knowledge. An example of this will be found in *The Esoterism of Dante*, chap. 3.

reduced to means of a purely human order. From this simple obser-vation, and without even going to the heart of the matter, it can therefore be immediately concluded that the presence of a 'non-human' element is necessary, such indeed being the character of the spiritual influence whose transmission constitutes initiation strictly speaking.

6

SYNTHESIS
AND SYNCRETISM

WE WERE JUST SAYING that it is not only useless but sometimes even dangerous to mix ritual elements belonging to different traditional forms, and that this is true not only for the initiatic domain, which was what we first had in mind, but in reality is so for the entire traditional domain. We believe it will not be without interest to consider this question in all its generality, although it may seem to divert us somewhat from considerations relating more directly to initiation. Since the mixing in question represents moreover only a particular case of what can properly be called 'syncretism', we should begin by clarifying what is meant by this word, all the more so in that those of our contemporaries who claim to study traditional doctrines—without at all getting to their essence, especially those who consider them historically and in a purely scholarly way—very often have the irksome tendency of confusing 'synthesis' with 'syncretism'. This observation applies generally to the 'profane' study of doctrines of the exoteric order as well as to those of the esoteric order; moreover, the distinction between them is rarely made as it should be, and thus the so-called 'science of religions' treats of a multitude of things that in reality have nothing 'religious' about them, as, for example, the initiatic mysteries of antiquity mentioned above. This 'science' clearly affirms its 'profane' character, in the worst sense of the word, by asserting in principle that only someone outside all religions and so having only an altogether external understanding of them (we should rather say 'outside of tradition', without specifying any of its particular modalities), is qualified to consider religion 'scientifically'. The truth is that under the pretext of disinterested knowledge there hides a clearly anti-traditional motive, a 'criticism' that for its promoters, and perhaps less consciously for their followers, is meant to destroy all tradition, and of which the prejudice is to see in tradition only a collection of psychological, social, or other purely human facts. We will not dwell on this further, for besides the fact that we have often spoken of it elsewhere, our present intention is only to point out a confusion that, although very characteristic of this special mentality, can obviously also exist independently of this anti-traditional motive.

'Syncretism' in its true sense is nothing more than a simple juxtaposition of elements of diverse provenance brought together 'from the outside' so to speak, without any principle of a more profound order to unite them. Obviously such an aggregation cannot really constitute a doctrine any more than a heap of stones makes a building, and if it sometimes gives the impression of doctrine to those who look at it only superficially, this is an illusion that cannot stand up under even modest scrutiny. One need not look very far to find good examples of such syncretism. Modern counterfeits of tradition like occultism and Theosophy are basically nothing else,[1] fragmentary notions borrowed from different traditional forms, generally poorly understood and more or less deformed, are herein mixed with ideas belonging to philosophy and to profane science. There are also philosophical theories patched together almost entirely from fragments of other theories, where syncretism usually takes the name of 'eclecticism', but in the final analysis this is less serious than the preceding situation since it is, after all, only philosophy, that is to say profane thought, which at least does not pretend do be something it is not.

In every case syncretism is an essentially profane process by virtue of its very 'exteriority'; not only is it not synthesis, but in a certain sense it is even the contrary, for synthesis by definition starts from principles, that is to say from what is most interior; it goes, one might say, from center to circumference, whereas syncretism remains on the circumference itself, in the pure and as it were 'atomic' multiplicity of an indefinite multitude of elements taken

1. Cf. *Reign of Quantity*, chap. 36.

one by one and considered in themselves, for themselves, and apart from their principle, that is from their true raison d'être. Syncretism thus has willy-nilly a wholly analytic character. It is true that none speak so often or so readily of synthesis as certain 'syncretists', but this proves only that they sense that if they were to recognize the true nature of their composite theories they would thereby have to admit that they are not the depositories of any tradition and that the task to which they have devoted themselves in no way differs from what any 'researcher' who happened along could do by piecing together various notions he has taken from books.

If such people have an evident interest in passing their syncretism off as a synthesis, the error of those of whom we spoke earlier is generally the reverse: finding themselves in the presence of a true synthesis, they rarely refrain from calling it syncretism. The explanation for such an attitude is in essence quite simple. Clinging to the most narrowly profane and exterior point of view that can be imagined, they have no notion of anything pertaining to another order, and since they will not or cannot admit that some things elude them, they naturally try to reduce everything to procedures they can understand. Imagining that all doctrine is no more than the work of one or several individuals without any intervention of higher elements (for it must not be forgotten that this is the fundamental postulate of all their 'science'), they attribute to these individuals what they themselves would be capable of doing in like case; and it hardly needs saying that they take no pains at all to ascertain whether or not the doctrine they are investigating after their own fashion is the expression of the truth, for since such a question is not 'historical' it never occurs to them. It is even doubtful whether they have ever suspected that there may be a higher truth than the mere 'factual truth' that is the sole object of their erudition; as for the interest that this kind of investigation seems to hold for them under such conditions, we must admit that it is quite impossible for us to comprehend, so foreign is this mentality to ours.

However that may be, what is particularly important to note is that the false conception that sees syncretism in traditional doctrines has as a direct and inevitable consequence what can be called the theory of 'borrowings': when the existence of similar elements is noted in two different doctrinal forms it is immediately supposed that one must have borrowed them from the other. This, of course, has nothing to do with the question of the common origin of traditions, or of their authentic filiation and the regular transmission and successive adaptation that this implies, all of which entirely elude the methods of investigation at the disposal of the profane historian and therefore literally do not exist for him. Those who hold this theory think only of borrowings in the crudest sense of the word, of a sort of copying or plagiarizing of one tradition by another with which it happens to come into contact through entirely contingent circumstances, and of an accidental incorporation of unconnected elements answering to no deeper cause;[2] and this is in fact precisely what the very definition of syncretism implies. Furthermore, it is never asked whether one and the same truth should not normally have more or less similar or at least comparable expressions, apart from any question of borrowing; but this cannot even be asked because, as we have just said, the existence of this truth is itself resolutely ignored. This last explanation would be insufficient in any case without the notion of the primordial unity of tradition, but it would at least convey a certain aspect of reality; and let us add that this explanation must never be confused with another theory, no less profane than that of 'borrowing' although differing in kind, which appeals to what is called by some the 'unity of the human spirit', taking this in an exclusively psychological sense (although in fact no such unity exists) and implying further that all doctrine is simply a product of the 'human spirit', so that this 'psychologism' no more considers the question of doctrinal truth than does the 'historicism' of the partisans of the syncretistic explanation.[3]

2. An example of how this way of seeing things is applied to the esoteric and initiatic domain is furnished by the theory that sees in the *taṣawwuf* of Islam a borrowing from India on the grounds that similar methods are found in both. The orientalists who maintain this theory have evidently never thought of asking themselves whether these methods were not equally required in both cases by the very nature of things, something that nonetheless seems rather easy to understand, at least for anyone who has no preconceived ideas.

3. Cf. *Reign of Quantity*, chap. 13.

A further point is that when this same idea of syncretism and 'borrowing' is applied to the traditional scriptures, it gives birth to the search for hypothetical 'sources' and supposed 'interpolations' which, as we know, is one of the greatest resources of 'criticism' in its work of destruction, a work the only real aim of which is the negation of any 'supra-human' inspiration.[4] This is closely connected with the anti-traditional motive that we noted at the beginning, and what we must keep especially in mind here is the incompatibility of any 'humanist' explanation with the traditional spirit, an incompatibility, moreover, that is obvious, since not to take into account the 'non-human' element is strictly to misunderstand the very essence of tradition, without which there is nothing left worthy to bear this name. On the other hand, in order to refute the syncretistic idea it suffices to recall that every traditional doctrine necessarily has a knowledge of metaphysical principles as its center and point of departure, and that everything else it may include in a more or less secondary way is, in the final analysis, only the application of these principles to different domains; this amounts to saying that it is essentially synthetic, and, as we said above, synthesis by its very nature excludes all syncretism.

One can take this still further: if it is impossible that there should be syncretism within traditional doctrines themselves, it is equally impossible that it should find a place among those who have truly understood these doctrines and who by this fact have perforce understood the vanity of such a procedure, as well as of all others proper to profane thought, and thus have no need of it. Whatever is truly inspired by traditional knowledge always proceeds from 'within' and not from 'without'; whoever is aware of the essential unity of all traditions can, according to the case, use different traditional forms to expound and interpret doctrine, if there happens to be some advantage in doing so, but this will never even remotely resemble any sort of syncretism or the 'comparative

---

4. The multiple-source theory of the early books of the Old Testament does not in itself contradict the view that the material is of supra-human inspiration. Furthermore, the evidence for this theory is overwhelming, and to call it syncretistic would be too much of a simplification. ED.

method' of scholars. On the one hand, the central and principial unity illuminates and dominates all; on the other, if this unity is absent or, better, hidden from the sight of the profane 'scholar', he can do no more than grope in the 'outer darkness', vainly busying himself amid a chaos that can be put to order only by the initiatic *Fiat Lux*, which, failing the necessary 'qualification', will never be uttered for him.

7

AGAINST MIXING
TRADITIONAL FORMS

As we have said elsewhere, according to the Hindu tradition there are two ways of being outside caste, one higher and the other lower.[1] One can be 'without caste' (*avarna*) in the 'privative' sense, that is below it, or, on the contrary, one can be 'beyond caste' (*ativarna*), that is above it, although this second case is incomparably more rare than the first, especially in the conditions of the present age.[2] In a similar way, one can be beneath or beyond traditional forms: the man 'without religion' for example, as found today in the modern West, is unquestionably in the first situation; the second, on the contrary, applies exclusively to those who have obtained an effective understanding of the fundamental unity and identity of all traditions; and here again this latter situation can only be very exceptional at present. It must be understood, however, that in speaking of an effective understanding we mean that merely theoretical notions of this unity and this identity, while surely far from negligible, are altogether insufficient for someone to consider himself beyond the need of adhering and strictly conforming to a given form. This does not mean, of course, that such a person must not try to understand other forms as completely and profoundly as possible, but only that, practically speaking, he must not use ritual or other means that belong to different forms, which as we said above

1. *Reign of Quantity*, chap. 9.
2. On the contrary, as we said in an earlier note, this was the norm for men in the primordial age.

would not only be useless and vain but harmful and dangerous in various respects.[3]

Traditional forms may be compared to paths that, though they lead to the same goal,[4] are nonetheless distinct. One obviously cannot follow several at once, and once one has been taken it ought to be followed without detour to its end, for passing from one to another is the surest way to impede one's progress and even risk losing one's way completely. Only someone who has persevered to the path's end can by that very fact stand above all paths, because he no longer needs to follow them; he is thenceforth able, should the need arise, to practice all the forms impartially, but this is precisely because he has gone beyond them and because, for him, they are now united in their common principle. Moreover, he will generally continue to confine himself outwardly to a given form even if only as an 'example' to those around him who have not yet reached the same point; but if particular circumstances should require it, he could just as well follow other forms since from his standpoint there is no longer any real difference among them. Furthermore, once these forms are thus unified for him, mingling or confusion of any kind is no longer possible since this presupposes the existence of diversity as such, and, once again, we are speaking only of someone who is effectively above this diversity. For him forms no longer have the character of paths or means, for which he has no further use, and remain only as expressions of the one Truth, expressions of which it is just as legitimate to make use, should circumstances require it, as it is to speak different languages in order to make oneself understood by those to whom one is speaking.[5]

3. This should clarify what we said above about the 'jurisdiction' of initiatic organizations deriving from a given traditional form. Since initiation in the strict sense, obtained by affiliation with such an organization, is a 'beginning', he who receives it is obviously far from being effectively above traditional forms.

4. To be quite exact it is appropriate to add: on the condition that they are complete, that is, that they include not only the exoteric part but also the esoteric and initiatic part. It is always thus in principle, but in fact it may happen that, by a sort of degeneration, the second part is forgotten and as it were lost.

5. This is precisely what is meant, from the initiatic point of view, by the 'gift of tongues', something to which we shall return.

In brief, between the situation above and that of an illegitimate mingling of traditional forms there is all the difference that we have noted as existing in a general way between synthesis and syncretism, which is why it was necessary to clarify this distinction at the outset. Indeed, anyone who considers all forms in the very unity of their principle thereby has, as we have just said, a view that is essentially synthetic in the most rigorous sense; he is within all forms equally, and we ought even to say at the most interior point of all, since this point is truly their common center. To return to the simile just used, all paths start from different points but gradually converge, always remaining distinct until they reach this unique center;[6] but seen from the center itself they are really only so many radii emanating from it and linking it with the many points on the circumference.[7] These two opposite points of view on the same paths correspond exactly to those respectively of one who is 'on the way' toward the center and one who has arrived there, states often described in traditional symbolism as those of the 'traveler' and of the 'sedentary', the latter also being compared to someone standing at the summit of a mountain who, without having to move, likewise sees all its slopes, whereas the one climbing the same mountain only sees the part nearest him; and it is quite obvious that only the view of the first can be called synthetic.

On the other hand, the one who is not at the center is perforce always in a more or less 'exterior' position even with regard to his own traditional form, all the more so with regard to the others; if he then should wish to perform rites belonging to many different forms, claiming to use them concurrently as means and 'supports' of his spiritual development, he will not really be able to combine them except 'from the outside', which amounts to saying that what he accomplishes will be nothing else than syncretism, which consists precisely in this kind of mingling of disparate elements that nothing

6. As we explained above in the case of a traditional form that has become incomplete, it could be said that the path has come to an end at some point before reaching the center, or, perhaps more exactly still, that it is impracticable to set out from this point, which marks the passage from the exoteric to the esoteric domain.

7. Of course from this central point of view the paths that are no longer practicable as such—those just referred to in the preceding note—are no exception.

really unifies. All that we have said against syncretism in general, therefore, applies in this particular situation, and, one could say, even more so in certain respects: as long as it is only a question of theories this sort of mingling can indeed be relatively inoffensive, even if it is to no purpose; but in the case under consideration, because of the direct contact with deeper realities implied, it risks leading the one who so acts to a deviation or an arresting of that interior development for which, on the contrary, he believed quite wrongly that he would thereby procure the greatest facility. This situation is similar to that of someone who, hoping to secure his health the more effectively, makes use at one and the same time of many different medicines the effects of which neutralize and destroy each other and sometimes even provoke unforeseen reactions harmful to his organism. There are things that are efficacious when used separately but that are nonetheless radically incompatible.

This leads us to clarify another point. Besides the properly doctrinal reason for denying the validity of any mingling of traditional forms there is one consideration that, while more contingent, is no less important from what one might call the 'technical' point of view. Suppose that someone finds himself in the conditions required for accomplishing the rites belonging to several forms in such a way that they have real effects, which naturally implies that he has at least some effective link with each of these forms. It could happen—indeed, it is almost inevitable in most cases—that these rites usher in not only spiritual influences but also, and even first and foremost, psychic influences that, not being in harmony among themselves, will clash and provoke a state of disorder and disequilibrium more or less seriously affecting the one who has imprudently aroused them, clearly a kind of danger to which one should not expose oneself carelessly. Moreover, the clash of psychic influences is more especially to be feared when these latter are the result of using the most outward rites, that is, those belonging to the exoteric side of the different traditions, since it is obviously these above all that exclude each other, the different paths diverging all the more the further they move from the center. On the other hand, although this may seem paradoxical to someone who has not reflected on it sufficiently, the opposition is then all the more violent as the traditions to which they belong have more in common, as for example with those exoterisms that assume a religious form in the strict sense of the word, for things that are very different enter into conflict only with difficulty by reason of this very difference. In this domain as in every other there can be conflict only on condition that similar ground be occupied. We will not dwell further on this, but it is to be hoped that this warning suffices for those who might be tempted to set such discordant methods in motion. Let them not forget that only in the purely spiritual domain is one safe from all harm because it is there alone that opposition itself has no more meaning, and that as long as the psychic domain has not been completely and definitively surpassed the worst mishaps always remain possible, even, and perhaps we should say especially, for those who so resolutely profess not to believe in them.

8

INITIATIC
TRANSMISSION

WE HAVE PREVIOUSLY STATED that initiation is essentially the transmission of a spiritual influence, a transmission that can only take place through a regular, traditional organization, so that one cannot speak of initiation outside of an affiliation with an organization of this kind. We have explained that 'regularity' must be understood to exclude all pseudo-initiatic organizations, which, regardless of pretension and outward appearance, in no way possess any spiritual influence and thus are incapable of really transmitting anything. It is therefore easy to understand the supreme importance that all traditions attach to what is called the initiatic 'chain',[1] a succession that ensures the uninterrupted transmission in question; outside of this succession even the observance of ritual forms is in vain, for the element essential to their efficacy is lacking.

Later we shall consider the matter of initiatic rites in more detail, but first we must answer an objection that could be raised here: do not rites themselves have an intrinsic efficacy? Our reply is that they do indeed, for if they are not properly observed, or if any one of their essential elements is altered, no effective result can be obtained; yet even if these are necessary conditions for the efficacy of rites, they still are not sufficient, for it is also necessary that they be accomplished by those with the proper qualifications. This, it may be noted, is not at all peculiar to initiatic rites but applies to exoteric

1. The word 'chain' translates the Hebrew *shelsheleth*, the Arabic *silsilah*, and the Sanskrit *paramparā*, all of which express essentially the notion of a regular and uninterrupted transmission.

rites as well, to religious rites, for example, which have their own particular efficacy yet cannot be validly accomplished by just anyone. Thus, if a religious rite should require priestly ordination, anyone who has not received this ordination would observe all the proper forms in vain, and even if he brought the correct intention to the rite[2] he would obtain no result, for he does not bear the spiritual influence that is to act taking these ritual forms as its support.[3]

Even in rites of a very inferior order that concern only secondary traditional applications, such as magical rites, where the intervening influence is in no way spiritual but merely psychic (understanding thereby in the most general sense, the subtle elements of human individuality and their counterparts in the 'macrocosmic' order), the production of a real effect is also conditioned in many cases by an unambiguous transmission, common country witchcraft furnishing numerous examples in this regard.[4] We will not however emphasize this point, which lies outside our subject, and mention it only to show more clearly that in rites involving the action of influences of a superior order (an order that can properly be called 'non-human' and that includes both initiatic and religious rites), a regular transmission is even more indispensable to permit their valid accomplishment.

This is the essential point, and we must again insist upon it: we have already said that the constitution of regular initiatic organizations is not a matter of merely individual initiatives, and exactly the same can be said for religious organizations, for in both cases the presence of something beyond human possibilities is necessary.

2. We expressly formulate this condition of intention here in order to make it very clear that rites can never be the object of 'experiments' in the profane sense of the word; anyone who would accomplish a rite, of whatever order, merely out of curiosity and to 'experience' its effects can be assured in advance that its effect will be nil.

3. Even rites that do not expressly require this sort of ordination cannot be accomplished by just anyone, for explicit adherence to the traditional form to which the rites belong is always an indispensable condition of their efficacy.

4. This condition of transmission is thus also found in deviations from tradition or in its degenerated remnants, and even, we may add, in its subversion properly so called, in what we have called the 'counter-initiation'. On this subject see *Reign of Quantity*, chaps. 34 and 38.

Moreover, we can bring these two cases together by saying that both involve the totality of organizations that truly qualify as traditional; it can then be understood without further reflection why we have refused to apply the name tradition to things that are purely human, as profane language mistakenly does. It would not be without benefit to note that in its original sense the word 'tradition' expresses the very idea of transmission that we now have in mind, a point to which we shall return later.

Now, for the sake of convenience we could divide traditional organizations into the 'exoteric' and the 'esoteric', although these two terms understood in their most precise sense cannot perhaps be applied with equal exactitude; for our present purposes, however, it will suffice to understand by 'exoteric' those organizations that in certain forms of civilization are open to all without distinction, and by 'esoteric' those organizations reserved for an elite that admits only those possessing a particular 'qualification'. Only the last are initiatic organizations, while the former comprise not only specifically religious organizations but also, as seen in Eastern civilizations, social organizations that lack a religious character, though they are also attached to principles of a superior order, which is always the indispensable condition for recognizing them as traditional. Since we do not need to consider exoteric organizations in themselves, but only to compare them with esoteric or initiatic organizations, we can limit ourselves to a consideration of religious organizations, for these are the only traditional exoteric organizations known in the West, so that what pertains to them will be immediately comprehensible to our readers.

In light of the above we can say that all religion in the true sense of the word has a 'non-human' origin and is organized so as to preserve the deposit of an equally 'non-human' element which it retains from this origin. This element, which belongs to the order of spiritual influences and exerts its effective action by means of the appropriate rites, of which the valid accomplishment furnishes a real support to the influences involved, requires a direct and uninterrupted transmission at the core of the religious organization. If this is true of the merely exoteric order (it is understood, of course, that we are not addressing those negating 'critics' to whom we have previously referred, who try to reduce religion to a 'human fact' and whose opinions we need not consider any more than anything else that similarly proceeds from anti-traditional prejudices), it must be even more true of a higher order, that is, of the esoteric order. The terms we have just used are broad enough to be retained when we substitute the word initiation for the word religion, in which case the whole difference will lie in the nature of the spiritual influences that enter into play (for there are still many distinctions to make within this domain, in which latter we would include all that pertains to possibilities of a supra-individual order), and especially in the respective ends of their action.

If to make ourselves better understood we focus on the case of Christianity in the religious order, we can then add that the rites of initiation, which have as their immediate aim the transmission of a spiritual influence from one individual to another individual who, in principle at least, can continue the transmission in turn, are precisely analogous in this respect to the rites of ordination.[5] And we may even note that both can contain several degrees, for the plenitude of the spiritual influence is not necessarily communicated at a single stroke with all its implied prerogatives, especially as concerns the actual capacity to exercise particular functions in the traditional organization.[6] Now we know how important the question of 'apostolic succession' is for the Christian churches, and this is not difficult to understand, since, if that succession were somehow interrupted,

---

5. We say 'in this respect' because from another point of view the first initiation, insofar as it is a 'second birth', would be comparable to the rite of baptism; it follows that the correspondence one might envisage between things appertaining to such different orders must necessarily be complex and not easily reducible to a sort of unilinear schema.

6. We say 'actual capacity' to specify that what is involved here is something more than the preliminary 'qualification', which can also be designated as a capacity. Thus one can say that an individual is qualified for the exercise of sacerdotal functions if he suffers from none of the impediments that preclude access to them, but he will not possess an actual capacity for it unless he has received ordination. And let us note in this connection that ordination is the only sacrament for which particular qualifications are required, in which respect it is again comparable to initiation, on condition naturally that we always bear in mind the essential difference between the exoteric and the esoteric domains.

ordination would no longer be valid and most rites would then be no more than empty formalities, lacking any effective influence.[7] Those who rightly admit the necessity of this in the religious order should not have the least difficulty understanding its no less rigorous imposition in the initiatic order; in other words, that a regular transmission, constituting the 'chain' of which we have spoken, is also strictly indispensable there.

We have just remarked that initiation must have a 'non-human' origin, for without this it can never attain its final end, which extends beyond the domain of individual possibilities. That is why truly initiatic rites cannot be attributed to human authors; in fact, we can no more know the authors than we can know the inventors of traditional symbols,[8] and for the same reason, for these symbols are equally 'non-human' in their origin and essence.[9] Moreover, there are very strong links between rites and symbols, which we will examine later. Strictly speaking, one can say that in such cases there is no 'historical' origin, since the real origin is situated in a world to which the conditions of time and space, defining historical facts, do not apply, which is why such things will inevitably escape profane methods of research that by definition, as it were, can lead to relatively valid results only within the purely human order.[10]

In such circumstances it is easy to understand that the role of the individual who confers initiation on another is veritably one of 'transmitter' in the most exact sense of the word. Such a person does not act as an individual, but as the support of an influence not

---

7. In fact, the Protestant churches that do not acknowledge sacerdotal functions have suppressed almost all rites or have kept them merely as 'commemorative' simulacra; and given the constitution proper to the Christian tradition, under such circumstances they could be nothing more. On the other hand, the discussions to which the question of the legitimacy of the Anglican church give rise are well known, and it is curious that even when the Theosophists wished to form their 'Liberal Catholic church', they sought before all else to assure it the benefit of regular 'apostolic succession'.

8. Attributions to legendary or generally symbolic personages cannot be considered at all as 'historical', but on the contrary fully confirm what we are saying here.

9. Islamic esoteric organizations transmit a sign of recognition that, according to tradition, was communicated to the Prophet by the archangel Gabriel himself.

10. Let us note here that people who for 'apologetic' reasons insist on what they rather barbarously call the 'historicity' of a religion, to the point of seeing in this something essential and sometimes even subordinating doctrinal considerations to

belonging to the individual order; he is only a link in the 'chain' of which the starting-point lies outside and beyond humanity. This is why he acts not in his own name but in the name of the organization to which he is attached and from which he holds his powers; or, more exactly still, he acts in the name of the principle that the organization visibly represents. This also explains how the efficacy of the rite accomplished by an individual can be independent of the true merit of the individual as such, something that is equally true of religious rites. We do not intend this in any 'moral' sense, which would clearly have no importance to an exclusively 'technical' question, but in the sense that even if the individual lacks the degree of knowledge necessary to comprehend the profound meaning of the rite and the essential reason for its diverse elements, that rite will nonetheless be fully effective if the individual is properly invested with the function of 'transmitter' and accomplishes it while observing all the prescribed rules and with an intention that suffices to determine his consciousness of attachment to the traditional organization. From this it immediately follows that even an organization that at any given time has only what we have called 'virtual' initiates (and we will return to this question later) is nonetheless capable of really transmitting the spiritual influence of which it is the repository. For this to be the case, it is sufficient that the 'chain' be unbroken; in this regard the well-known fable of 'the ass bearing relics' is susceptible to an initiatic interpretation well worth meditating on.[11]

On the other hand, even the complete knowledge of a rite is entirely devoid of any effective value if it has been obtained outside

it (whereas historical facts themselves are, on the contrary, only valuable when they can be taken as symbols of spiritual realities), commit a serious error to the detriment of the 'transcendence' of this religion. Such an error, which evinces moreover a highly 'materialized' conception and an incapacity to raise oneself to a higher order, can be regarded as a harmful concession to the 'humanist', that is to say the individualistic and anti-traditional, point of view that characterizes the modern Western mind.

11. In this connection it is worth noting that relics are precisely vehicles of spiritual influences, which is the true reason for the cult of which they are the object. This is true even if the representatives of the exoteric religions are not always aware of it, for these representatives sometimes seem oblivious to the very 'positive' character of the forces they handle, which nevertheless does not prevent these forces from acting effectively even without their knowledge, although perhaps with less scope than if they were better managed 'technically'.

of regular conditions. It is for this reason—to take a simple example where the rite is reduced essentially to the pronunciation of a word or formula—that in the Hindu tradition a *mantra* learned otherwise than from the mouth of an authorized *guru* is without effect because it is not 'vivified' by the presence of the spiritual influence whose vehicle it is uniquely destined to be.[12] This applies in some degree to everything to which a spiritual influence is attached; thus study of the sacred texts of a tradition can never substitute for their direct communication; and this is why, even where traditional teachings are more or less completely available in written form, they still continue to be transmitted orally, for this is indispensable for their full effect (we are not restricting ourselves here to a merely theoretical knowledge) and also guarantees the perpetuation of the 'chain' to which the very life of the tradition is linked. Otherwise, one would be facing a dead tradition to which effective attachment is no longer possible; and although knowledge of what remains of a tradition can still have a certain theoretical interest (beyond merely profane erudition of course, which latter has no value here except insofar as it is capable of aiding the comprehension of certain doctrinal truths), it can in no way promote 'realization' of any kind whatsoever.[13]

In all this it is so completely a matter of communicating something 'vital' that in India no disciple may ever sit facing his *guru*, in order that the action of *prana*, linked to the breath and to the voice, not be exercised on him too directly, for it might produce a violent shock that could be dangerous psychically, and even physically.[14] This action is all the more powerful because in such a case the *prana* itself is only the vehicle or subtle support for the spiritual influence transmitted from *guru* to disciple; and in the exercise of his proper

12. In connection with this 'vivification' so to speak, let us note in passing that the essential purpose of consecrating temples, images, and ritual objects is to make them effective receptacles of spiritual influences without whose presence the rites for which they serve would be inefficacious.

13. This completes and clarifies what we said above of the vanity of a so-called 'ideal' attachment to the forms of a vanished tradition.

14. This is also the explanation of the special arrangement of seats in a Masonic lodge, something that most Masons today are surely far from suspecting.

function the *guru* must not be considered as an individuality (individuality, except as a mere support, truly disappearing at such time) but only as the representative of the tradition itself, which he incarnates as it were with respect to his disciple, this being exactly the role of 'transmitter' referred to above.

9

TRADITION
AND TRANSMISSION

WE HAVE PREVIOUSLY NOTED that, etymologically, 'tradition' expresses no idea except transmission; when one speaks of 'tradition' in the sense we intend, its meaning really does not extend beyond this perfectly normal usage, as our previous explanations should make clear. Nonetheless, some have raised an objection in this regard, so that we must dwell upon this point further in order that no ambiguity may remain. The objection runs thus: anything at all can be the object of a transmission, even things of the most profane order; why then could one not just as well speak of 'tradition' for everything transmitted, regardless of its nature, instead of restricting this word to that domain called 'sacred'?

A preliminary remark will greatly reduce the scope of this question. If one returned to primordial conditions, the objection would never arise, for the distinction it implies between 'sacred' and 'profane' did not then exist. Indeed, as we have often explained, there is no such thing as a profane order to which certain things could belong by their very nature; there is in reality only a profane point of view, which is the consequence and product of a particular degeneration that itself results from the descending march of the human cycle and its gradual movement away from the principial state. One can therefore say that before this degeneration, that is to say in the normal state of a not yet fallen humanity, all things possessed a traditional character, for all things were envisaged in their essential dependence on and conformity to principles, so that a profane activity, separate from and ignorant of these principles, would have been altogether inconceivable, even in what we presently call 'ordinary life', or rather in what would have corresponded to it at that time. This life, however, had an aspect quite different from that which our contemporaries understand by the term,[1] and this was even more true for the sciences and the arts and crafts, the traditional character of which was long maintained and is still found in every normal civilization, so much so that one could say that the profane conception is, excepting 'classical' antiquity to a certain degree, exclusive to modern civilization, which itself represents the final degree of degeneration.

If we now consider the state of things following the onset of this degeneration, we can ask why the idea of tradition excludes what thereafter was considered to belong to the profane order (that is, what no longer has any conscious link with principles), and is applied only to what has kept its original character and retains its 'transcendent' aspect. It is not sufficient to say that usage required this, at least as long as those confusions and altogether modern deviations to which we have previously called attention had not yet been produced;[2] it is true that usage can often modify the original meaning of words, especially by broadening or restricting them, but for such usage to be legitimate it must have its raison d'être, and especially in such a case as this the reason cannot be unimportant. Let us observe, moreover, that this situation is not limited only to those languages that employ derivatives of the Latin word 'tradition'; in Hebrew, *kabbalah*, which has exactly the same meaning of transmission, is similarly reserved to designate tradition as we have understood it, and even ordinarily its strictly esoteric and initiatic aspect, that is, what is most 'inward' and elevated in that tradition and thus what constitutes its very spirit as it were; and this again demonstrates that here is surely something more important and more significant than a simple question of usage in the sense of mere modifications in current language.

What first follows from this is that what the term tradition can be applied to remains fundamentally, though not necessarily in its outward expression, what it was originally, that is, something that has

---

1. Cf. *The Reign of Quantity,* chap. 15.
2. See especially ibid., chap. 31.

been transmitted from a previous state of humanity to its present state. At the same time we can see that the 'transcendent' character of everything traditional also implies a transmission in another sense, starting with the very principles that are communicated to the human state; this sense thus joins with the preceding one and obviously completes it. Again calling on terms we have used elsewhere,[3] we could speak of a 'vertical' transmission from the suprahuman to the human and a 'horizontal' transmission across the states or successive stages of humanity; the vertical transmission is of course essentially 'non-temporal', the horizontal transmission alone implying chronological succession. We might add that the vertical transmission, which we have just envisaged as from above, when taken in the reverse direction from below, becomes a 'participation' by humanity in realities of the principial order, indeed, a participation assured by tradition in all its forms since it is precisely through it that humanity is put into effective contact with a superior order. For its part, horizontal transmission, if considered as a re-ascent over the course of time, becomes a 'return to origins', a restoration of the 'primordial state'; and we have already indicated that this restoration is precisely a necessary condition for man to raise himself effectively to the superior states.

But there is still more to be said on this point. To the character of 'transcendence', which essentially belongs to principles and in which everything effectively linked to them participates to some degree (this participation expressing itself as the presence of a 'non-human' element in all that is properly traditional), is added a character of 'permanence', which explains the immutability of these same principles and which is similarly communicated, in the measure possible, to their applications, even when these belong to contingent domains. Of course, this is not to say that tradition is not susceptible of conditioned adaptations in certain circumstances; yet beneath these modifications there is always permanence in what is essential, and even where contingencies are involved, they are, as it were, surpassed and 'transformed' through their attachment to principles. On the contrary, when we place ourselves at the profane point of

---

3. See *The Symbolism of the Cross.*

view, which is characterized in an entirely negative way by the absence of any such attachment, we are, as it were, within pure contingency, with all the consequent instability and incessant change, and with no possibility of extricating ourselves; in a certain way this is 'becoming' reduced to itself, and it is not difficult to see that every profane idea is subject to continual change, as are the modes of activity deriving from such ideas, of which what is called 'fashion' is the most striking example. From this we may conclude that tradition includes not only everything worthy of transmission but also everything capable of it, since all that lacks a traditional character and that consequently falls within the profane point of view is so dominated by change that all transmission soon becomes a pure and simple 'anachronism', or a 'superstition' in the etymological sense of the word and no longer corresponds to anything real or valid.

We should now understand why tradition and transmission without any abuse of language may be regarded as nearly synonymous, or at least why in every respect tradition can be called transmission par excellence. Moreover, if the idea of transmission so essentially inheres in the traditional point of view that this latter could legitimately derive its very name from it, our remarks about the need for a regular transmission in what pertains to the traditional order (and more especially the initiatic order, which is not only an integral but even an 'eminent' part of it) are thereby reinforced and even acquire the kind of immediate evidence that should, by the simplest logic and without further appeal to more profound considerations, decisively preclude any argument on this point concerning which only pseudo-initiatic organizations could have an interest in maintaining ambiguity and confusion, precisely because they lack this transmission.

10

INITIATIC CENTERS

WE CONSIDER OUR REMARKS sufficient to demonstrate the necessity for initiatic transmission and to make clear that what we are dealing with is not at all nebulous but on the contrary extremely precise and well-defined, something in which dreams and fancy have no role, any more than does what current fashion calls 'subjective' and 'ideal'. In order to complete our consideration of this subject we still must speak of the spiritual centers from which all regular transmission directly or indirectly proceeds, centers themselves connected to the supreme center that preserves the immutable deposit of the primordial tradition from which each traditional form is derived through an adaptation to particular circumstances of time and place. In a previous work[1] we indicated how these spiritual centers are constituted in the image of the supreme center itself, of which they are, as it were, so many reflections; we will therefore not return to that here, but will limit ourselves to examining certain points more immediately related to our present subject.

To begin with, the link to the supreme center is clearly indispensable for the continuity of transmission of spiritual influences from the very origins of present humanity (or, rather, from beyond these origins, since what is involved is 'non-human') and throughout the entire duration of its cycle of existence. This is true for everything of a traditional character, even for exoteric organizations, religious or otherwise, at least regarding their point of departure, and it is all the more true for the initiatic order. In addition, this link maintains the inner and essential unity present under diverse formal appearances,

---

1. *The King of the World.*

and is consequently the fundamental guarantee of 'orthodoxy' in the true sense. But it must be understood that this link does not always remain conscious, something only too evident in the exoteric order; on the other hand, it would seem that it must always be conscious in initiatic organizations, one of the purposes of which is precisely to allow passage beyond a particular traditional form and thus to proceed from diversity to unity, while taking the specific forms as starting-point. Naturally, this does not mean that such a consciousness must exist among all the members of an initiatic organization, which is manifestly impossible and furthermore would render its hierarchy of degrees useless, though normally it would exist at the summit of that hierarchy if all who had attained it were truly 'adepts', that is, beings that have effectively realized the fullness of initiation;[2] for such 'adepts' would constitute an initiatic center in uninterrupted conscious communication with the supreme center. This is not always the case in fact, however, if only because a distancing from the origins permits a certain degeneration which, as we mentioned previously, can reach a point where an organization comes to include only what we have called 'virtual' initiates, yet continues all the same to transmit, albeit unknowingly, the spiritual influence of which it is the repository. The link subsists in that case despite everything, thanks to the fact of uninterrupted transmission, and this is sufficient to allow those who receive the spiritual influence under these conditions to recover the necessary consciousness of this link if they have the requisite potential for it. Even in this case, then, membership in an initiatic organization is far from a mere formality with no real import, as is the case with membership in some profane association, although this is all too willingly believed by those who, rather than looking further, prefer to let themselves be deceived by purely outward similarities which are

---

2. This is the only true and legitimate meaning of the word, which originally belonged exclusively to initiatic terminology, particularly that of the Rosicrucians; but it is still necessary to point out one of those strange abuses of language so prevalent in our era. In popular usage 'adepts' has come to be a synonym of 'adherents', to the extent that this is applied to the entire membership of any organization whatsoever, even the most profane ones that can be imagined.

in fact due to the degeneration of the only initiatic organizations that they may know more or less superficially.

On the other hand, it is important to note that an initiatic organization can proceed from the supreme center not directly but through the intermediary of secondary and subordinate centers, and this is even the most usual situation. Just as within each organization there is a hierarchy of degrees, so among the organizations themselves there are what could be called degrees of relative 'interiority' and 'exteriority'; and clearly those most exterior, that is, most distant from the supreme center, are also those where an awareness of the link to this center is most easily lost. Although all initiatic organizations have essentially the same goal, they participate at different levels, as it were, in the primordial tradition, though this fact does not exclude certain members of each from reaching the same degree of effective knowledge; and this is no reason for surprise if one remembers that the various traditional forms are not immediately derived from the same original source, for the 'chain' can consist of a greater or lesser number of intermediate links without this implying for all that any break in continuity. This superposition is not among the least reasons for the difficulty and complexity of even a moderately detailed examination of how initiatic organizations are constituted; again, we should add that such a superposition can also be found within a single traditional form, as is particularly evident in the Far-Eastern tradition. This example, which we refer to only in passing, will perhaps allow us to understand better how continuity is assured across the many levels of superposed organizations, from those that, engaged in the domain of action, are only temporary formations meant to play a relatively external role, to those of a more profound order that, while remaining in principial 'non-action', or rather, precisely because of this, give to all the others their real direction. In this regard we must especially call attention to the fact that, even if certain of the former are sometimes opposed to each other, this in no way prevents an effective unity of direction, for this direction is beyond such opposition and outside its domain. In sum, what we have here is something comparable to the roles of various actors in the same play, which, although opposing one another, nonetheless cooperate in advancing the whole. Each organization likewise plays its appointed role in a larger plan; and this can be extended to include even the exoteric domain, where in such conditions the contending elements nonetheless yield, though perhaps unconsciously and involuntarily, to a sole direction, the existence of which is not even suspected.[3]

These considerations also explain how, within a single organization, a kind of double hierarchy can exist, especially when the apparent leaders are themselves unaware of any link to a spiritual center. In such cases there may exist beside the visible hierarchy made up by those apparent leaders, an invisible hierarchy of which the members may not fulfill any 'official' function but who, by their presence alone, nonetheless assure an effective liaison with this center. In the more exterior organizations these representatives of the spiritual centers obviously need not reveal themselves as such and can adopt the appearance most suitable to the action 'of presence' that they must exercise; they may be either ordinary members of the organization with a fixed and permanent role or, if it is a case of an influence that is temporary or that is to be communicated to different places, they may appear as those mysterious 'travelers' of whom history has preserved more than one example and whose outward pose is often chosen so as to best put off inquiry, either by attracting attention for particular purposes, or on the contrary by passing

---

3. According to the Islamic tradition, every being is naturally and necessarily *muslim*, that is, in submission to the divine Will, from which indeed nothing can withdraw; differences among beings lie in the degree to which they conform to the universal order, some doing so voluntarily while others remain unaware of it, even claiming to oppose it (see *The Symbolism of the Cross*, chap. 25). To fully understand how this relates to what we have just said, it should be noted that authentic spiritual centers must be considered to represent the divine Will in the world, so that those who are affiliated with them can be regarded as collaborating consciously in the realization of what Masonic initiation calls the 'plan of the Great Architect of the Universe'. As for the two other categories we have just alluded to, those who are purely and simply unaware are the profane (among whom of course must be numbered 'pseudo-initiates' of every stripe), and those who entertain the illusory claim of being able to oppose the accepted pre-established order make up under one or another name what we have called the 'counter-initiation'.

unnoticed.[4] From this one can recognize the identity of those who, without belonging to any known organization (by which we mean one clothed in sensible forms), nevertheless presided in certain instances over their formation or subsequently inspired and directed them invisibly. This was notably the role of the Brotherhood of the Rose-Cross during a certain period[5] in the West, and this was also the real meaning of what eighteenth-century Masonry called the 'Unknown Superiors'.

All this permits us to glimpse among the many possibilities of spiritual centers certain means of acting which are quite different from those ordinarily attributed to them, and which are especially evident in abnormal circumstances, that is to say circumstances that do not permit of more direct procedures and a more apparent regularity. Aside from an immediate intervention of the supreme center—which is always and everywhere possible—a spiritual center of any kind may thus also act outside its normal sphere of influence, whether in favor of individuals particularly 'qualified' but isolated in a milieu where the darkness has reached such a point that almost nothing of tradition remains and initiation is precluded, or in view of a more general but more exceptional goal, such as reforging an initiatic 'chain' that has been accidentally broken. When such an action occurs in a period or civilization where spirituality has almost entirely disappeared and where things pertaining to the initiatic order are consequently more hidden than ever, we should not be surprised if its modalities are extremely difficult to determine, all the more so since the ordinary conditions of place and sometimes even of time here become nonexistent so to speak. We need not dwell on this point, but it is essential to remember that even if an

4. As an example of the former class, which inevitably escapes the attention of historians but is without doubt the most frequent, we will cite just two typical examples well known in the Taoist tradition and the equivalents of which are also to be found in the West: jugglers and horse traders.

5. Granted that not much precision is possible here, we may consider this period to extend from the fourteenth to the seventeenth century. One can therefore say that it corresponds to the beginning of the modern age, from which it is evident that their concern was above all to conserve whatever could be salvaged of the traditional knowledge of the Middle Ages, despite the new conditions in the West.

apparently isolated individual succeeds in gaining a real initiation, this initiation is spontaneous in appearance only and will in fact always involve some kind of attachment to an effective center,[6] for outside of such an attachment the question of initiation cannot even be raised.

Returning to a consideration of normal cases, we must first forestall any misunderstanding by stating that when we referred above to certain oppositions, we did not have in mind the multiple paths that can be represented by as many particular initiatic organizations, whether among different traditional forms or within one and the same form. This multiplicity is made necessary by the difference in individual natures, and allows each to find a way conformable to his own nature and that permits the development of his own possibilities. If the goal is the same for all, the starting-points are nonetheless indefinitely diverse and comparable to the multitude of points on a circumference, from each of which proceeds a radius terminating in the unique center, which radii thus represent the very paths in question. Here there is no opposition, but, on the contrary, a perfect harmony; and indeed there could be no opposition except where for contingent reasons certain organizations are called upon to play an as it were accidental role, one that is therefore outside the essential goal of initiation and that does not affect it in any way.

Certain appearances make it possible to believe, as is often done, that some initiations are inherently opposed to each other; but this is an error, and it is rather easy to see why this could not really be the case. Since in principle there is but one unique Tradition from which every orthodox traditional form is derived, there can be only one initiation, equally unique in its essence although present under diverse forms and with multiple modalities; where 'regularity' is lacking, that is, where there is no attachment to an orthodox traditional center, there is no longer true initiation, and the word is abused when used of such a case. We are referring here not only to those pseudo-initiatic organizations touched upon previously, which are truly nothing, but there is something else that presents a

---

6. Certain mysterious incidents in the life of Jacob Boehme for example can in fact be explained only in this way.

more serious character and which is precisely what gives a reasonable appearance to the illusion we have just noted. If there appear to be opposing initiations, this is because, outside of authentic initiation, there is what could be called 'counter-initiation' on condition that we specify the exact sense in which such an expression should be understood and the limits within which something can be truly opposed to initiation. But as we have explained the matter sufficiently elsewhere, it is unnecessary to devote special attention to it here.[7]

7. See *Reign of Quantity*, chap. 38.

11

INITIATIC
ORGANIZATIONS
AND RELIGIOUS SECTS

As WE HAVE SAID, the study of initiatic organizations is a particularly complex matter, and we must add that it is further complicated by too frequent errors that usually proceed from a more or less complete misunderstanding of their real nature. Among these errors the first we should note is the application of the term 'sects' to such organizations, for this is much more than a simple impropriety of language. Indeed, in such a case this expression should be rejected not only because it is disagreeable and offensive but also because it is apparently the work of adversaries, even though some may use it without an especially hostile intention through imitation or habit, just as there are those who describe the doctrines of antiquity as 'paganism' without even suspecting that this is quite an abusive term belonging to a low order of polemics.[1] This is in truth a serious confusion of things of entirely different orders, a confusion

---

1. In his *The Golden Verses of Pythagoras*, Fabre d'Olivet very justly says in this regard: 'The name "pagan" is an offensive and base term deriving from the Latin *paganus*, which means a lout, a peasant. When Christianity had fully triumphed over Greek and Roman polytheism, and when by the order of the Emperor Theodosius the last temples dedicated to the Gods of the Nations had been cast down, the country people for a long time still persisted in the old cult, so that those who imitated them were in derision also called *pagani*. This denomination, which might have been appropriate for Greeks and Romans in the sixth century, is false and ridiculous when extended to other times and peoples.'

that hardly seems inadvertent on the part of those who create or maintain it. In the Christian world, and occasionally even in the Islamic world,[2] this confusion is chiefly due to enemies or negators of esoterism, who wish by a false assimilation to project upon esoterism something of the disrepute attached to 'sects' properly speaking, that is, to 'heresies' in the specifically religious sense.[3]

Now by the very fact that it is a question of esoterism and initiation, it has nothing whatsoever to do with religion but rather with pure knowledge and 'sacred science'. Though this latter possesses a sacred character (certainly not the monopoly of religion, as some wrongly believe),[4] it is nonetheless essentially a science, though in a sense quite different from that given this word by those moderns who know of nothing but profane science, which is devoid of all value from the traditional point of view, since, as we have often explained, it stems from a change in the very idea of science. Doubtless this confusion is facilitated by the fact that esoterism has more direct links with religion than with anything else in the exterior order by reason of the traditional character common to both; and as noted previously, esoterism can in certain cases even assume a base and support in a specific religious form; but it is nonetheless related to a domain quite different from this, and thus can enter neither into opposition nor competition with it. By definition, moreover, it involves an order of knowledge reserved for an elite, whereas, also by definition, religion (as well as the exoteric aspect of every tradition, even if it be without a specifically religious form) is addressed to all without distinction; initiation in the true sense of the word implies particular 'qualifications', and thus cannot be of a religious

2. The Arabic term corresponding to the word 'sect' is *firqah*, which also specifically expresses an idea of 'division'.

3. Although it is in either case a matter of confusing the esoteric and the exoteric domains, this is quite different from the false assimilation of esoterism to mysticism discussed earlier, for this latter, which seems to be of more recent date, tends rather to 'annex' esoterism than to discredit it, which is certainly more clever, and which might lead one to believe that some have come to realize the insufficiency of a crudely scornful attitude and of pure and simple denial.

4. There are some who go so far in this direction as to claim there is no other 'sacred science' than theology!

order.[5] Even without looking any further, the supposition that an initiatic organization could compete with a religious organization is truly absurd, for its 'closed' character and restricted recruitment place it at too great a disadvantage in such a case;[6] but that is neither its role nor its aim.

Etymologically, whoever says 'sect' necessarily says scission or division; and 'sects' are indeed divisions engendered at the heart of a religion by more or less profound differences among its members. Consequently, sects are inevitably numerous[7] and their existence implies a departure from the principle, to which, on the contrary, esoterism is by its very nature closer than is religion and than is exoterism in general, even when these latter are free from any deviation. It is through esoterism that all traditional doctrines are in fact unified, beyond the differences of their outward forms, in certain respects necessary in their own order; and from this point of view not only are initiatic organizations not 'sects', but they are even exactly the opposite.

Sects, whether schisms or heresies, are always derived from a particular religion, of which they constitute irregular branches so to speak. On the contrary, esoterism can never be derived from religion; even where it takes religion as a support, that is, as a means of expression and of realization, it does nothing but effectively join it to its principle, and in reality, with respect to religion, it represents

---

5. One might object that, as we said above, there are also 'qualifications' required for priestly ordination; but in that case it is only a matter of exercising certain particular functions while in this the 'qualifications' are necessary not only for exercising a function in an initiatic organization, but indeed for receiving the initiation itself, which is something completely different.

6. On the contrary, there is every reason for the initiatic organization as such to restrict its recruitment as much as possible, for in this order a too great extension is generally one of the principal causes of a certain degeneration, as we shall explain below.

7. This shows the radical falsity of the ideas of those who, as is frequently the case especially among 'anti-Masonic' writers, speak of 'The Sect' in the singular and with an initial capital, as a kind of 'entity' in which their imagination incarnates all toward which they have some aversion. The fact that words come thus to lose completely their legitimate meaning is, let us say it again, one of the characteristics of the mental disorder of our time.

the Tradition anterior to all particular exterior forms, religious or otherwise. The inner cannot proceed from the outer any more than the center can proceed from its circumference; nor can the greater proceed from the less, any more than the spirit can proceed from the body. The influences presiding over traditional organizations always move in a descending direction and never re-ascend, any more than a river can return to its source. To claim that initiation could have issued from religion, and even more so from a 'sect', is to reverse all the normal relationships resulting from the very nature of things.[8] What the spirit is to the body, so truly is esoterism to religious exoterism, so much so that when a religion has lost all points of contact with esoterism[9] nothing remains but a 'dead letter' and a misunderstood formalism, for what had invigorated it was an effective communication with the spiritual center of the world, which can be established and consciously maintained only by esoterism and by the presence of a true and regular initiatic organization.

Now, to explain how the confusion we are attempting to dispel was able to assume an appearance convincing enough to be accepted by a rather large number of those who see things only superficially, we must note the following: it does seem that in some instances religious sects could have sprung from the thoughtless diffusion of fragments of misunderstood esoteric doctrine; but esoterism itself could in no way be held responsible for this kind of 'popularization' or 'profanation', in its etymological sense, which is contrary to its very essence and has never occurred except at the expense of doctrinal purity. Such a thing could happen only where these teachings were received with such little comprehension—due to a lack of preparation or perhaps even of 'qualification'—as to attribute to them a religious character entirely denaturing them;

8. A similar but more egregious error is to make initiation originate in something still more outward, as in a philosophy for example. The initiatic world exerts its 'invisible' influence on the profane world, directly or indirectly, but it can on the contrary never be influenced by it, apart from the abnormal case of certain seriously degenerate organizations.

9. It is necessary to add that when we say 'points of contact', this implies the existence of a limit common to both domains, by which their communication is established but which does not involve any confusion between them.

after all, does not error always proceed from an incomprehension or deformation of truth? Such was probably the case of the Albigensians, to give an example from the Middle Ages; yet if these were 'heretics', Dante and the Fedeli d'Amore, who kept strictly to the initiatic domain, were surely not;[10] and this example further elucidates the principal difference between sects and initiatic organizations. We should add that even if certain sects thus may have arisen out of a deviation from initiatic teaching, this very fact assumes the prior existence of this teaching and its independence with regard to the deviation; historically, as well as logically, the contrary opinion would seem to be completely untenable.

One question still remains to be examined: how and why have such deviations come about? This risks taking us too far afield, for obviously a complete answer would necessitate examining each particular case in detail; but we can say in general that on the surface it appears nearly impossible to prevent completely all divulging of initiatic doctrine regardless of the precautions taken; and if such disclosure is in any case only partial and fragmentary (bearing after all only on what is relatively most accessible) the resultant deformations are therefore all the more accentuated. But from another and more far-reaching point of view one could perhaps say that such things are necessary in certain circumstances as a mode of action that must be exerted on the march of events; in human history sects also have a role to play, even if only an inferior one, and we must not forget that every apparent disorder is in reality only one element in the total order of the universe. In any case, the disputes of the outside world lose much of their importance when seen from the point of view where all the oppositions that provoke them are reconciled, which is the case for the strictly esoteric and initiatic point of view; but precisely on this account it could never be the role of initiatic organizations to become involved in disputes, or, as it is commonly put, to 'take sides' in them, whereas sects, on the contrary, find themselves inevitably engaged in them by their very nature, and in the final analysis this is even perhaps their entire raison d'être.

10. Concerning this, see *The Esoterism of Dante*, especially chaps. 1 and 3.

12

INITIATIC
ORGANIZATIONS
AND SECRET SOCIETIES

THERE IS ANOTHER very frequent error concerning the nature of initiatic organizations that deserves closer attention than does the error of assimilating them to religious 'sects', for it relates to a point that seems particularly difficult for most of our contemporaries to understand, but is one that we consider absolutely essential. This is that initiatic organizations differ entirely in nature from all that in our day are called 'societies' or 'associations', these being defined by outward characteristics that may be completely absent from initiatic organizations, for even if such characteristics are sometimes introduced therein, they remain altogether accidental and, as we have said from the beginning, must not be regarded as anything but the effect of a kind of degeneration, or, if one prefers, of a contamination, in the sense of adopting profane or at least very exoteric forms with no real relation to the true aim of these organizations. Thus it is altogether erroneous to identify 'initiatic organizations' with 'secret societies', as is commonly done. First of all, it is very evident that the two expressions cannot in any way coincide in their application, for in fact there are many kinds of secret societies that have nothing initiatic about them since they can be formed by mere individual initiative and for any goal whatsoever, a point to which we shall have to return later. On the other hand, if it happens that an initiatic organization should accidentally take on the form of a society (and this is doubtless the principal cause of the error just mentioned), it would necessarily be secret in at least one of the meanings of this word, meanings not always distinguished with sufficient precision.

Indeed, it must be said that current usage appears to attach to the expression 'secret societies' several rather different meanings that do not seem necessarily connected, hence the divergence of opinion when it comes to knowing whether a designation really fits in this or that particular case. Some wish to restrict the expression to organizations that conceal their existence, or at least the names of their members; others extend it to organizations that are merely 'closed' or that keep secret only certain special forms, ritual or not, adopted as means of recognition for their members, or other things of this kind; and naturally the first group will protest when the second qualify as secret an association that cannot meet their own definition. We say 'protest' because all too often discussions of this kind are not at all of an entirely disinterested nature. When more or less openly declared adversaries of some organization call it secret, rightly or wrongly, they obviously have a polemical and more or less insulting intention, as if in their eyes the secret could only have 'unavowed' motives, and one can sometimes even discern a sort of thinly-veiled threat in the guise of a deliberate allusion to the 'illegality' of such an organization, for it is hardly necessary to say that it is always on the 'social' if not on the merely 'political' aspect of things that such discussions dwell. It is quite understandable under such conditions that members or partisans of the organization in question do their best to prove that the epithet 'secret' could not really be applied to it, and that for this reason they wish to accept only the most restricted definition, which most evidently cannot be applied to them. Furthermore, one can say in a general way that most of these discussions have no other cause than a lack of agreement about the meanings of the terms employed; but when, as is the case here, any interests are involved underneath this divergence in the use of words, it is very likely that the discussion will be pursued indefinitely without the adversaries ever arriving at an agreement. In any case, the contingencies that occur in such cases are surely very far from the initiatic domain, which is the only one to concern us; if we have felt obliged to say a few words about this here it is solely to clear the ground, as it were, and also to demonstrate that in all of the quarrels relating to secret societies, or to what are so called, either initiatic organizations are not involved, or at least it is not their initiatic character as such that is involved, something, moreover, that would be impossible for other more profound reasons that the rest of our account will better explain.

Placing ourselves entirely outside of such discussions and at the point of view of disinterested knowledge, we can say that whether or not an organization clothes itself in the particular and moreover wholly outward forms that permit it to be defined as a society, it can be qualified as secret in the widest sense of this word, and without attaching to it the least unfavorable intention,[1] when it possesses a secret of any kind whatsoever, whether by the very force of things or only in virtue of a more or less artificial and explicit convention. We think this definition is wide enough to include all the possible cases, from initiatic organizations furthest removed from any outward manifestation to mere societies of any purpose, political or otherwise, which, as we said above, have no initiatic or even traditional character at all. It is thus from within the domain it embraces, and basing ourselves as much as possible on its own terms, that we must make the necessary distinctions, and this in a twofold way: on the one hand, between organizations that are societies and those that are not; and on the other, between those that have an initiatic character and those that do not; for owing to the 'contamination' we have pointed out, the two distinctions do not exactly coincide; they would coincide only if historical contingencies had not led in certain cases to an intrusion of profane forms into organizations that by their origin and essential purpose are nonetheless of an incontestably initiatic nature.

There is no need to dwell at great length on the first of the two points just noted, for everyone knows well enough what a 'society' is, that is to say an association having statutes, rules, and meetings at fixed times and places, keeping a roll of its members, possessing archives, minutes of meetings, and other written documents; in a

---

1. In fact, the unfavorable intention commonly attached here proceeds solely from that characteristic trait of the modern mentality that we have elsewhere defined as the 'hatred of secrecy' under all its forms (*Reign of Quantity*, chap. 12).

word, hedged round by a more or less cumbersome exterior apparatus.[2] All of this, we repeat, is perfectly useless for an initiatic organization, which in the matter of outward forms and symbols has need of nothing but a certain collection of rites and symbols which, as with the teaching accompanying and explaining them, must be transmitted in a regular fashion by oral tradition. In this connection we will again recall that even if these things are sometimes set down in writing, this can only be as a mere 'mnemonic device' and could in no case obviate direct and oral transmission, since this latter alone permits communication of a spiritual influence which is the fundamental purpose of every initiatic organization. A profane person who knew all the rites from having read their descriptions in books would still not be initiated in any way, for it is quite evident that the spiritual influence attached to these rites would in no way have been transmitted to him.

An immediate consequence of what we have just said is that, as long as it does not take on the contingent form of a society with all the exterior manifestations that this implies, an initiatic organization is as it were 'ungraspable' by the profane world; and one can understand without difficulty that it leaves no trace accessible to the investigations of ordinary historians whose essential method is to refer solely to written documents, which in this case are nonexistent. On the other hand, every society, no matter how secret it may be, presents an 'outside' that is necessarily open to investigation by the profane, and through which it is always possible for them to acquire some measure of knowledge about it, even if they are incapable of penetrating to its more profound nature. It goes without saying that this last proviso concerns initiatic organizations that have taken on such a form, or, let us say freely, have degenerated into societies because of their circumstances and the environment in which they find themselves; and we will add that this phenomenon has never occurred so plainly as in the West, where it affects all

---

2. We must not forget to mention the 'financial' side required by this very apparatus, for it is all too well known that the question of 'dues' takes on considerable importance in all societies, including Western initiatic organizations that have acquired an exterior form.

that remains of organizations still able to claim an authentically initiatic character, even if, as cannot be pointed out too often, in their present state most of their members themselves have come to misunderstand this. We do not wish to investigate here the causes of this misunderstanding, which are diverse and numerous and derive in great part from the special nature of the modern mentality; we will only point out that this form of society may well be a factor, for since in this form the exterior inevitably takes on an importance out of proportion with its real value, the accidental ends up completely masking the essential; and what is more, the apparent similarities with profane societies can also occasion many errors concerning the true nature of these initiatic organizations.

We will give only one example of such misunderstandings, one that touches the very heart of our subject. Where a profane society is concerned, one can leave it as one entered it and thereupon find oneself purely and simply what one was before; a resignation or a dismissal suffices to break all ties which are obviously of a wholly outward nature and imply no profound modification of the being. On the contrary, once one has been admitted into an initiatic organization, whatever it may be, one can never by any means cease to be attached to it, for by the very fact that it consists essentially in the transmission of a spiritual influence, initiation is necessarily conferred once and for all and possesses a strictly ineffaceable character. Here we have a fact of an 'interior' order against which no administrative formality can do a thing. But wherever there is a society there are by that very fact administrative formalities through which there can be resignations and dismissals, by means of which one ceases to all appearances to be a part of the society in question; and one sees immediately the ambiguity that results when the society represents only the 'exteriority' of an initiatic organization. Thus it is necessary in all strictness to make a distinction between the society and the initiatic organization as such; and since, as we have said, the first is merely a contingent and 'superadded' form of which the second—in itself and in all that constitutes its essence—remains entirely independent, the application of this distinction really presents much less of a difficulty than might at first appear.

Another consequence to which we are logically led by these considerations is this: every society, even a secret one, can always be the target of attacks coming from the outside because it has in its makeup elements that situate it, so to speak, on the same level as these attacks; thus, in particular, it can be dissolved by the action of a political power. On the contrary, the initiatic organization by its very nature escapes such contingencies, and no external force can suppress it; in this sense, too, it is truly 'ungraspable'. In fact, since the quality inhering in its members cannot be lost nor the existence of the members be taken away, the organization preserves an effective existence as long as even one single member remains alive, and only the death of the last one will bring about its disappearance. But even this eventuality supposes that its authorized representatives, for reasons of which they alone can judge, will have decided not to ensure the continuation of the transmission of which they are the depositaries; and thus the sole possible cause of its suppression, or rather of its extinction, is necessarily found only within itself.

Finally, every initiatic organization is also 'ungraspable' from the point of view of its secret, this secret being such by nature and not by convention and consequently impenetrable by the profane; the converse is a self-contradictory hypothesis, for the true initiatic secret is nothing other than the 'incommunicable' of which initiation alone can give knowledge. But this relates rather to the second of the two distinctions indicated above, that between initiatic organizations and those secret societies devoid of any initiatic character at all. Moreover, this distinction seems apparent enough when we consider the different ends that each kind of organization proposes, though in fact the question is more complex than it may seem at first glance. There is one case, however, that brooks no doubt: if the origin of any organization whatsoever is fully documented as the work of individuals whose names can be cited and which thus possesses no link to tradition, one may rest assured, despite the claims, that there is absolutely nothing initiatic about the organization. The existence of ritual forms in some of these organizations changes nothing in this regard, for such forms, borrowed or imitated from initiatic organizations, are merely a parody lacking any real value;

and this applies not only to organizations of which the ends are wholly political or, more generally, 'social', in whatever sense can be attributed to this word, but also to all those modern constructions that we have called pseudo-initiatic, including those claiming a vague 'ideal' affiliation with some tradition.

On the other hand, there may be some doubt in the case of an organization of which the origin has something enigmatic and which cannot be linked to definite individuals; for even if its manifestations clearly have no initiatic character it may nonetheless be a deviation or a degeneration of something that was originally initiatic. This deviation, which occurs especially under the influence of social preoccupations, implies that incomprehension of the organization's primary and essential end has become general among its members; in practice, this incomprehension can be of a greater or lesser degree, and what still remains of initiatic organizations in the West represents in a certain way an intermediate stage in this respect. The extreme case is where the ritual and symbolic forms are preserved but no awareness remains of their true initiatic character, so much so that they are no longer interpreted except according to some contingent application. Whether this function be legitimate or not is in any case not the question, for degeneration consists precisely in the fact that nothing is envisaged beyond this application and the more or less exterior domain to which it is particularly related. It is quite clear that in such cases those who see things only 'from the outside' are unable to discern what is really involved or to distinguish between this kind of degenerate initiatic organization and the kind we first spoke about [that is, between initiatic organizations that have degenerated into mere societies and those, pseudo-initiatic or not, having origins that can be traced to individuals], all the more so in that once the former have lost all comprehension of any purpose except one similar to that for which the latter were artificially created, there results a sort of de facto 'affinity' by virtue of which both can find themselves in more or less direct contact, and even sometimes more or less inextricably mixed.

To better understand this point let us consider a pair of organizations that seem outwardly similar but nonetheless clearly differ in origin, and belong respectively to each of the two categories we have just distinguished: the Illuminati of Bavaria and the Carbonari. Regarding the first, their founders are known, as is the manner in which they elaborated its 'system' on their own initiative and with no connection whatsoever to anything already existing; and we also know the successive stages by which the grades and rituals were transmitted—though some of these were never practiced and existed only on paper—for everything was written down from the beginning as the founders' ideas developed and became more precise; this, indeed, was what led to the miscarriage of their plans, which, of course, referred exclusively to the social domain and did not in any respect go beyond it. There is thus no doubt that all of this was only the artificial production of certain individuals and that the forms they adopted were only a simulacrum or parody of initiation, for a traditional affiliation was lacking and a truly initiatic purpose was foreign to their preoccupations. With Carbonarism, on the contrary, it is obvious both that it is impossible to assign it an 'historical' origin of this sort and that its rituals clearly present the character of a 'craft initiation', as such akin to Masonry and the Compagnonnage. But whereas the latter have always retained a certain understanding of their initiatic character, however diminished through the intrusion of preoccupations of a contingent order and the ever greater part accorded them, it does seem—although one cannot be certain, since a few members who are not necessarily the apparent leaders can always prove an exception to the general incomprehension, without it being obvious[3]—that the degeneration of Carbonarism finally reached such a degree that it became no more than an association of political conspirators whose activities in the history of the nineteenth century are well known. The Carbonari then mingled with other organizations of quite recent formation that had never possessed any initiatic character at all, while, on the other hand, many of them at the same time also belonged to Masonry, which can be explained both by the affinity of these two organizations and by a certain degeneration of Masonry itself in the same direction, though not carried as far, as that of Carbonarism.

3. They cannot be reproached for such an attitude if the incomprehension had become such that it was in practical terms impossible to react against it.

As for the Illuminati, their relationship with Masonry had a completely different character: those who joined did so only with the firm intention of acquiring a preponderant influence and using it as an instrument for realizing their particular designs, an attempt that also failed, as did everything else; and one can see well enough by this how far from the truth are those who claim to make of the Illuminati themselves a 'Masonic' organization. Let us add further that the ambiguity of the name 'Illuminati' should give us no illusions. It is used here only in a strictly 'rationalist' sense, and it must not be forgotten that in eighteenth-century Germany the term 'enlightenment' had a meaning almost equivalent to that of 'philosophy' in France, which is to say that nothing more profane and even more formally contrary to any initiatic or even merely traditional spirit than this can be conceived.

Let us open yet another parenthesis regarding this last remark. If it happens that some 'philosophical' and more or less 'rationalist' ideas infiltrate an initiatic organization, this must be seen only as the effect of individual or collective error on the part of its members due to their incapacity to understand the true nature of the organization and thus to secure themselves from all profane 'contamination'. This error of course in no way affects the very principle of the organization, but is one of the symptoms of that actual degeneration of which we have spoken, regardless of how far this may have advanced. And we can say as much of 'sentimentalism' and of 'moralism' in all their forms, which are no less profane in nature, all of this being generally linked more or less closely to a predominance of social preoccupations. But it is especially when these preoccupations take on a specifically 'political' form in the narrowest sense of the word that the degeneration risks becoming practically irremediable. One of the strangest phenomena of this kind is the penetration of 'democratic' ideas into Western initiatic organizations (here we are naturally thinking of Masonry above all, or at least of certain of its factions) without their members appearing to recognize that this is a pure and simple contradiction, and indeed in two respects, for by very definition every initiatic organization is formally opposed to the notion of the 'democratic' or the 'egalitarian', firstly with respect to the profane world, in regard to which it is, in the most exact acceptation of the word, a separate and closed 'elite', and secondly in itself, by virtue of the hierarchy of grades and functions that it nec-essarily establishes among its own members. This phenomenon is but one of the manifestations of the deviation of the modern West-ern spirit which spreads and penetrates everywhere, even where it ought to encounter the most unyielding resistance; moreover, this does not apply to the initiatic point of view alone, but applies equally to the religious point of view, that is, in sum, to all that has a truly traditional character.

Thus, in addition to organizations that have remained purely initiatic there are others that for one or another reason have degenerated or deviated more or less completely but that nonetheless remain initiatic at their core, however misunderstood this core may be in the present conditions. Then there are the counterfeits or caricatures, that is to say the pseudo-initiatic organizations; and finally there are the more or less secret organizations that harbor no initiatic claims and of which the ends obviously have nothing to do with this domain. But it must be understood that pseudo-initiatic organizations, whatever the appearances, are really just as profane as this last group and that both belong together and stand in opposition to initiatic organizations, whether these be pure or 'contaminated' with profane influences.

But to all this it is necessary to add still another category, that of organizations belonging to the 'counter-initiation', which in the contemporary world certainly have a much more considerable importance than is commonly supposed. We shall limit ourselves here simply to mentioning them—failing which our enumeration would be gravely lacking—and only note a new complication that results from their existence. In certain cases it happens that they exercise a more or less direct influence on profane organizations, especially pseudo-initiatic organizations,[4] and this raises one more difficulty in determining the true character of this or that organization. But of course we do not have to occupy ourselves here with the examination of particular cases, and it suffices to explain clearly the general classification that was to be established.

4. Cf. *Reign of Quantity,* chap. 36.

However, this is not all, for there are organizations that, despite having only a contingent purpose, nonetheless possess a true traditional affiliation because they proceed from initiatic organizations of which they are, as it were, only an emanation, and by which they are 'invisibly' directed even when their apparent leaders are unaware of it. This is particularly true among Far-Eastern secret organizations: formed solely for a special purpose, these organizations generally have only a temporary existence and disappear without trace once their mission is accomplished. But they really represent the last and most outward rung of a hierarchy that rises ever closer to those initiatic organizations that are purest and most inaccessible to the gaze of the profane world. Here there is no longer any question of a degeneration of initiatic organizations, but rather of formations expressly willed by them—although they themselves do not descend to this contingent level and intervene in the action exercised there—for ends that are naturally very different from what a superficial observer might see or suppose. Recalling what was already said above on this subject, we see that the most exterior of these organizations can sometimes find themselves opposed to and even struggling against each other while nonetheless sharing a common direction or inspiration, for this direction lies beyond the domain of their opposition, in which alone it is valid; and perhaps this situation is found in places other than the Far East, although such a hierarchization of superposed organizations is found nowhere more clearly or more completely than in the Taoist tradition. In this tradition there are organizations of 'mixed' character, if one may so express it, which cannot be said to be either strictly initiatic or merely profane since their affiliation with superior organizations confers on them a participation, even if indirect and unconscious, in a tradition whose essence is purely initiatic;[5] and something of this essence is always present in their rites and symbols for those who know how to penetrate their deepest meaning.

All the categories of organizations that we have considered have nothing in common but the sole fact of harboring a secret, whatever

---

5. Let us recall that Taoism represents solely the esoteric side of the Far-Eastern tradition, its exoteric side being represented by Confucianism.

its nature may be; and it goes without saying that this secret can differ greatly from one category of organization to another. There is obviously no possible comparison between the true initiatic secret and a political project that is kept hidden, or the dissembling of an organization's existence and that of the names of its members for reasons of mere prudence. And let us not even speak of the many fantastic groups of our day, especially in Anglo-Saxon countries, which 'ape' the forms of initiatic organizations but conceal absolutely nothing and which truly lack any importance and even any meaning, pretending to keep a secret that has no serious justification. This last case holds no interest except to illustrate clearly the current misunderstanding in the mind of the general public about the nature of the initiatic secret, which they imagine refers simply to rituals and to words and signs used as means of recognition, which would make it as outward and artificial a secret as any other, that is to say, a secret that exists finally only by convention. Now, if such a secret in fact exists in most initiatic organizations, it is only a wholly secondary and accidental element and in reality has no value except as a symbol of the true initiatic secret, which is itself such by the very nature of things and which in consequence could never be betrayed in any way since it is of a purely interior order and, as we have already said, lies strictly in the 'incommunicable'.

13

THE INITIATIC SECRET

ALTHOUGH we have just indicated the essential nature of the initiatic secret,[1] we must be even more precise in order to distinguish it without any possible ambiguity from all other kinds of more or less outward secrets that are encountered in the many organizations that can for this reason be qualified as 'secret' in a more general sense. We have said that, for us, this designation signifies only that such organizations possess a secret of some sort, and also that, depending on the goal they propose for themselves, this secret can naturally refer to the most diverse things and take the most varied forms; but in all cases, secrets of any kind other than the properly initiatic secret always have a conventional character, by which we mean that they are secrets only by virtue of a more or less formal convention and not by the very nature of things. The initiatic secret, on the contrary, is such because it cannot but be so, since it consists exclusively of the 'inexpressible', which consequently is necessarily also the 'incommunicable'; thus, if initiatic organizations are secret, this character has nothing artificial about it and does not result from a more or less arbitrary decision by anyone. This point is particularly important for distinguishing, on the one hand, initiatic organizations from all other secret organizations of whatever kind, and on the other, within initiatic organizations themselves, what is essential from all that might accidentally attach itself thereto. Let us therefore develop the consequences of this a little.

The first of these consequences, which we have already noted, is that whereas every secret of an exterior order can always be betrayed,

1. See also *Reign of Quantity*, chap. 12.

the initiatic secret can never be betrayed since in itself and in a way by definition it is inaccessible to and ungraspable by the profane and so cannot be penetrated by them, since knowledge of it can only be the consequence of initiation itself. In fact this secret is of such a nature that words cannot express it, which is why, as we shall explain more completely in what follows, the initiatic teaching can only use rites and symbols that suggest rather than express, in the ordinary sense of the word. Properly speaking, what is transmitted by initiation is not the secret itself, since this is incommunicable, but the spiritual influence that the rites vehicle and that makes possible the interior work by means of which, with the symbols as base and support, each one will attain that secret and penetrate it more or less completely, more or less profoundly, according to the measure of his own possibilities of comprehension and realization.

Whatever one may think of other secret organizations, initiatic organizations can in any case not be reproached for having this character, since their secret is not something that they hide voluntarily for some reason, legitimate or otherwise, and always more or less subject to discussion and evaluation as is all that proceeds from the profane point of view, but is something no one is empowered to unveil and communicate to another, even should he so wish. As for the fact that these organizations are 'closed', that is, that they do not admit everyone indiscriminately, this is explained simply by the first condition of initiation described above, the necessity of possessing certain particular 'qualifications' lacking which no real benefit can be derived from attachment to such an organization. Moreover, when an initiatic organization becomes too 'open' and insufficiently strict in this respect, it runs the risk of degenerating through the incomprehension of those whom it thus thoughtlessly admits, who, especially when they become the majority, do not fail to introduce all sorts of profane opinions and to divert its activity toward goals that have nothing in common with the initiatic domain, as one sees only too often in what still remains of this kind of organization in the Western world today.

Thus a second consequence of what we stated at the beginning is that the initiatic secret in itself, and the 'closed' character of the organizations that possess it (or, to speak more exactly, that possess the means whereby it is possible for those who are 'qualified' to gain access to it), are two completely different things and must never be confused. Concerning the first, its essence and importance are completely misunderstood if reasons of 'prudence' are invoked, as is sometimes done; as to the second, which pertains to the nature of men in general and not to that of initiatic organizations, one can, on the contrary, speak of 'prudence' up to a certain point in the sense of an organization defending itself, not against 'indiscretions', which are impossible in regard to its essential nature, but against that danger of degeneration of which we have just spoken. Still, this is not the primary reason, which is nothing other than the perfect uselessness of admitting individuals for whom initiation would never be anything but a 'dead letter' or empty formality without any real effect because they are, as it were, impervious to the spiritual influence. As for 'prudence' toward the outer world, as it is most often understood, this can only be an altogether accessory consideration, even though it may certainly be legitimate in the face of a more or less consciously hostile environment, for profane incomprehension rarely stops short at a kind of indifference and changes only too easily into a hatred of which the manifestations present a danger that certainly has nothing illusory about it. But this could not affect the initiatic organization itself, which, as we have said, is truly 'ungraspable' as such. Thus, precautions in this regard will impose themselves to the extent that the organization becomes more 'exteriorized' and therefore less purely initiatic; moreover, it is evident that it is only in this case that it can find itself in direct contact with the profane world, which otherwise would only ignore it purely and simply. We will not speak here of a danger of another order that can result from the existence of what we have called the counter-initiation and that mere external measures of prudence could not prevent in any case; such measures are effective only against the profane world, whose reactions, we repeat, are only to be feared to the extent that the organization has adopted an outward form such as that of a 'society', or has been drawn more or less completely into an activity exercised outside the initiatic domain, all of which can only be regarded as having a merely accidental and contingent character.[2]

This brings us to yet another consequence of the nature of the initiatic secret. It can in fact happen that, besides the secret that alone is essential to it, an initiatic organization may also possess, secondarily and without in any way losing its own character, other secrets that are not of the same order but are more or less exterior and contingent; and it is these purely accessory secrets that, being perforce the only ones apparent to the outside observer, are most likely to provoke various confusions. These secrets can come from the 'contamination' we spoke of, understanding by this the accretion of goals having nothing to do with initiation and which may be given more or less importance since in this kind of degeneration all degrees are obviously possible; but this is not the only case, and it may just as well happen that such secrets are related to contingent though legitimate applications of the initiatic doctrine itself, applications that it is judged well to 'reserve' for reasons that can be very different and that would have to be determined for each particular case. The secrets we allude to here are more particularly those concerning the traditional arts and sciences, and what can be said most generally in this regard is that, since these arts and sciences cannot be truly understood outside of the initiation that constitutes their principle, their 'vulgarization' can only lead to problems, for it would amount inevitably to a deformation or even a denaturation of precisely the kind that gave birth to the profane arts and sciences, as we have explained on other occasions.

In this same category of accessory and non-essential secrets must be placed another kind, one very widespread in initiatic organizations and which most commonly occasions among the profane an error to which we have previously called attention. This is the secret that relates either to the entirety of the rites and symbols in use in

---

2. What we have just said applies to the profane world reduced to itself, if we may express ourselves thus; but it is appropriate to add that in certain cases it can also serve as the unconscious instrument for action by the representatives of the counter-initiation.

these organizations, or still more particularly, and also in a stricter manner than usual, to certain words and signs used as 'means of recognition' to permit members to distinguish one another from the profane. It goes without saying that any secret of this nature has only a conventional and wholly relative value, and that by the very fact that it concerns itself with exterior forms it can always be discovered or betrayed, a risk that naturally occurs all the more easily as the organization is less rigorously 'closed'. Thus we must emphasize not only that this secret can never be confused with the true initiatic secret except by those who lack even the slightest idea of its nature, but even that it has nothing essential about it, so much so that its presence or absence could not define an organization as either possessing or lacking an initiatic character. In fact, the same thing or something equivalent also exists in most other secret organizations that are in no way initiatic, although the reasons for this are then different. It may be a matter of imitating the most outward appearance of initiatic organizations, as with those organizations we have qualified as pseudo-initiatic and certain fantastic groups that do not even merit this name; or it may simply be a matter of safeguarding themselves against indiscretions in the most common sense of this word, as happens especially with political associations, something that can be understood without the least difficulty. On the other hand, the existence of a secret of this kind is in no way necessary for initiatic organizations, for which its importance is all the less to the degree that they have a purer and more elevated character because they are then the freer from all outward forms and from all that is not truly essential. Something thus occurs that might at first appear paradoxical, though it is really quite logical: an organization uses such 'means of recognition' because of its 'closed' character, but it is precisely in those organizations that are most 'closed' that these means are sometimes reduced to the point of disappearing altogether because they are no longer needed, their usefulness being directly linked to a certain degree of 'exteriority' in the organization having recourse to them. This usefulness attains its maximum, as it were, when the organization acquires a 'semi-profane' aspect, of which the form of a 'society' is the most typical example, for it is then that its occasions for contact with the exterior world are most numerous and extensive, and, consequently, that it is most important for it to distinguish itself therefrom by means that are themselves outward.

The existence of such an exterior and secondary secret in the most widespread initiatic organizations is justified by yet other reasons. Some attribute to it above all a 'pedagogical' role, so to speak; in other words, the 'discipline of the secret' constitutes a sort of 'training' or exercise that is part of the method of these organizations—and this can be seen in a way as an attenuated and restricted form of the 'discipline of silence' that was used in certain ancient esoteric schools, particularly among the Pythagoreans.[3] This point of view is certainly correct, on condition that it not be exclusive; and it should be remarked that in this respect the value of the secret is completely independent of the value of the things it bears upon. As far as 'discipline' is concerned, keeping a secret about the most insignificant things will be just as efficacious as keeping a secret that is really important in itself. This should be a sufficient response to the profane who, in this connection, accuse initiatic organizations of 'puerility' since they fail to understand that the words or signs on which secrecy is imposed have their own symbolic value. If they cannot follow as far as this last consideration, at least the foregoing should be within their reach and certainly does not require a great effort to comprehend.

But in reality there is a deeper reason based precisely on the symbolic character just mentioned which makes what are called 'means of recognition' not merely this but also something more. They are truly symbols like any other, and their meaning must be meditated on and penetrated in the same way; thus they form an integral part

---

3. *Disciplina secreti* or *disciplina arcani*, as it was also called in the Church of the first centuries, something that certain enemies of the 'secret' seem to forget; but it should be noted that in Latin the word *disciplina* usually signifies 'teaching', which is its etymological meaning, and even, by derivation, 'science' or 'doctrine', whereas what is called 'discipline' in French has value only as a preparatory means for an end which may be knowledge, as is the case here, but which may also be something completely different, for example, something merely 'moral'. In fact it is this last meaning that it is in fact most commonly given in the profane world. [The same can be said of the word 'discipline' in current English. ED.]

of the initiatic teaching. It is the same, moreover, for all the forms used by initiatic organizations and, more generally yet, for all that have a traditional character (including religious forms): they are fundamentally always something other than they appear from the outside, and this is what essentially distinguishes them from profane forms, where the outward appearance is everything and does not conceal any reality of another order. From this point of view the secret in question is itself a symbol of the true initiatic secret, which is obviously much more than a mere 'pedagogical' means;[4] but here, of course, no less than elsewhere, the symbol must not be confused with what is symbolized, and this is the confusion effected by profane ignorance because it does not see beyond appearances and does not even imagine that there can be anything besides what strikes the senses, which is practically equivalent to the pure and simple negation of all symbolism.

In conclusion, let us point out a final consideration that we may yet develop further. The outward secret, where it exists in initiatic organizations, is properly part of the ritual since its object is communicated, under the corresponding obligation of silence, in the very course of the initiation into or at the completion of each degree. Thus this secret is not only a symbol, as we have just said, but also a true rite, with all the virtue belonging to it as such; and besides, rite and symbol are in truth always closely linked by their very nature, as we shall explain more amply in what follows.

---

4. It would be possible to go into this in somewhat more detail if one wished; for example, the 'sacred words', which must never be uttered, are a particularly clear symbol of the 'ineffable' or the 'inexpressible'. Moreover, something similar can be found in exoterism, for example the Tetragrammaton in the Jewish tradition. In the same order of ideas one could also show that certain signs are related to the 'localization' of subtle centers in the human being of which the awakening constitutes one of the means of acquiring effective initiatic knowledge according to certain methods (notably the 'tantric' methods in the Hindu tradition).

14

INITIATIC
QUALIFICATIONS

WE MUST NOW come back to the questions concerning the first and preliminary condition of initiation, that is to what are called initiatic 'qualifications'. Indeed, it is hard to treat this subject completely, but we can at least bring to it a few clarifications. First of all, it must be well understood that these qualifications belong exclusively to the individual domain. Indeed, if only the personality or the 'Self' were considered,[1] there would be no difference between beings in this respect, and all without exception would be equally qualified. But the question presents quite another face by the fact that the individuality must necessarily be taken as a means and a support of initiatic realization, and thus must possess the necessary aptitudes for this role, which is not always the case. The individuality in a way is only the instrument of the true being, though if this instrument has certain defects it can be somewhat or even altogether unusable for what is needed. Besides, there is nothing to be astonished at if one reflects that, even in profane activities (or at least what have become such in the present epoch), what is possible for one individual is not possible for another, and that, for example, the exercise of any particular craft requires certain special aptitudes, both mental and physical. The essential difference in this case is that the activity in question belongs exclusively to the individual domain which it does not transcend in any way or in any respect, whereas with initiation the result to be attained is, on the contrary, beyond

---

1. On Guénon's use of the terms 'personality', 'Self', 'individuality', and 'ego' see *Man and His Becoming according to the Vedānta*, chap. 2. ED.

the limits of the individuality; but again, this must be taken as the starting-point, and this is an inescapable precondition.

We can also say that the individual undertaking the work of initiatic realization must perforce start from a certain state of manifestation, the one in which he is presently situated, and that this state includes a whole cluster of determinate conditions, both those inherent to that state and generally defining it, and those within this same state that are particular to the individual and distinguish him from all others. It is evident that it is the latter that must be considered with respect to initiatic qualifications because they are by very definition not common to all individuals but properly characterize only those who belong, at least virtually, to the 'elite' understood in the sense in which we have often used this word elsewhere, a sense that we will explain even more precisely later in order to show how it is directly related to the question of initiation.

Now it should be clearly understood that the individuality must be taken here as it is in fact, with all its constituent elements, and that there may be qualifications that concern each of these elements, including the corporeal element itself, which from this point of view must in no way be treated as something indifferent or negligible. Perhaps there would be no need to stress this were we not confronted by the grossly oversimplified idea of the human being held by modern Westerners. Not only do they consider the individuality to be the whole being, but they reduce it to two parts that they suppose to be separate from each other, one being the body and the other something rather ill-defined that is indifferently designated by the most varied and sometimes least appropriate names. But the reality is altogether different: the multiple elements of the individuality, however one may wish to classify them, are not at all thus isolated from each other but form a whole in which there cannot be a radical and irreducible heterogeneity; and all these elements, the body as well as the others, are in the same way manifestations or expressions of the being in the different modalities of the individual domain. Among these modalities there are correspondences, so that what happens in one normally has repercussion in the others, with the result that on the one hand the state of the body can favorably or unfavorably influence the other modalities, and on the other, since the inverse is just as true (and even truer, since the possibilities of the corporeal modality are the most restricted), the body can furnish signs that manifest states of the other modalities,[2] and it is clear that each of these two complementary considerations has its importance in regard to initiatic qualifications. All of this would be perfectly obvious if the specifically Western and modern notion of 'matter', Cartesian dualism, and more or less 'mechanistic' ideas had not so obscured these things for most of our contemporaries,[3] and these are the contingent circumstances that oblige us to tarry over such elementary considerations which otherwise could be stated in a few words without having to add the least explanation.

It goes without saying that the essential qualification, which takes precedence over all the others, is that of a greater or lesser 'intellectual horizon'; but it can happen that intellectual possibilities existing virtually in an individual are prevented from developing, either temporarily or even definitively, because of the individual's inferior elements (elements at once psychic and corporeal). This is the first reason for what one could call secondary qualifications; and there is also a second reason following immediately from what was just said: in these inferior elements, which are the most accessible to observation, one may find marks of certain intellectual limitations, and in this case the secondary qualifications become, as it were, the symbolic equivalents of the fundamental qualification itself. In the first case, on the contrary, it may happen that they do not always have an equal importance; thus there may be impediments opposing any initiation, even simply virtual, or only an effective initiation, or again the passage to particular more or less elevated degrees, or finally only the exercise of certain functions within an initiatic organization (for one can be qualified to receive a spiritual influence without being for this reason necessarily qualified to transmit it); and it must also be added that there are special impediments that concern only certain forms of initiation.

On this last point it suffices to recall that the diversity of modes of initiation, whether among different traditional forms or within one

---

2. Whence the science that, in the Islamic tradition, is called *ilm-ul-firāsah*.
3. On all these questions see *Reign of Quantity.*

and the same traditional form, has for its goal precisely a response to the diversity of individual aptitudes; such a diversity of modes would obviously be to no purpose if a single mode were equally suitable to all who were generally qualified to receive initiation. Since things are not so, each initiatic organization must have its particular 'technique', and it can naturally admit only those able to conform to it and receive from it an effective benefit, which implies, with respect to qualifications, the application of a whole order of special rules valid only for the organization in question, and which, for those who will be rejected thereby, in no way excludes the possibility of finding an equivalent initiation elsewhere, provided that they possess the general qualifications that are strictly indispensable in all cases. One of the clearest examples we can give of this is the fact that there exist forms of initiation that are exclusively masculine, while there are others to which women can be admitted in the same way as men,[4] from which it follows that there is a certain qualification required in one case but not in the other, and that this difference belongs to the particular modes of initiation in question, a point to which we shall return later, for we have noted that this fact is generally very poorly understood in our time.

Where a traditional social organization exists, even in the outward order, each person occupies the place that befits his own individual nature, and, if he is qualified, this very fact allows him more easily to find the mode of initiation that corresponds to his own possibilities. Thus if we consider the caste system from this point of view, the initiation of the Kshatriyas cannot be identical with that of the Brahmins, and so forth;[5] and in a yet more particular way, a certain form of initiation can be linked to the practice of a given craft and cannot be completely effective unless the craft practiced by the individual is indeed that to which he is destined by the aptitudes inherent in his very nature, so that these aptitudes will also be at the same time an integral part of the special qualifications required for the corresponding form of initiation.

4. In antiquity there were also exclusively feminine forms of initiation.
5. We shall return to this further on in connection with sacerdotal and royal initiation.

On the contrary, where nothing is any longer organized according to traditional and normal rules, as with the modern West, there results a confusion that extends to all domains and that inevitably entails many complications and difficulties regarding the precise determination of initiatic qualifications, since the place of the individual in society no longer has, then, anything but a remote connection to his nature, with only its most outward and least important aspects most often taken into consideration, that is to say those aspects that really have no value, even a secondary one, from the initiatic point of view. Another cause of difficulties, one somewhat responsible for this situation, is the loss of the traditional sciences, for the information supplied by some of them could furnish the means of recognizing an individual's true nature, and once these criteria are lacking, no other means can make up for them entirely and with perfect exactitude, since whatever else may be done will always include a greater or lesser share of 'empiricism', which can lead to many errors. In the final analysis, one of the principal reasons for the degeneration of certain initiatic organizations is the admission of unqualified individuals, whether through mere ignorance of the rules that should eliminate them or through the impossibility of applying these rules with any certainty. The latter is indeed one of the factors that most contributes to this degeneration, and if it becomes general it can even finally lead to the complete ruin of the organization.

After these general considerations, we ought to give some well-defined examples of the conditions required for gaining access to a given initiatic form, and to show in each case their meaning and true importance in order to further clarify the real significance of secondary qualifications. But, when it must be addressed to Westerners, such an exposition becomes very difficult in view of the fact that even in the most favorable cases they are familiar with only a very limited number of initiatic forms, and references to all others risk remaining almost wholly misunderstood. Again, all that remains in the West of ancient organizations of this kind is in all respects very much diminished, as we have already said many times before, and it is easy to confirm this more particularly in regard to the question now at hand. If certain qualifications are still required in these organizations, it is more out of habit than from any understanding of their purpose; and in these conditions it is not surprising if the members of these organizations sometimes protest against the retention of such qualifications in which their ignorance sees only a sort of historical remnant, a vestige from a state of things that has long since disappeared—in a word, a pure and simple 'anachronism'. Nonetheless, since one is obliged to take as a starting-point what is most immediately to hand, even this might provide the occasion for information that, despite everything, is not without interest, and that, although having in our eyes only an 'illustrative' value, can still provoke reflections of a broader application than might at first appear.

There are scarcely any initiatic organizations in the West that can still claim an authentic traditional affiliation (outside of which condition, let us recall once more, there can only be a question of pseudo-initiation) other than the Compagnonnage and Masonry, that is to say initiatic forms based, at least at their origins, essentially on the practice of a craft and consequently characterized by particular symbolic and ritual methods directly related to this craft itself.[6] However, there is a distinction to be made here: in the Compagnonnage, the initial link with the craft has always been maintained, whereas in Masonry it has in fact disappeared, whence the danger in this case of a complete misunderstanding of the need for certain conditions that are nonetheless inherent to this initiatic form itself. Indeed, in the former case it is evident that the conditions necessary for the craft to be effectively and indeed fully practiced can never have been forgotten, even if nothing more than this is considered— that is, even if one takes into account only its outward purpose and forgets its more profound and properly initiatic purpose. On the contrary, where this deeper purpose is no less forgotten and where the outward purpose itself no longer exists, it is natural enough (which, of course, is not to say legitimate) that the persistence of such conditions comes to be seen as an altogether unnecessary and annoying restriction, even an injustice (a notion much abused in

---

6. We have described the principles underlying the relationships between initiation and the crafts in *Reign of Quantity*, chap. 8.

our day in consequence of an 'egalitarianism' destructive to the notion of the 'elite') imposed on recruitment, a recruitment that the mania for 'proselytism' and the democratic superstition of the majority—traits very characteristic of the modern Western mind— wishes to make as broad as possible, something that, as we have already said, is truly one of the most certain and most irremediable causes of degeneration for an initiatic organization.

In the final analysis, what is forgotten in such cases is simply this: if the initiatic ritual takes the craft as a 'support' in such a way that it is so to speak derived from it by an appropriate transposition (though in the beginning things were no doubt envisaged in reverse, for from the traditional point of view the craft is really only a contingent application of the principles to which the initiation directly relates), then in order to be really and fully valid the accomplishment of this ritual requires conditions that include those required by the practice of the craft itself, for the same transposition applies equally here in virtue of the correspondences that exist between different modalities of the being; and from this it is clear that, as we said above, whoever is qualified for initiation in a general way is not thereby qualified unreservedly for any initiatic form whatsoever. We should add to this that the misunderstanding of this fundamental point, which leads to the wholly profane reduction of such qualifications to mere corporative rules, appears, at least in Masonry, to be linked rather closely to a misunderstanding of the true meaning of the word 'operative', regarding which we will later have to provide the necessary clarification, for it raises quite broad questions about initiation.

Thus, if Masonic initiation excludes women in particular (which, as we have already said, does not mean that they are unqualified for every initiation) as well as men with certain infirmities, this is not merely because those who are admitted used to have to carry burdens or climb scaffolds, as some assure us with a disconcerting naiveté; rather, the Masonic initiation itself could not be valid for such people and could have no effect because of their lack of qualification. The first thing that can be said here is that even if the link with the craft has been broken with respect to outward practice, it nonetheless continues in a more essential way insofar as it remains necessarily inscribed in the very form of this initiation, for if this connection were eliminated, the initiation would no longer be Masonic but something completely different; moreover, since it would be impossible to substitute legitimately another traditional filiation for the one that actually exists, there would really no longer be any initiation at all. This is why, wherever there still exists at least a certain more or less obscure consciousness—for lack of a more effective understanding—of the true value of ritual forms, the conditions we are speaking of continue to be considered as integral parts of the *landmarks* (this English term, in its 'technical' acceptation, has no exact equivalent in French) that can in no circumstances be modified, and the suppression or neglect of which would risk entailing a veritable initiatic nullity.[7]

There is still more: if we closely examine the list of bodily defects considered to be impediments to initiation, it will be noted how some do not seem outwardly very serious and, in any case, would not prevent a man from practicing the craft of the builder.[8] And so this, too, is only a partial explanation, although exact in the measure to which it applies, for, besides the conditions required by the craft, the initiation requires others having nothing to do with these but relating solely to the modalities of the ritual work considered not only in its 'materiality', so to speak, but above all as having to produce effective results for the one who accomplishes them. This will appear all the more clearly when, from among the diverse formulations of the *landmarks* (for although in principle not written down, they have nevertheless often been the object of more or less detailed enumerations), we go back to the most ancient ones, that is, to an epoch when the things in question were still known, and even, for some at least, known in a way that was not merely theoretical or 'speculative' but really 'operative' in the true sense to which we alluded above. This examination reveals something that many today would surely think altogether extraordinary if they were capable of

---

7. These *landmarks* are considered to have existed *from time immemorial*, that is, it is impossible to assign to them any definite historical origin.

8. Thus, to give a precise example of this type, it is hard to see how a stutterer could be impeded by his infirmity in the practice of this craft.

noticing it: the impediments to initiation in Masonry coincide almost exactly with what constitute impediments to ordination in the Catholic church.[9]

This last point is one that requires some commentary in order to be well understood, for at first one might be tempted to suppose that we have here a certain confusion between things of different orders, all the more so in that we have often insisted on the essential distinction that exists between the initiatic and religious domains, and that consequently must also be found between the rites belonging to each respectively. However, there is no need to reflect very long in order to understand that there must be general laws conditioning the accomplishment of rites of whatever order they may be, for in the end it is always a matter of bringing into play certain spiritual influences, although the goals naturally differ according to the case. Moreover, it could also be objected that in the case of ordination what is important is the aptitude for fulfilling certain functions,[10] whereas the qualifications required for receiving initiation are distinct from those that might be necessary to exercise in addition a function in the initiatic organization (a function that principally concerns the transmission of the spiritual influence); and it is precisely not from the point of view of functions that the similarity is really applicable. What must be taken into account is that, in a religious organization like Catholicism, only the priest actively accomplishes the rites, whereas the lay people participate in them only in a 'receptive' mode; on the contrary, activity in the ritual is always and without any exception an essential element of every initiatic method, so that this method necessarily implies the possibility of accomplishing such an activity. In the final analysis, then, it is this active accomplishment of rites that, besides the properly intellectual qualification, requires certain secondary qualifications, varying in part according to the special character assumed by these rites in this

9. This is so in particular for what in the eighteenth century was called the 'rule of the letter B', that is, for impediments that in both cases consist of a series of infirmities and bodily defects of which the names in French, by a rather curious coincidence, all begin with the letter 'B'.

10. As we said before, this case is the only one where particular qualifications are required in a traditional organization of the exoteric type.

or that initiatic form, but among which the absence of certain bodily defects always plays an important role, whether these defects be a direct impediment to the accomplishment of the rites or the outward sign of corresponding defects in the subtle elements of the being. It is this latter conclusion above all that we wished to draw from all these considerations, and what seems to relate more particularly to the case of Masonic initiation has been only the most convenient way for us to explain these things, which we must make even clearer with the help of some particular examples of impediments due to bodily defects or to psychic defects outwardly manifested by them.

If we are to consider infirmities or merely bodily defects as outward signs of certain psychic imperfections, it will be fitting to make a distinction between defects that the being exhibits from birth or that develop naturally over the course of its existence as a consequence of a certain predisposition, and those that are merely the result of some accident. It is evident that the first reveal something that more strictly inheres in the very nature of the being, and that consequently is more serious from our present point of view, although, since nothing can happen to a being that does not really correspond to some more or less essential element of its nature, even apparently accidental infirmities cannot be considered entirely indifferent in this respect. From another point of view, if these same defects are considered as direct impediments to the accomplishment of rites or to their effective action on the being, the distinction we have just made no longer applies; but it must be clearly understood that defects that do not constitute impediments of this kind are nonetheless impediments to initiation for the first reason, and sometimes even more absolute impediments, for they express an inward 'deficiency' that makes the being unfit for any initiation, whereas there can be infirmities that impede only the 'technical' methods peculiar to this or that initiatic form.

Some may be astonished that accidental infirmities thus correspond to something in the very nature of the being affected by them; but this is after all only a direct consequence of the real relationships the being has with the environment in which it manifests itself: all the relationships among beings manifested in one and the same world, or what comes to the same thing, all their reciprocal actions and reactions, can only be real if they are the expression of something that belongs to the nature of each of them. In other words, everything a being undergoes, as well as all that it does, constitutes a 'modification' of that being, and must necessarily correspond to one of the possibilities in its nature, so that there can be nothing that is purely accidental if this word be understood in the sense of 'extrinsic', as it commonly is. The difference is thus only one of degree, for certain modifications represent something more important or deeper than others, so that there are as it were hierarchical values to observe in this respect among the different possibilities of the individual domain; but strictly speaking, nothing is indifferent or without meaning because, in the end, a being can receive from outside only 'occasions' for realizing, in manifested mode, the virtualities that it first carries within itself.

It might also seem strange to those who judge by appearances that certain infirmities that are hardly serious from an outward point of view should always and everywhere have been considered as impediments to initiation, a typical case of this kind being stuttering. It suffices to reflect only a little to realize that in this case we find both impediments we have mentioned. First there is the fact that the ritual 'technique' almost always includes the pronunciation of certain verbal formulas which must naturally be correct above all in order to be valid, something stuttering does not permit in those afflicted by it; and, secondly, there is in this infirmity the manifest sign of a certain 'arrhythmia' in the being, if we can use this word; indeed, the two things are closely linked, for the very use of the formulas we have just alluded to is really only one application of the 'science of rhythm' to the initiatic method, so that the incapacity to pronounce them correctly depends in the final analysis on an internal 'arrhythmia' of the being.

This 'arrhythmia' is itself only one particular case of disharmony or disequilibrium in the constitution of the individual, and one can say in a general way that if all bodily anomalies that are the mark of a more or less accentuated disequilibrium are not always absolute impediments (for obviously there are many degrees to observe), they are at least unfavorable signs in a candidate for initiation.

Moreover, it can happen that such anomalies, which are not properly speaking infirmities, are not of a nature to oppose the accomplishment of the ritual work, but if they become serious enough to indicate a deep and irremediable disequilibrium, this may itself suffice to disqualify the candidate, as we have already explained above. Examples are noticeable asymmetries of the face or limbs; but of course, if it were a matter of very minor asymmetries, they might not even really be considered anomalies, for in fact no one exhibits an exact bodily symmetry in every respect. Besides, this can be interpreted to signify that, at least in the present state of humanity, no individual is perfectly balanced in all respects; and indeed, the realization of the perfect equilibrium of the individuality, which implies the complete neutralization of all the opposing tendencies acting in it and thus their fixation in its very center—the only point where these oppositions cease to manifest themselves—is, by this very fact, purely and simply equivalent to the restoration of the 'primordial state'. It is clear, then, that nothing should be exaggerated, and that if there are individuals qualified for initiation, they are so despite a certain state of relative disequilibrium that is inevitable but which initiation precisely can and must attenuate if it is to produce an effective result, and which it must even remove entirely if it is to be carried to the degree that corresponds to the perfection of the individual possibilities, that is, as we shall explain a bit further, to the term of the 'lesser mysteries'.[11]

We must also note that there are certain defects which, though not opposed to a virtual initiation, may prevent it from becoming effective, and it goes without saying that here, especially, one must take into account differences of method among the diverse initiatic forms; but in every case there will be conditions of this kind to consider once we pass from the 'speculative' to the 'operative'. One of the most general of these cases consists notably in such defects as curvatures of the spinal column that hinder the normal circulation

---

11. We have pointed out elsewhere in connection with descriptions of the Antichrist, and precisely in what concerns his bodily asymmetries, that certain initiatic disqualifications of this kind can, on the contrary, constitute qualifications for the counter-initiation.

of subtle currents in the organism, for it is hardly necessary to recall the important role that these currents play in most processes of realization even from the outset, and up to the point where the individual possibilities have been surpassed. In order to avoid any misunderstanding in this regard it is appropriate to add that if the effectuation of these currents is accomplished consciously in certain methods,[12] there are others where it is not, but where such an action no less effectively exists and is no less important; a thorough-going examination of certain ritual particularities, of certain 'signs of recognition', for example, which are at the same time something altogether different when truly understood, could furnish very clear although assuredly unexpected evidence of this for those unaccustomed to consider things from this point of view, which is specifically that of initiatic 'technique'.

As we must limit our remarks, we will content ourselves with these examples, which are doubtless few, but are deliberately chosen as most characteristic and instructive so as best to explain what is really involved; after all, it would be of little use and would even be quite tedious to multiply them indefinitely. If we have dwelt so much on the bodily side of initiatic qualifications it is because this is certainly what risks being least visible to many and what our contemporaries are generally most disposed to misunderstand, so that it requires their attention all the more; and here we have also found an opportunity to illustrate as clearly as possible how far is what relates to initiation from the more or less vague theories read into it by those who, because of the all too common modern confusions, claim to speak of things about which they have not the least real knowledge, but which they believe themselves no less able to 'reconstruct' at the whim of their imagination. And finally, it is particularly easy to see, through 'technical' considerations of this sort, that initiation is something altogether different from mysticism and could not really have the least connection with it.

12. Particularly in 'tantric' methods, to which we have already alluded in an earlier note.

15

INITIATIC RITES

IN PRECEDING CHAPTERS we have been obliged almost continually to refer to rites, for they constitute the essential element in the transmission of the spiritual influence and attachment to the initiatic 'chain', so much so that it can be said that without rites initiation is not possible. We must now return to this question in order to clarify certain particularly important points, but it should be understood that here we are not claiming to treat exhaustively of rites in general—their purpose, their role, the diverse types into which they are divided—for that is a subject which would demand a complete volume in itself.

It is important to note at the outset that the presence of rites is a characteristic common to all traditional institutions of whatever order, exoteric as well as esoteric, taking these terms in their broadest sense as we have already done earlier. This characteristic is a consequence of the 'non-human' element that is essentially implied in such institutions, for it can be said that the purpose of rites is always to put the human being in contact, directly or indirectly, with something that goes beyond his individuality and which belongs to other states of existence. It is obvious however that it is not always necessary for the communication so established to be conscious in order to be real, for it is most often effected by means of certain subtle modalities of the individual, into which most men today can no longer transfer their center of consciousness. However this may be, whether the effect is apparent or not, or whether it be immediate or deferred, the rite always carries its efficacy in itself, on the condition of course that it be accomplished in conformity with the traditional rules that ensure its validity and outside of which it would only be an empty form and a useless imitation; and this efficacy has nothing 'marvelous' or 'magical' about it, as some people occasionally say with the clear intention of denigration and negation, for it results simply from the clearly defined laws according to which spiritual influences act and of which the ritual 'technique' is, at root, nothing but the application and implementation.[1]

This inherent efficacy, founded on laws that allow no place for fantasy or for the arbitrary, is common to all rites without exception, and it holds for rites of the exoteric order as well as for initiatic rites, and, among the former, for rites belonging to non-religious traditional forms as well as for religious rites. In this connection we must again recall, for it is a most important point, that this efficacy is, as has been said, entirely independent of the worth of the individual who accomplishes the rite, for it is the function alone that counts here and not the individual as such. In other words, the necessary and sufficient condition is that the officiant should have regularly received the power to accomplish the rite, and it makes little difference if he does not truly understand its significance and even if he does not believe in its efficacy, for this cannot prevent the rite from being valid if all the prescribed rules have been properly observed.[2]

Having said this, we can now speak more particularly about initiation, and we will remark first of all that its ritual character brings

---

1. There is hardly need to say that the observations set out here concern true rites exclusively, those possessing an authentically traditional character, and that we absolutely refuse to give the name of rite to anything that is only a parody of these, that is, to ceremonies established through purely human customs and of which the effect, if indeed they have one, could never go beyond the 'psychological' domain in the most profane meaning of this word. The distinction of rites from ceremonies is in any case important enough for us to treat it more particularly in what follows.

2. It is thus a grave error to use the expression 'playing at ritual', which we have often seen used by a certain Masonic writer, apparently quite pleased with this rather unfortunate 'discovery', when speaking of the accomplishment of initiatic rites by individuals who are ignorant of their meaning, a meaning they do not even seek to penetrate. Such an expression would only be appropriate of the profane who imitate rites while having no capacity to accomplish them validly; but in an initiatic organization, however degenerate it may be with respect to the qualification of its present members, ritual is not something to be played with; it is and always remains something serious and truly efficacious, even when those taking part in it are unaware of this.

out one of the fundamental differences that separate it from mysticism, which has no such character, something easily understood if one refers to what we have said about its 'irregularity'. It might perhaps be objected that mysticism sometimes seems to be more or less directly linked to the observance of certain rites, but these rites do not in any way belong to it as such since they are nothing other than ordinary religious rites; moreover this link has no necessary character, for it is in fact hardly present in every case, whereas, we repeat, there is no initiation without special and particular rites. Indeed, unlike mystical initiations, initiation is not something that falls from the clouds, so to speak, without it being known how or why; on the contrary, it rests on positive scientific laws and on rigorous technical rules.[3] We cannot insist too much on this whenever the occasion presents itself, in order to avoid every possibility of misunderstanding as to its true nature.

As for the distinction between initiatic and exoteric rites, we can indicate it here only rather summarily, for entering into detail on this subject would risk taking us very far afield. In particular, it would be necessary to draw all the consequences from the fact that initiatic rites are reserved solely for an elite possessing certain qualifications, whereas exoteric rites are public and addressed indifferently to all the members of a given social milieu, which well shows that, despite their sometimes apparent similarities, their goals cannot really be the same.[4] Unlike initiatic rites, exoteric rites do not in fact have as their goal the opening of the being to certain possibilities of knowledge for which all cannot be qualified; on the other

3. Expressions like 'sacerdotal art' and 'royal art' properly refer to this technique of handling spiritual influences, for they designate the respective applications of the corresponding initiations. On the other hand, in this case it is a matter of sacred and traditional science, which, while certainly of an altogether different order than profane science, is no less 'positive' and even much more so, if one understands this word in its true meaning instead of abusively misappropriating it as do modern 'scientists'.

4. Let us point out in this connection the error of ethnologists and sociologists, who very improperly qualify as 'rites of initiation' certain procedures that relate simply to the admission of the individual to an exterior social organization, one for which the attainment of a certain age is the sole qualification required, a point to which we shall return later.

hand, it is essential to note that, although they also necessarily involve the intervention of an element of the supra-individual order, their action is never meant to go beyond the domain of individuality. This is very apparent in the case of religious rites, which we can take more particularly as a term of comparison because they are the only exoteric rites that the West knows at present; every religion intends solely the 'salvation' of its adherents, which is a finality that still relates to the individual order and, by definition as it were, its point of view does not extend beyond this; even the mystics always envisage only 'salvation' and never 'deliverance', even though the latter is, on the contrary, the final and supreme goal of all initiation.[5]

Another point of capital importance is the following: initiation of any degree represents for the being who receives it a permanent acquisition, a state that virtually or effectively it has reached once and for all and that nothing can ever take away.[6] Let us note that this is one more very clear difference from mystical states, which are passing and even fugitive and from which the being returns as it entered, and which it may even never find again, all of which is explained by the 'phenomenal' character of these states, received from outside as it were rather than proceeding from the very 'interior' of the being.[7] From this the consequence immediately follows that rites of initiation confer a definitive and ineffaceable character;

5. If, following the distinction that we will clarify later, it is said that this is true only of the 'greater mysteries', we answer that the 'lesser mysteries', which effectively stop at the limits of human possibilities, constitute in respect of the latter only a preparatory stage and are not themselves their own proper end, whereas religion presents itself as a self-sufficient whole that does not require any further complement.

6. So as to leave no room for ambiguity, let us clarify that this must be understood only of the degrees of initiation and not of the various functions that may be conferred only temporarily on an individual or that he may become unfit to exercise for multiple reasons. These are two entirely distinct things, and one must be very careful not to confuse them, for the first is of a purely inward order whereas the second concerns an outward activity of the being, which explains the difference that we have just noted.

7. This touches on the question of the 'duality' necessary to the religious point of view by the very fact that it relates essentially to what Hindu terminology designates as the 'non-supreme'.

moreover, it is the same in another order with certain religious rites, which, for this reason, could never be renewed for the same individual and thus present the closest analogy to initiatic rites, to the point that one could in a certain sense consider them a sort of transposition of these latter into the exoteric domain.[8]

Another consequence of what we have just said is something we have already noted in passing, but which merits more emphasis: once received, the initiatic quality[9] is in no way bound to the fact of the recipient's active membership in this or that organization; once the attachment to a traditional organization has been effected, it cannot be broken by anything at all, and it continues even when the individual no longer has any apparent relationship with that organization, which then has only a wholly secondary importance in this regard. In the absence of any other consideration, this alone would suffice to show how profoundly initiatic organizations differ from profane associations to which they cannot be assimilated or even compared in any way, for whereas one who resigns or is expelled from a profane association no longer has any link to it and becomes again exactly what he was before he became part of it, the link established by the initiatic character on the contrary does not in any way depend on contingencies such as a resignation or expulsion, which are of a merely 'administrative' order, as we have already said, and affect only outward relationships; and if these relationships are entirely in the profane order, as is the case with associations having nothing else to offer their members, in the initiatic order, on the contrary, they are only an altogether accessory and nowise necessary

8. We know that among the seven sacraments of Catholicism three fit this case and can be received only once: baptism, confirmation, and ordination. The analogy of baptism with an initiation, insofar as it is a 'second birth', is obvious enough, and confirmation represents in principle the accession to a superior degree; as for ordination, we have already pointed out the similarities that can be found in it regarding the transmission of spiritual influences, and which are all the more striking in that this sacrament is not received by all and requires, as we said, certain special qualifications.

9. As was pointed out in an earlier note, 'quality' here designates an acquired but thenceforth permanent effect on the being that receives it, in Scholastic terminology this kind of *qualitas* being called *habitus*. ED.

means in relation to the inward realities that are alone of real importance. A little reflection suffices, we think, to make this perfectly evident; what is astonishing is to note, as we have many times had occasion to do, an almost universal misunderstanding of such simple and elementary ideas as these.[10]

10. Taking as an application of this the simplest and most common example from among initiatic organizations, it is wholly inexact to speak of an 'ex-Mason' as is currently done; a resigned or even an expelled Mason may no longer be attached to any Lodge or Obedience, but remains no less a Mason for all that, and whether he wishes it or not nothing is changed; the proof is that, should he later be reinstated, he is not initiated again or required to repeat the grades he has already received, so that only the English expression *unattached Mason* is appropriate in such a case.

16

RITE AND SYMBOL

WE HAVE SHOWN THAT rites and symbols, both of which are essential elements of every initiation, and, more generally are associated with everything traditional, are in fact closely linked by their very nature. All the constituent elements of a rite necessarily have a symbolic sense, whereas, inversely, a symbol produces—and this indeed is its essential purpose—in one who meditates upon it with the requisite aptitudes and disposition, effects rigorously comparable to those of rites properly speaking, with the reservation of course that when this meditation is undertaken there be, as a preliminary condition, that regular initiatic transmission failing which the rites would be in any case nothing more than a vain counterfeit, as with their pseudo-initiatic parodies. We must also add that the origin of authentic rites and symbols (anything less does not deserve the name, since it amounts in the end to entirely profane and fraudulent imitations) is likewise 'non-human'. Thus the impossibility of assigning to them any definite author or maker is not due to a lack of information, as profane historians suppose (that is, if for want of a better solution they have not been driven to look on them as the product of a sort of 'collective consciousness', which, even if it existed, would in any case be quite incapable of producing things of a transcendent order, such as these), but is a necessary consequence of that very origin, something that can only be contested by those who completely misunderstand the true nature of tradition and of all its integral parts, as is evidently the case with rites and symbols.

If the fundamental identity of rites and symbols is more closely examined, it will first be noted that a symbol, understood as a 'graphic' figuration, as it is most commonly, is only as it were the fixation of a ritual gesture.[1] In fact it often happens that for a symbol to be regular, its actual tracing must be accomplished under conditions that confer upon it all the characteristics of a true rite. A very clear example of this in a lower domain, that of magic (which is nonetheless a traditional science), is provided by the preparation of talismanic figures; and in the order that more immediately concerns us the tracing of *yantras* in the Hindu tradition provides a no less striking example.[2]

But this is not all, for the above-mentioned concept of the symbol is really much too narrow: there are not only figurative or visual symbols but also auditory symbols, two fundamental categories that in the Hindu doctrine are called the *yantra* and the *mantra*.[3] Their respective predominance characterizes the two categories of rites that originally related to the traditions of sedentary peoples in the case of visual symbols and to those of nomadic peoples in the case of auditory ones; it should of course be understood that no absolute separation can be made between the two (for which reason we speak only of predominance), for every combination is possible as a result of the multiple adaptations that have arisen with the passage of time and produced the various traditional forms we know today. These considerations clearly show the bond that exists in general between rites and symbols, but we may add that in the case of *mantras* this bond is more immediately apparent, for once it has been traced out, the visual symbol remains or may remain in a permanent state (which is why we have spoken of a fixed gesture), while the auditory symbol, on the contrary, is manifested only in the actual performance of the rite. This difference is attenuated, however, when a correspondence is established between visual and

1. These considerations relate directly to what we have called the 'theory of gestures', to which we have alluded on several occasions but have not had occasion to explain until now.

2. This can be likened to the *tracing board* of the Lodge in early Masonry (and also, perhaps by corruption, to the *trestle-board*), which in effect constituted a true *yantra*. The rites concerned with the construction of monuments intended for traditional uses might also be cited as an example here, for monuments of this sort necessarily have a symbolic character.

3. See *Reign of Quantity*, chap. 21.

auditory symbols, as in writing, which represents a true fixation of sound (not of sound as such, of course, but of a permanent possibility of reproducing it); and it need hardly be recalled in this connection that all writing, at least in its origin, is essentially symbolic figuration. The same is true of speech itself, in which the symbolic character is no less inherent by its very nature, for it is quite clear that every word is nothing more than a symbol of the idea it is intended to express. Thus all language, whether spoken or written, is truly a body of symbols, and it is precisely for this reason that language, despite all the 'naturalistic' theories contrived in modern times to explain it, cannot be a more or less artificial human creation nor a simple product of man's individual faculties.[4]

Among visual symbols themselves there is an example very similar to that of auditory symbols. These are symbols that are not permanently traced but only employed as signs in initiatic rites (notably the 'signs of recognition' mentioned earlier)[5] and even in religious ones (the 'sign of the cross' is a typical example known to all),[6] where the symbols are truly one with the ritual gesture itself.[7] It would in any case be altogether futile to make of these signs yet a third category of symbols distinct from those of which we have already spoken; certain psychologists would probably consider them to be such, and call them 'active' symbols, or some such thing, but

4. It goes without saying that the distinction between 'sacred languages' and 'profane languages' arises only secondarily; for languages as well as for the sciences and the arts, the profane character is only the result of a degeneration that arose earlier and more readily in the case of languages on account of their more current and more general use.

5. 'Words' that serve a similar purpose, passwords for example, naturally fall into the category of auditory symbols.

6. This sign was, moreover, a veritable 'sign of recognition' for the early Christians.

7. A sort of intermediate case is that of the symbolical figures traced at the beginning of a rite or preparatory to it and effaced immediately after its accomplishment; this is true with many *yantras*, and was formerly so with the *tracing board* of the Lodge in Masonry. This practice does not represent a mere precaution against profane curiosity, which as an explanation is far too 'simple' and superficial, for it should be regarded above all as a consequence of the intimate bond uniting symbols and rites, which implies that the former have no reason for visual existence apart from the latter.

they are obviously made to be visually perceptible and thus belong to the category of visual symbols; among these, by reason of their 'instantaneity', if one may put it so, are those that are most similar to the complementary category of auditory symbols. In any case, a 'graphic' symbol, we repeat, is itself the fixation of a gesture or a movement (that is, the actual movement, or the totality of more or less complex movements, required to trace it, which in their specialized jargon psychologists would no doubt call an 'action gestalt'),[8] and with auditory symbols one can also say the movement of the vocal organs required to produce them, whether it be a matter of uttering ordinary words or musical sounds, is as much a gesture as all the other kinds of bodily movement, from which in fact it can never be entirely isolated.[9] Thus the notion of the gesture, in its widest meaning (which indeed accords better with the real meaning of the word than the more restricted meanings currently allowed), brings all these different cases back to unity, so that we can discern in them their common principle; and this fact has a profound significance in the metaphysical order which we cannot enlarge upon without straying far from the subject of our present study.

It will now be easy to understand that every rite is literally made up of a group of symbols which include not only the objects used or the figures represented, as we might be tempted to think if we stopped at the most superficial meaning, but also the gestures effected and the words pronounced (the latter, as we have said, really constituting moreover only a particular case of the former); in a word, all the elements of the rite without exception; and these elements then have a symbolic value by their very nature and not by

8. This is especially evident in a case such as that of the 'sign of recognition' among the Pythagoreans, where the pentagram was traced out at one stroke.

9. On the subject of the correspondences between language and gesture (the latter taken in its ordinary and restricted sense) it should be remarked that the works of Marcel Jousse, though their point of departure is quite different from ours, are nonetheless in our opinion worthy of interest insofar as they touch on the question of certain traditional modes of expression related, in a general way, to the constitution and usage of the sacred languages, but are almost lost or entirely forgotten in the vernacular languages, which have in fact been diminished to the most narrowly restricted of all forms of language.

virtue of any superadded meaning that might attach to them from outward circumstances without really being inherent to them. Again, it might be said that rites are symbols 'put into action', or that every ritual gesture is a symbol 'enacted',[10] but this is only another way of saying the same thing, highlighting more particularly the rite's characteristic that, like every action, it is something necessarily accomplished in time,[11] whereas the symbol as such can be envisaged from a timeless point of view. In this sense one could speak of a certain pre-eminence of symbols over rites; but rites and symbols are fundamentally only two aspects of a single reality, which is, after all, none other than the 'correspondence' that binds together all the degrees of universal Existence in such a way that by means of it our human state can enter into communication with the higher states of being.

10. Note especially in this connection the role played in rites by gestures called *mudrās* in the Hindu tradition, which constitute a veritable language of movements and attitudes; the 'handclasps' used as 'means of recognition' in initiatic organizations in the West as well as in the East are really only a particular case of *mudrās*.

11. In Sanskrit the word *karma*, of which the primary meaning is 'action' in general, is also used in a 'technical' sense to mean 'ritual action' in particular; what it then expresses directly is this same characteristic of the rite we are here indicating.

17

MYTHS, MYSTERIES, AND SYMBOLS

OUR PREVIOUS CONSIDERATIONS quite naturally lead us to examine another related question, the relationship of the symbol to what is called 'myth'. On this subject it first should be pointed out that we have occasionally spoken of a certain degeneration of symbolism that has given birth to 'mythology', taking this last word in its usual sense. This is in fact accurate when applied to 'classical' antiquity but it is perhaps invalid when applied outside this period of the Greek and Latin civilizations. Thus, since the term can only provoke troublesome ambiguities and unjustified comparisons, it is best to avoid it altogether; but if correct usage imposes this restriction, we should nevertheless say that, in itself and in its original meaning, the word 'myth' has nothing to do with a degeneration that was moreover of relatively late origin and due only to a more or less complete misunderstanding of what remained of an earlier tradition. It is fitting to add that if we can speak of 'myths' in connection with this tradition (on condition that its true meaning be reinstated and everything 'pejorative' attached to it in current usage be ruled out), in any case there was at that time no 'mythology' as moderns understand the term, for this amounts to no more than a study undertaken 'from the outside' and hence implies a misunderstanding raised, one might say, to the second power.

Nor is the distinction sometimes made between 'myths' and 'symbols' based on reality. While some people consider a myth to be a narrative having a meaning other than that which is directly and literally expressed by the words composing it, for others a symbol would essentially be a figurative representation of certain ideas by a geometric diagram or by some design or other; the symbol would then be a graphic mode of expression and myth a verbal mode. But from what we have explained earlier regarding the meaning of the word 'symbol', this is an altogether unacceptable restriction, for every image taken to represent an idea, that is, to express or suggest it in any way and to any degree, is by that very fact a sign or, what amounts to the same thing, a symbol of that idea; and it hardly matters whether a visual image or any other is involved, for this introduces no essential difference and changes absolutely nothing as to the principle of symbolism itself. In every case, symbolism is based on a relationship of analogy or correspondence between the idea to be expressed and the image, graphic, verbal, or any other, by which it is expressed. From this quite general point of view words themselves, as we have already stated, are not and cannot be anything but symbols. Instead of talking about an idea and an image, as we have just done, one could even speak still more generally of a correspondence between any two realities of different orders, a correspondence based on the nature of both at once; under these conditions a reality of a certain order can be represented by a reality of another order, the latter then being a symbol of the former.

With this principle of symbolism in mind, we see that it is evidently susceptible of a great variety of modalities; myth is simply a particular case, one of these modes; one could say that symbol is the genus and myth is one of its species. In other words, a symbolic narrative can be envisioned just as well, and by the same right, as a symbolic design, or, by the same right, as many other things that have the same character or play the same role; myths are symbolic recitals, as also are 'parables', which are essentially the same thing.[1] It does not seem to us that this point should present any difficulty

---

1. It is interesting to note that what the Masons call the 'legends' of the different grades fall under this definition of myth, and that the 'enacting' of these 'legends' shows quite well that they are really incorporated into these rites themselves, from which it is absolutely impossible to separate them. What we have said about the essential identity of rite and symbol, therefore, once more applies very clearly in such a case.

once we have understood the general and fundamental notions of symbolism.

Having established this much, we will clarify now the proper meaning of the word 'myth' itself, which can lead us to certain not unimportant remarks relating to the character and function of symbolism taken in its most specific sense, which not only differs from the ordinary sense, but even opposes it in certain respects. The word 'myth' is commonly regarded as a synonym for 'fable', taking this simply as any fiction, and usually a fiction clothed in more or less poetic dress. This is the result of the degeneration we spoke about at the beginning, and the Greeks, from whose language this term is borrowed, certainly share in the responsibility for what is really a profound alteration and deviation from the original meaning. Indeed, early on in all Greek forms of art, individual fantasy was given free rein, so that the arts, instead of remaining properly hieratic and symbolic, as among the Egyptians and the peoples of the East, soon took an altogether different direction, aiming less at instructing than at pleasing, and resulting for the most part in works almost devoid of any real and profound meaning (except for the elements that still subsisted, even if only unconsciously, from the previous tradition), in which we no longer find any trace of the eminently 'exact' science that true symbolism is. In short, this was the beginning of what can be called profane art, and it coincides noticeably with the beginning of that equally profane thought which, due to the exercise of the same individual fantasy in another domain, was to become known under the name of 'philosophy'. This fantasizing was exercised especially on pre-existing myths. Poets, who from this point on were no longer sacred writers as at the beginning, nor retrained any 'supra-human' inspiration, so obscured and denatured these myths by developing them at the whim of their imagination and surrounding them with superfluous ornamentation that it becomes very difficult to uncover their meaning and to extract their essential elements, except perhaps by comparing them with similar symbols found elsewhere which have not suffered the same distortion. Thus, at least for most people, myth finally became nothing more than a misconstrued symbol, which it remains for us moderns. But this is only an abuse and, we could say, a 'profanation' in the proper sense of the word; what we need to see is that before its deformation myth was essentially a symbolic recital, as we said above, and that this was its unique purpose; and from this point of view myth is not entirely synonymous with fable, for this last word (in Latin *fabula*, from *fari*, 'to speak') etymologically designates any recital whatsoever without specifying its intention or character, and even here the idea of a 'fiction' became attached to it only later. Thus these two terms, myth and fable, which have come to be seen as equivalent, are derived from roots that in fact have altogether opposite meanings, for whereas the root of 'fable' designates the spoken word, that of 'myth' on the contrary, strange as it may seem at first glance since a recital is involved, designates silence.

In fact, the Greek word *muthos*, 'myth', comes from the root *mu* (found also in the Latin *mutus*, 'mute'), which represents a closed mouth and hence silence.[2] This is the meaning of the verb *muein*, 'to shut the mouth', 'to be silent' (which by extension also comes to mean 'to shut the eyes', both actually and figuratively). An examination of some of the derivatives of this verb is especially instructive. Thus from *muo* (infinitive *muein*) are immediately derived two other verbs with only slight differences in form, *muao* and *mueo*; the first has the same meanings as *muo*, and we must join to this another derivative, *mullo*, again meaning 'to shut the lips', and so to murmur without opening the mouth.[3] As for *mueo*—and this is most important—it signifies 'to initiate' (into the 'mysteries', a word derived from the same root, as we shall soon see, specifically

---

2. The *Mutus Liber* of the Hermeticists is literally the 'mute book', a book, that is, without verbal commentary; but it is also, at the same time, a book of symbols insofar as symbolism can truly be regarded as the 'language of silence'. [The *Mutus Liber*, a collection of plates depicting stages in the alchemical work, first published in 1677, was influential in later alchemical and Hermetic writings, particularly those of the French occult schools. See Adam McLean, *A Commentary on the Mutus Liber* (Grand Rapids: Phanes Press, 1991). ED.]

3. The Latin *murmur* is in any case only the root *mu* prolonged by the letter *r* and repeated, so as to represent a muffled and continuous sound produced with the mouth shut.

through the intermediary of *mueo* and *mustes*) and hence both 'to instruct' (though at first to instruct without spoken words, as was indeed the case in the mysteries) and 'to consecrate'; we might even have said 'to consecrate' first, if consecration meant, as it normally ought, the transmission of a spiritual influence, or the rite by which the latter is regularly transmitted. Later, in Christian ecclesiastical language, this same word came to mean the conferring of ordination, which is also very much a 'consecration' in this sense, although in an order differing from the initiatic order.

But, some will say, if the word 'myth' has such an origin, how could it designate a certain kind of narrative? It is because here the idea of 'silence' must be related to things that by their very nature are inexpressible, at least directly and in ordinary language, for one of the general functions of symbolism is effectively to suggest the inexpressible, to give a presentiment of it, or better said, to render it 'accessible' by virtue of the transpositions it makes possible from one order to another—from an inferior order to a superior one, from what can be grasped immediately to what can be grasped only with much greater difficulty—such being precisely the primary goal of myths. Besides, even in the 'classical' period, Plato still appealed to myths in order to expound concepts that went beyond the range of his habitual dialectical means; and these myths, which he certainly did not 'invent' but only 'adapted' (for they bear the unmistakable mark of a traditional teaching, something also evident in certain procedures he employs for the interpretation of words that compare to the *nirukta* in Hindu tradition),[4] are far from being merely the more or less negligible literary ornaments that commentators and modern 'critics' all too often see in them simply because it is so much easier thus to brush them aside without further inspection than to provide even an approximate explanation. On the contrary, they represent all that is most profound in Plato's thought, all that is most free from individual contingencies, and which, because of this very profundity, he cannot express in any other way than by symbols. With Plato, dialectic often includes a certain amount of 'playfulness', which is quite in keeping with the Greek mentality, but

---

4. For examples of this type of interpretation see especially the *Cratylus*.

when he abandons this for myth one may be sure that this playfulness has come to an end and that what is now at issue has as it were a 'sacred' character.

In myth, then, what is said is something other than what is meant; and let us note in passing that this is also the etymological meaning of 'allegory' (from *allo agoreuein*, literally 'to say something else'), which provides us another example of the deviations of meaning in current usage, for at present this word in fact designates only a conventional and literary representation with a merely moral or psychological intention, one that most often falls under the category of what is commonly called 'personified abstractions', and this, it hardly needs saying, could not be further from true symbolism. But coming back to myth, although it does not say what it means, it does suggest it by that analogical correspondence which is the very basis and essence of all symbolism, so that we could say one keeps silent in the very act of speaking, and that it is from this that myth draws its name.[5]

It remains to draw attention to the kinship of the words 'myth' and 'mystery', both deriving from the same root, the Greek word *musterion*, 'mystery', which is also directly related to the idea of 'silence'; and this can be interpreted in several different but related ways, each with its own raison d'être from a certain point of view. Let us note first of all that according to the derivation (from *mueo*) indicated above, the principal meaning of the word refers to initiation, and indeed, what were called 'mysteries' in Greek antiquity should be so understood. On the other hand, and this shows the truly peculiar destiny of certain words, the word 'mystical', closely related to the words just mentioned, applies etymologically

---

5. Note that this is also the meaning of the following words of Christ, which surely confirm the basic identity of 'myth' and 'parable' pointed out above: 'To them that are without [an expression exactly equivalent to 'profane'], all things are done in parables, because seeing they see not and hearing they hear not' (Matt. 13:13, Mark 4:11–12, Luke 8:10). This is the case of those who grasp only what is said literally, who are incapable of going further to reach the inexpressible, and to whom, consequently, it was not given to 'know the mystery of the kingdom of God'; and the use of the word 'mystery' in this last phrase of the Gospel text is to be especially noted with respect to the considerations that follow.

to everything concerning the mysteries; *mustikos* is in fact the adjectival form of *mustes*, 'initiated', and was therefore originally equivalent to 'initiatic' and designated everything related to initiation, to its doctrine and even to its goal (though in this ancient sense it was never applied to persons); now among moderns the same word 'mystical', alone among the terms derived from this common root, has come to designate solely something which, as we saw, has absolutely nothing to do with initiation, and is in certain respects even opposed to it.

Let us now return to the different meanings of the word 'mystery'. In its most immediate sense—in our opinion the crudest or at least the most outward —mystery is what we should not speak of, what we should keep silent about, what we are forbidden to disclose to the outside world. This is how it is ordinarily understood even when the ancient mysteries are in question, and in its present use the word hardly retains any other meaning than this. Nevertheless, even taking into account questions of opportuneness that must certainly have played a role from time to time but which were never anything but purely contingent, this prohibition against revealing rites and teachings must above all be seen as having a symbolic value, something we have already explained above in connection with the true nature of the initiatic secret. As we said, what was called the 'discipline of the secret' (which was just as obligatory in the primitive Christian church as in the ancient mysteries, something the religious adversaries of esoterism would do well to remember) seems to us to have been far from a mere precaution against hostility, as real and often dangerous as this hostility may have been due to the incomprehension of the profane world. We see other reasons of a much more profound order, reasons indicated by the other meanings of the word 'mystery'. We might also add that the close similarity between the words 'sacred' (*sacratum*) and 'secret' (*secretum*) is not simply coincidence; both involve something 'put aside' (*secernere*, 'to place apart', from which is derived the participle *secretum*), 'reserved', separated from the profane realm; similarly, a consecrated place is called *templum*, of which the root *tem* (found in the Greek *temno*, 'to cut', 'to cut off from', 'to separate', from which *temenos*, 'a sacred enclosure', is derived) also expresses the same idea; and 'contemplation', derived from the same root, is again related to this idea by its strictly 'inward' character.[6]

The second meaning of the word 'mystery', which is already less outward, designates what must be received in silence,[7] what it is unsuitable to speak of; from this point of view all traditional doctrines, including religious dogmas, which constitute a particular case, may be called mysteries (the use of the word being then extended to domains other than the initiatic, though they too are domains in which a 'non-human' influence is exerted) because they are truths that by their essentially supra-individual and supra-rational nature are above all discussion.[8] Now, to link this meaning to the first, one might say that to lavish mysteries, so understood, indiscriminately on the profane is inevitably to expose them to discussion, a profane method par excellence, with all the resultant drawbacks, a method perfectly described by the word 'profanation', a term previously applied to something else but which here must be taken in both its most literal and most complete sense. The destructive work of modern 'criticism' with respect to all traditions is too eloquent an example of what we mean to require further emphasis.[9]

Finally, there is a third meaning, the most profound of all, according to which the mystery is strictly inexpressible, something one can only contemplate in silence (and here it is fitting to recall what was just said about the origin of the word contemplation); and since the inexpressible is also incommunicable, the prohibition against revealing the sacred teaching symbolizes, from this new

---

6. So it is etymologically absurd to speak of 'contemplating' any external spectacle whatever, as is done by the moderns, for whom the true meaning of words seems in so many cases to be completely lost.

7. We are reminded here of the silence formerly imposed on disciples in certain initiatic schools, notably the Pythagorean.

8. This is nothing other than the infallibility inherent in every traditional doctrine.

9. This meaning of the word 'mystery', which is also inherent to the word 'sacred' for the reasons stated above, is most clearly recorded in the Gospel precept: 'Give not that which is holy to dogs. Neither cast ye your pearls before swine; lest perhaps they trample them under their feet; and, turning upon you, they tear you' (Matt. 7:6). Note that the profane are here symbolically represented by animals considered 'impure' in the ritual meaning of this word.

point of view, the impossibility of expressing by spoken words the real mystery for which this teaching is only, so to speak, a garment that both reveals and veils it.[10] Obviously, a teaching that concerns the inexpressible can only suggest it with the help of appropriate images, which then become supports for contemplation; from what we have explained, this amounts to saying that such a teaching necessarily acquires a symbolic form. This was always and among all peoples one of the essential characteristics of initiation into the mysteries, whatever name may have been given it, and we can therefore say that symbols, and particularly myths when the teaching is conveyed by words, truly constitute, according to their primary purpose, the very language of initiation.

10. The common notion of the 'mysteries', especially when applied to the religious domain, implies an obvious confusion of the 'inexpressible' with the 'incomprehensible', a confusion altogether unjustified except in relation to the intellectual limitations of certain individuals.

18

SYMBOLISM
AND PHILOSOPHY

IF, AS WE HAVE JUST EXPLAINED, symbolism is inherent to everything of a traditional character, it is also one of the features by which traditional doctrines in their totality (for this applies to both the esoteric and exoteric domains) differ at first glance from profane thought, to which such symbolism is necessarily wholly foreign since it expresses something 'non-human', which can never be present in such thought. Nevertheless, philosophers, who are, as it were, the pre-eminent representatives of profane thought but who claim to involve themselves with the most diverse matters as if their competence knew no bounds, sometimes dabble with symbolism and formulate rather strange theories; for instance, some have tried to create a 'psychology of symbolism', something connected to that specifically modern error of 'psychologism' which is itself only a particular case of the tendency to reduce everything to exclusively human elements. Others, however, do recognize that symbolism is not dependent on philosophy, but they then attach a clearly unfavorable interpretation to this assertion, as if symbolism were an inferior and even a negligible thing; listening to them, one suspects that they are simply confusing it with the pseudo-symbolism of certain literati and are thus mistaking an entirely abusive and misleading use of the word for its true meaning. In reality, if symbolism is, as they say, a 'form of thought' (which is true in a certain sense, although this does not preclude its being primarily something else), philosophy is so too, though one that is radically different from symbolism and opposed to it in several respects. One can go further: that form of thought represented by philosophy corresponds only to a quite special point of view, of which the greatest failing, inherent to all profane thought, is not knowing or wishing to recognize any limits, and which, even in the most favorable cases, is valid only within a very restricted domain. Even if one should fail to recognize here anything more than two forms of thought (which amounts to confusing the use of symbolism with its very essence), it would be a serious error to put them on the same level, for symbolism, as should be clear now, has an altogether different value. That philosophers may not share this opinion proves nothing, for to situate things correctly one must first consider them impartially, which, under the circumstances, they cannot do; as for us, we are firmly of the opinion that, as philosophers, they will never succeed in penetrating to the deeper meaning of even the least important symbol, because symbolism goes entirely beyond their manner of thinking and thus inevitably eludes their grasp.

Those acquainted with our frequent remarks concerning philosophy will not be surprised to see it accorded only a very modest importance; in order to recognize its subordinate position it suffices simply to recall that every mode of expression necessarily has a symbolic character, in the most general sense of this term, with respect to what it expresses. Philosophers cannot but use words, and these words are in themselves nothing other than symbols; it is therefore philosophy that in a certain way, albeit quite unconsciously, enters the domain of symbolism, and not the reverse.

However, in another respect there is an opposition between philosophy and symbolism, if one understands this latter in its usual more restricted sense, which is what is intended when we consider it as characterizing traditional doctrines; philosophy, like everything expressed in ordinary forms of language, is essentially analytic, whereas symbolism is essentially synthetic. The form of language is by very definition 'discursive', as is human reason, of which it is the proper instrument, and of which it follows or reproduces every step as exactly as possible; symbolism in its strict sense is, on the contrary, truly 'intuitive', which quite naturally renders it incomparably more suitable than language to serve as a support for intellectual and supra-rational intuition, which is precisely why it constitutes the mode of expression par excellence of all initiatic teaching. As to philosophy, it in a way represents the type of discursive thought (which, of course, does not mean that all discursive thought has a specifically philosophical character), and it is this that imposes limitations on it from which it cannot free itself; symbolism on the other hand, as a support of transcendent intuition, opens truly unlimited possibilities.

The discursive character of philosophy makes it exclusively rational since this characteristic is peculiar to reason in itself; therefore the domain of philosophy and its possibilities cannot in any case extend beyond the capacity of reason; moreover, it represents only a certain rather particular use of that faculty, for it is evident, even if only from the mere existence of independent sciences, that in the domain of rational knowledge itself there are many things that do not fall within the competence of philosophy. This is not in any way to contest the value of reason, as long as it does not try to exceed its proper domain,[1] but this value, as also this domain, can only be relative; moreover, did not the word *ratio* itself originally have the meaning of 'relation'? We have no dispute with the legitimacy of dialectic within certain limits, even though it is frequently misused by philosophers; still, dialectic can never be an end in itself, but only a means, and perhaps even a means that is not universally applicable; but to realize this implies going beyond the limits of dialectic, and it is this that the philosopher as such cannot do.

Even if we extend philosophy as far as is theoretically possible, that is, to the extreme limits of the domain of reason, in truth it still includes very little, for, to use a Gospel expression, 'one thing alone is needful,' and it is precisely this that will always remain inaccessible to philosophy since it lies above and beyond all rational knowledge. In the face of the inexpressible, that is, of 'mystery' in the truest and most profound sense of the word, of what use are the discursive methods of philosophy? On the contrary, the essential function of symbolism, let us repeat, is to make the inexpressible 'accessible', to furnish the support that effectively permits intellectual intuition to reach it. Who, having understood this, could still deny the immense

---

1. It is worth noting in this connection that 'supra-rational' is in no way a synonym for 'irrational'; what is above reason is not contrary to it, but purely and simply escapes it.

superiority of symbolism and contest that its scope is incomparably greater than that of any possible philosophy? However excellent and perfect in its kind a philosophy may be (and we are certainly not thinking of the modern philosophies in making such a proviso), it remains 'only straw', to use an expression from Saint Thomas Aquinas himself, who, though not inclined to overly disparage philosophical thought, at least understood its limitations.

There is however something else: to consider symbolism as a 'form of thought' is to envisage it only in a purely human respect, which indeed is clearly the only way it can be compared to philosophy; doubtless it must be so considered insofar as it is a mode of expression available to man, yet in truth this is far from sufficient and in no way touches its essence, representing only the most outward aspect of the matter. We have emphasized the 'non-human' side of symbolism enough so that we need not return to it here; it will suffice, in short, to state that its foundation is in the very nature of beings and things, and is in perfect conformity with the laws of that nature, and to reflect on how natural laws themselves are ultimately only an expression and a kind of exteriorization, as it were, of the divine or principial Will. The true foundation of symbolism is the correspondence that exists among all orders of reality, that links one to another, and that therefore extends from the natural order taken in its entirety to the supernatural order itself. By virtue of this correspondence all of nature is itself only a symbol, that is to say it receives its true meaning only if seen as a support to raise us to the knowledge of supernatural or 'metaphysical' (in its proper and etymological sense) truths, which is precisely the essential function of symbolism as well as the fundamental purpose of all traditional science.[2] For this very reason symbolism necessarily contains something of which the origin extends beyond humanity, and one can say that this origin lies in the very Divine Word. It is first of all in universal manifestation itself, and then, with respect more especially to humanity, in the primordial tradition—which is also very much a 'revelation' of the Word—that Tradition, from

2. This is why the world is like a divine language to those who can understand it; according to the biblical expression, *Coeli enarrant gloriam Dei* (Ps. 19:2) [The heavens proclaim the glory of God].

which all other traditional forms are derived, is incorporated, so to speak, in symbols transmitted from age to age without our being able to assign them any 'historical' origin; and the process of this symbolic incorporation is analogous in its own order to that of manifestation.[3]

Faced with these prerogatives which establish the transcendent value of symbolism, what can philosophy ever really lay claim to? The origin of symbolism is truly identical with the origin of time, if it does not in a sense even lie beyond time, since in reality this comprises only one particular mode of manifestation;[4] and since we have already indicated that no authentically traditional symbol can be traced to human invention—attributed, that is, to the ingenuity of some particular individual—should not this very fact be cause for reflection? The provenance of all philosophy is, on the contrary, always some definite and in fact recent epoch, even if it is a matter of 'classical' antiquity, which is only a very relative antiquity (which proves quite well that even in human terms this special form of thought pertains to nothing essential);[5] it is always the work of a man whose name and dates are known to us, and his name is usually used to designate it, clearly demonstrating that there is nothing here but the individual and the human. This is why we have just said that we can compare philosophy and symbolism only on the condition that we restrict ourselves to considering symbolism in its human aspect, since for everything else we can find in the philosophic order neither equivalence nor even correspondence of any kind.

In the most favorable light, philosophy is thus 'human wisdom', or one of its forms, but in any case it remains just that, which is why we can say that it is ultimately a very meagre thing, an altogether

3. In order not to leave room for any ambiguity, we will once more recall in this connection that we absolutely refuse to give the name of tradition to anything that is purely human and profane, and in particular to any philosophical doctrine.

4. It is therefore scarcely comprehensible that a certain Masonic rite, of very questionable regularity, claims to date its documents from an era reckoned *Ab Origine Symbolismi* [from the Origin of Symbolism].

5. There are perhaps grounds for asking why philosophy was born precisely in the sixth century before the Christian era, an epoch that presents rather singular characteristics in many respects, as we have pointed out on several occasions.

rational speculation grounded in a purely human faculty, that by which individual human nature is essentially defined. To say 'human wisdom' is to say 'worldly wisdom', in the sense in which 'world' is used in the Gospels;[6] we could as well say 'profane wisdom', for all these expressions are basically synonymous and indicate clearly that what is involved is not true wisdom but at most only its somewhat ineffectual shadow, one that is all too often 'inverted'.[7] Indeed, most philosophies are not even a shadow of wisdom, however distorted one may imagine this shadow to be; especially where modern philosophies are concerned, from which even the slightest vestiges of the ancient traditional knowledge have entirely disappeared, they are only constructions without a foundation, assemblages of more or less fantastic hypotheses, and finally, mere individual opinions without authority or real importance.

In order to conclude we can summarize in a few words our essential thoughts on this point. Properly speaking, philosophy is only 'profane knowledge' and can claim nothing more, whereas symbolism, understood in its true sense, is essentially part of 'sacred science', which could not really exist or make itself known without it, for it would then lack all appropriate means of expression. We are well aware that many, even most, of our contemporaries are unfortunately incapable of distinguishing between these two orders of knowledge (if indeed any profane knowledge really deserves this attribution), but it is, of course, not to them that our words are addressed, for, to repeat, it is solely with 'sacred science' that we intend to occupy ourselves.

---

6. In Sanskrit, the word *laukika*, 'worldly' (an adjective derived from *loka*, 'world'), is often given the same meaning as in the language of the Gospels—that is, 'profane'—and this agreement seems to us well worth remarking.

7. Even taking into account only the proper meaning of the words, it should be evident that *philosophia* is never *sophia*, 'wisdom'; with respect to this latter philosophy can normally be only a preparation or an approach. One could then say that philosophy becomes illegitimate when its aim is no longer to open the way to something beyond itself. And this is just what the scholastics of the Middle Ages recognized when they said *Philosophia ancilla theologiae* [Philosophy is the handmaiden of theology]; but as regards the latter, their point of view was far too limited, because theology, which is restricted to the exoteric domain, is a long way indeed from representing the integrality of traditional wisdom.

19

RITES AND CEREMONIES

HAVING CLARIFIED THE PRINCIPAL QUESTIONS relating to the true nature of symbolism as far as we are able, we now return to the question of rites, regarding which there remain a few unfortunate confusions to dispel. In our day it has become possible for the most extraordinary assertions to be made and routinely accepted, since both those expressing them and those giving ear to them are afflicted with the same lack of discernment. Anyone who observes the various manifestations of the contemporary mentality continually witnesses so many things of this kind, in all orders and in all domains, that he reaches a point where he is astonished at nothing. Still, it is very difficult to avoid a certain amazement upon seeing so-called spiritual teachers, whom some even believe to have special 'missions', entrench themselves behind their 'abhorrence of ceremonies' in order to reject all rites indiscriminately, no matter what their nature may be, and even declare their resolute hostility to them. In itself this abhorrence is perfectly allowable, perhaps even legitimate, on condition that it be understood largely as a matter of individual preference and that there be no insistence that all share it. For our part, we understand it without any difficulty, but we would never have thought that certain rites could be assimilated to 'ceremonies', nor that rites in general must have such a character in themselves. It is here that the confusion lies, and this seems truly strange when it appears in those who claim more or less explicitly to guide others in a domain where it is rites, precisely, that play an essential and most important role as indispensable 'vehicles' of spiritual influences, for without these influences there can be no question of any effective contact whatsoever with realities of a higher order, but only of vague and inconsistent aspirations, of a nebulous 'idealism' and speculations into the void.

We will not pause to investigate the origin of the word 'ceremony', which seems to be rather obscure and on which linguists are far from agreement.[1] We use it of course according to its current meaning, which all know too well to need further emphasis, since it always involves a greater or lesser display of outward pomp, whatever may be the circumstances that provide the occasion or pretext in any particular case. It is obvious that it can happen, and in fact often does happen, especially in the exoteric order, that rites are surrounded by such pomp; but then the ceremony is merely superadded to the rite itself and is thus accidental and in no way essential to it, a point to which we shall return shortly. On the other hand, it is no less obvious that there also exist, and today more than ever, a multitude of ceremonies of a purely profane character that are in no way connected to the accomplishment of any rite; and if these have come to be dignified with the name of 'rite' this is only due to one of those prodigious abuses of language we have so often denounced, which, moreover, is explained by the fact that behind all such things lies the intention of establishing 'pseudo-rites' meant to supplant true religious rites, but which naturally can only imitate them in a wholly outward fashion, that is, precisely according to their 'ceremonial' side alone. The rite itself, of which the ceremony is only a sort of 'envelope', would then be entirely non-existent, since there could never be a profane rite, which is a contradiction in terms; and it can be asked whether the conscious inspirers of these gross counterfeits simply count on the general ignorance and incomprehension to effect such a substitution or whether they themselves share them to some degree. We will not try to resolve this last question, and we will only remind those who might be astonished that it can even be raised, that a comprehension in whatever degree of properly spiritual realities is strictly closed to the 'counter-initiation'.[2] But all that concerns us at the moment is the fact that there exist ceremonies without rites as well as rites without ceremonies, and

1. Does this word come from the feast of Ceres among the Romans, or rather, as others have supposed, from the name of an ancient Italian city called Céré? It matters little in the end, for in any case this origin, like that of the word 'mystical', of which we spoke earlier, has little relationship with its current meaning, which is the only one that can now be used.

2. See *Reign of Quantity*, chaps. 38 and 40.

this suffices to show how wrong it is to identify or assimilate the two in any way.

We have often said that in a strictly traditional civilization everything has a truly ritual character, even including the activities of daily life; must we therefore suppose that traditional men live in a state of perpetual ceremony? This is literally unimaginable, and the question has only to be formulated to reveal its absurdity immediately. It even ought to be said that the contrary is true, for in a traditional civilization rites are something altogether natural and in no way exceptional, as they may seem to be when consciousness of the tradition weakens and the profane point of view grows in proportion to this weakening; in such a case, the ceremonies accompanying these rites and underlining as it were their exceptional character would surely have no raison d'être. If one goes back to its origins, a rite is nothing other than 'what conforms to order', according to the meaning of the Sanskrit *rita*;[3] it is this alone, therefore, that is really 'normal', whereas ceremony, on the contrary, always and inevitably gives the impression of something more or less abnormal, outside of the habitual and regular course of the events that fill the rest of existence. This impression, let us note in passing, might help to explain the very singular way in which modern Westerners, who now can scarcely separate religion from ceremonies, regard rites as something wholly isolated and having no real connection with all the other activities to which they 'consecrate' their lives.

Every ceremony has a character that is artificial, even conventional, so to speak, because it is, after all, a wholly human product; and though it may be meant to accompany a rite, this character is opposed to the rite itself, which, on the contrary, includes an essentially 'non-human' element. If the one who accomplishes a rite has attained a certain degree of effective knowledge, he can and must know that there is something about it that transcends him, that does not depend in any way on his own individual effort; but as for ceremonies, even if they overawe those who witness them (and whose role here is reduced to that of mere spectator rather than 'participant'), it is quite clear that those who organize them and

3. Ibid., chaps. 3 and 8.

oversee their execution know perfectly well what is going on, and clearly recognize that any efficacy depends entirely on the arrangements they themselves have made and the more or less satisfactory manner in which they are performed. In fact, precisely because it is no more than human, this efficacy cannot be of a truly profound order since in the final analysis it is purely 'psychological'. This is why it can be said that it is indeed a matter of impressing those present or of overawing them by all sorts of sensible means; and even in ordinary language, is not one of the greatest commendations that can be made of a ceremony precisely that it is 'imposing',[4] even if the true meaning of this epithet is generally not well understood? In this connection let us note further that those who see only 'psychological' effects in rites confuse these latter with ceremonies in this way as well, perhaps without being aware of doing so, and this because they are ignorant of that 'non-human' character in virtue of which the real effects of rites properly so called and independently of any accessory circumstance are, on the contrary, of a wholly different order from that of the psychological.

Now, it might be asked why ceremonies are thus attached to rites, as if the 'non-human' had need of this human assistance, when it should much rather remain as far removed as possible from such contingencies. The answer is that all of this is simply a consequence of the need to take into account the actual conditions of terrestrial humanity, at least in this or that period of its existence; it is a concession made to what is, from the spiritual point of view, a certain state of degeneration on the part of the men who are called to participate in the rites, for it is they and not the rites who need the help of ceremonies. There can be no question of reinforcing or intensifying the effect of the rites in their own domain, but solely of making them more accessible to the individuals to whom they are addressed, of preparing these individuals as much as possible by putting them into the appropriate emotional and mental state; this is all that ceremonies can do, and it must be admitted that they are far

---

4. Guénon's point here is clear in the French, where the same verb (*imposer*) is used for what the translation renders both as 'imposing' and, in the preceding sentence, 'overawing'. ED.

from useless in this respect since, for the generality of men, they fulfill this function quite well. This is also why they have no purpose except in the exoteric order, which is meant for all without distinction; as for the esoteric or initiatic order, the case is entirely different, since this is reserved for an elite that by very definition has no need of these wholly outward 'aids', its qualifications implying precisely that it is superior to the state of degeneracy affecting most people. Thus if ceremonies are sometimes introduced into the esoteric order, this can only be explained by a certain degeneration of the initiatic organizations where this has taken place.

What we have just said defines the legitimate role of ceremonies, but side by side with this there are also abuses and dangers. Since what is purely outward is also by the very force of things what is most immediately apparent, it is always to be feared that the accidental will obscure the essential, and that, in the eyes of those who witness them, ceremonies will acquire much more importance than rites, which they so to speak conceal under an accumulation of accessory forms. Even worse, those whose function as authorized representatives of the tradition is to accomplish rites may sometimes share this error if they themselves are affected by the general spiritual degeneracy of which we have spoken. Once true comprehension has disappeared, everything is reduced, at least at a conscious level, to an excessive and baseless 'formalism' that devotes itself primarily to maintaining the pomp of ceremonies, which it magnifies inordinately, while the rite, which alone should matter, is held to be almost negligible. For a traditional form, this is a kind of degeneration that borders on 'superstition', this being understood in its etymological sense, for concern with forms has here outlived the comprehension thereof, and thus the 'letter' completely stifles the 'spirit'. 'Ceremonialism' is by no means the observance of ritual but rather the forgetting of its profound value and real meaning, and in the end amounts to the more or less crude materialization of this or that individual's notions of its nature and role, and, finally, to the repudiation of the 'non-human' for the sake of the human.

20

CEREMONIAL MAGIC

To complete what has just been said about ceremonies and their essential differences from rites, we will consider a special case that we have intentionally left aside, that of 'magic ceremonies', and while this certainly lies outside the principal subject of our study, we think it will not be unprofitable to consider it in some detail since, as we have already said, it is magic that gives rise to the better part of the ambiguities created and sustained by a crowd of pseudo-initiates of every sort. Moreover, the word 'magic' is today constantly applied without rhyme or reason to the most diverse things, often without the least relation to what it really designates. Anything that seems more or less bizarre, anything out of the ordinary, or what is conventionally considered as such, becomes 'magic'. We have already pointed out how some apply this epithet to the efficacy proper to rites, though usually with the intention of denying its reality; and in truth, the word has come to have hardly any other meaning than this in ordinary language. For others, 'magic' has instead a 'literary' aspect, somewhat in the way that people currently speak of the 'magic of style'; and it is above all to poetry, or at least to a certain kind of poetry, if not to all, that they wish to attribute this 'magic' character. In this last case the confusion is perhaps less crude, but all the more important to dissipate. It is true that originally, and before it degenerated into mere 'literature' and the expression of purely individual fantasy, poetry was something quite different, and could in the final analysis be directly linked to *mantras*,[1] so that at that time there could indeed have been a real

1. Sacred books, or at least some of them, can be called 'poems' in this sense, but they certainly are not poems in the 'literary' sense as claimed by modern 'critics', who want thereby to reduce them to a purely human level.

magical poetry as well as a poetry intended to produce effects of a much higher order;[2] but as soon as it is a matter of profane poetry (and it is inevitably this that the moderns have in mind since they cannot recognize any other even if it stares them in the face, since they persist in regarding it merely as 'literature') there can no longer be any question of this, nor, whatever may be said (for this also is an abuse of language), can there be a question of 'inspiration' in the only true meaning of the word, that is, in the strictly supra-human sense, however much lip service it may be given. We are not of course denying that profane poetry, as indeed any other expression of ideas or sentiments, can produce psychological effects, but this is an entirely different question which, to be precise, has absolutely nothing to do with magic. Nonetheless, this point should be kept in mind because it can be the source of a confusion directly related to another error frequently made by the moderns about the nature of magic itself, to which we shall have to return later.

Having said this, let us recall that magic is properly a science, one could even say a 'physical' science in the etymological sense of the word, since it deals with the laws and production of certain phenomena (and as we have already noted, it is the 'phenomenal' character of magic that interests modern Westerners because it satisfies their 'experimentalist' tendencies); but it must be clearly understood that the forces intervening here belong to the subtle order and not to the corporeal order, for which reason it is completely false to try to assimilate this science to a 'physical' one in the restricted sense intended by the moderns, though this error is actually met with, since some people have thought that magical phenomena can be reduced to electricity or some sort of 'radiation' of the same order. Now if magic has this scientific character, one will perhaps ask how there can be a question of magic rites, and it must be admitted that this has to be rather embarrassing for moderns, given their idea of the sciences. Wherever they see rites they think they are dealing with something entirely different, something they almost always seek to

---

2. The only vestiges of magical poetry that can still be found today in the West are part of what our contemporaries are wont to call 'popular superstitions', something found especially in country witchcraft.

identify more or less completely with religion; but let us say at once and clearly that in reality magic rites have nothing in common with religious rites with respect to their end, nor moreover (and we are tempted to say 'with even more reason') with initiatic rites, as, from another point of view, the partisans of certain pseudo-initiatic notions current in our time wish to believe; and yet magic rites do indeed exist, although they stand entirely outside of these two categories.

The explanation is really quite simple. Magic is a science, as we have just said, but a traditional science; now in everything that has this character, be it a question of science, art, or the crafts, there is always something that, if properly understood, must be considered a true rite, at least as long as one is not limited to merely theoretical considerations; and there is no reason to be surprised at this, for every action accomplished according to traditional rules, whatever its domain, is really a ritual action, as we have already pointed out. Naturally, these rites must in each case be of a special kind, since their 'technique' is perforce suitable to the particular end for which they are intended; this is why every confusion and false assimilation such as those just mentioned must be scrupulously avoided, and this pertains to the rites themselves as well as to the different domains to which they respectively belong, the two, moreover, being closely linked; and magic rites will thus be nothing more than one kind among many others, such, for example, as healing rituals, which must also appear to the eyes of the moderns a very extraordinary and even incomprehensible thing although their existence in traditional civilizations is an incontestable fact.

It is appropriate to recall also that among the traditional sciences magic is one that belongs to the lowest order, for here, of course, everything must be considered in a strict hierarchy according to its nature and its proper domain, which is no doubt why it is subject, perhaps more than any other science, to many deviations and degenerations.[3] It sometimes happens that it is developed out of all proportion to its real importance, to the point of stifling, as it were, higher kinds of knowledge that are more worthy of interest; and

---

3. Cf. *Reign of Quantity*, chaps. 26 and 27.

certain ancient civilizations have perished from the spread of magic, just as modern civilization risks perishing from the spread of profane science, which moreover represents an even more serious deviation, since magic, despite everything, is still a form of traditional knowledge. Sometimes, too, magic outlives itself so to speak under the aspect of more or less crude and misunderstood vestiges, but remains capable of producing certain effective results; and it can then descend to the level of sorcery, which is the most common and widespread case, or degenerate in some other way. Until now we have not spoken of ceremonies, but we have come precisely to the point where they must be discussed, for ceremonies constitute the proper character of one of these degenerations of magic, so much so that it has even received the name of 'ceremonial magic'.

Surely, occultists are little disposed to admit that this 'ceremonial magic'—the only magic they try to practice—is only a degenerate form, yet this is the case; and even without wishing to assimilate it to sorcery, we can say that in certain respects it is even more degenerate than this latter, although in another fashion. Let us explain ourselves more clearly on this point. The sorcerer accomplishes certain rites and pronounces certain formulas, generally without understanding their meaning but content to repeat as exactly as possible what was passed on to him (this is a particularly important point when it is a question of anything of a traditional character, as can be easily understood from what we explained above); and these rites and formulas, which most frequently are only the more or less disfigured remnants of very ancient things and are certainly not accompanied by any ceremony, nonetheless have in many cases a certain efficacy (we are making no distinction here between the benefic and malefic intentions that may govern their use, since it is solely a question of the reality of the effects attained). On the contrary, the occultist who performs 'ceremonial magic' generally does not obtain any serious result, however careful he may be to conform to a multitude of minute and complicated prescriptions that he has merely learned from books and not received from any transmission; he may sometimes delude himself, but this is an altogether different affair, and one can say that between the practices of the sorcerer and his own there exists the same difference as that between a living thing, even if in a state of decrepitude, and something dead.

This failure of the 'magus' (for this is the word the occultists prefer to use, doubtless thinking it more honorable and less vulgar than 'magician') has two reasons. On the one hand, to the extent that in such a case there can still be a question of rites, he simulates rather than truly accomplishes them, for he lacks the transmission that would be necessary to 'vivify' them and which cannot be replaced by mere intention. On the other hand, these rites are literally stifled under the empty 'formalism' of the ceremonies, for, unable to distinguish the essential from the accidental (and the books he consults are far from helpful, for everything in them is usually mixed inextricably together, perhaps intentionally in some cases and unintentionally in others), the 'magus' will naturally give his attention to the outward aspect above all, which is what is most striking and 'impressive', and it is this which in the final analysis justifies the very name of 'ceremonial magic'. In fact, most of those who believe they are 'performing magic' really accomplish nothing more than a sort of autosuggestion purely and simply; and what is most curious here is that the ceremonies manage to impress not only the spectators, if there are any, but even those performing them, so that when they are sincere (and this is the only case that need occupy us, not that of charlatanism) they are like children taken in by their own game. These people only obtain, and can only obtain, exclusively psychological effects, that is to say effects of the same nature as those produced by ceremonies in general, which, after all, is their purpose; but even if they remain sufficiently conscious of what happens within them and around them to realize that everything reduces merely to this, they are very far from doubting that, even if this be so, it is only due to their incapacity and their ignorance. And so they rack their brains to concoct theories that agree with the most up to date notions, thereby rejoining willy-nilly the ideas of 'official science' itself to explain that magic and its effects belong entirely to the psychological domain, just as others do for rites in general. The sad thing is that what they speak of is in no way magic, from the perspective of which such psychological effects are perfectly null and void, and that in confusing rites with ceremonies they also confuse the reality with its caricature or parody. If the 'mages' themselves are so confused, how can one be astonished that similar confusions are current among the 'general public'?

These remarks will suffice on the one hand to establish a link between the case of magic ceremonies and what we said in the first place about ceremonies in general, and, on the other, to show whence some of the principal modern errors about magic derive. Surely 'performing magic', even if done as authentically as possible, is not an occupation that seems to us of much interest in itself; but we must still admit that it is a science of which the results, whatever one may think of their worth, are just as real in their own order as those of any other science, and have nothing in common with illusions and 'psychological' dreams. One must at least know how to determine the true nature of each thing and how to put it in the place it belongs, but it is precisely this that most of our contemporaries show themselves to be wholly incapable of, and what we have already called 'psychologism', that is to say the tendency to reduce everything to psychological interpretations, of which we have here a very clear example, is, among the characteristic manifestations of their mentality, not the least peculiar or the least significant. Moreover, this is at root only one of the most recent forms taken by 'humanism', that is to say the more general tendency of the modern spirit to try to reduce everything to purely human factors.

21

PSYCHIC 'POWERS'

IN ORDER TO COMPLETE our treatment of magic and other things of the same order, we must deal with yet another question, that of alleged psychic 'powers', which brings us back more directly to initiation, or rather to the errors made concerning it; for as we said at the beginning, there are those who expressly assign to initiation the purpose of 'developing those psychic powers latent in man'. What they so designate is really nothing other than a power to produce more or less extraordinary 'phenomena', and in fact most of the pseudo-esoteric or pseudo-initiatic schools of the modern West intend nothing else. This is a veritable obsession among the great majority of their adherents who deceive themselves about the value of these 'powers' to the point of taking them as the sign of spiritual development, or even as its result, whereas, even when they are not a mere figment of the imagination, they belong solely to the psychic domain—which in reality has nothing at all to do with the spiritual—and are most often an obstacle to the acquisition of any true spirituality.

This illusion about the nature and scope of the 'powers' in question is most often associated with an excessive interest in 'magic', which is also caused by the same passion for 'phenomena' so characteristic of the modern Western mentality. But here another error inserts itself which it is well to point out: the truth is that there are no 'magical powers', although one meets this expression everywhere, not only among those to whom we have alluded, but also, by a curiously coincident error, among those who attempt to combat the tendencies of these former while being no less ignorant than they concerning the real facts of the matter. Magic must be treated as the natural and experimental science that it really is; as bizarre or exceptional as the phenomena with which it occupies itself may be, they are no more 'transcendent' than any others, and when the magician produces such phenomena, he does so merely by applying the knowledge he has of certain natural laws, those of the subtle domain to which the forces he engages belong. Thus there is no extraordinary 'power' here, any more than with one who, having studied some science, applies its results. Would one say for example that a physician possesses 'powers' because, knowing that a certain remedy is good for this or that illness, he cures it by means of that remedy? Between the magician and the possessor of psychic 'powers' there is a difference comparable to that in the corporeal order between one who uses a machine to accomplish some work and another who does so solely by dint of his own strength or manual skill, both acting in the same domain but not in the same way. On the other hand, whether it be a matter of magic or of 'powers', in neither case is there anything, we repeat, of the spiritual or the initiatic; if we note the difference between these two things, it is not because one is worth any more than the other from our point of view, but because it is always necessary to know exactly what one is speaking of and to dispel any confusions that vex the subject.

With certain individuals psychic 'powers' are entirely spontaneous, the simple effect of a natural disposition that develops of itself. In this case it is obvious that there is no room for pride, any more than in the case of other natural aptitudes, since such aptitudes do not bear witness to any intended 'realization', the existence of which the possessor may not even suspect. If he has never heard of 'initiation', the idea of being 'initiated' will certainly never occur to him simply because he happens to see things that others do not see or because he sometimes has 'premonitory' dreams, or again because he heals a sick person by mere contact and without knowing how it comes about. But there is also the case where similar 'powers' are acquired or developed artificially as the result of special 'training'; this is something more dangerous, for it rarely happens without provoking a certain disequilibrium; and at the same time it is in such a case that illusion is most easily produced. There are people who are convinced that they have obtained 'powers', perfectly imaginary in fact, either because of their desire and a sort of 'obsession' [*idée fixe*], or because of a suggestion exercised over them by someone from those quarters where 'training' of this kind is commonly practiced. It is here above all that 'initiation' is carelessly spoken of and more or less identified with the acquisition of these all too well-known 'powers'; and it is therefore not surprising that weak minds or the ignorant allow themselves to be as it were spellbound by such claims, claims which the case of spontaneous powers suffices to reduce to nothing, since it involves 'powers' that are wholly similar and perhaps even more developed and more authentic, without requiring the least trace of any real or supposed 'initiation'. What is perhaps most strange and most difficult to understand is that when those who possess such spontaneous 'powers' happen to find themselves in contact with these same pseudo-initiatic groups, they are sometimes led to believe that they, too, are 'initiates'; they ought to know the true character of their powers, which are also found to one degree or another among many very ordinary children, although often these powers subsequently disappear more or less quickly. The only excuse for these illusions is that none of those who bring about these 'powers' in themselves or in others have the slightest idea of what true initiation is; but of course this does not in any way diminish the danger of the psychic and even physiological troubles that are the usual accompaniment of such things, or of the more remote and still more serious consequences of a disordered development of lower psychic possibilities which, as we have said elsewhere, runs directly counter to spirituality.[1]

It is particularly important to note that these 'powers' can very well coexist with the most complete doctrinal ignorance, as one can only too easily observe among most 'clairvoyants' and 'healers'; this alone should suffice to prove that they have not the least connection with initiation, of which the goal can never be anything but pure knowledge. At the same time, this shows that their acquisition is completely lacking in interest, since the possessor thereby advances no further in the realization of his own being, a realization that is one with effective knowledge itself; they are nothing but wholly contingent and transitory acquisitions, exactly comparable

1. See *Reign of Quantity*, chap. 35.

in this respect to powers acquired by bodily development, which latter at least do not present the same dangers; and even the few no less contingent advantages that their exercise may bring certainly do not compensate for the disadvantages to which we have just alluded. Besides, do not these advantages all too often consist in nothing better than astonishing the naïve and securing their admiration, or in other no less empty and puerile satisfactions? Indeed, to make a display of these 'powers' is already the proof of a mentality incompatible with any initiation, even the most elementary; what can one say then about those who use them in order to pass for 'great initiates'? Let us not dwell further on this, for such things arise out of nothing more than charlatanism, even if the 'powers' in question are real in their own order; indeed, it is not the reality of the phenomena as such that counts here, but rather the value and scope attributed to them.

There is no doubt that suggestion plays a great part in all of this, even among those whose good faith is undeniable. To be convinced of this one has only to consider the case of 'clairvoyants' whose alleged 'revelations' are as far as possible from agreeing with each other, and instead are always related to their own ideas or to those of their milieu or school. Let us suppose nonetheless that we are dealing with realities, which is more likely when the 'clairvoyance' is spontaneous than when it has been brought about artificially. Even in this case it is hard to see why what someone has seen or heard in the psychic world should, in general, have more interest or importance than what anyone might happen to see or hear in the corporeal world while walking down the street: people, most of whom are unknown or to whom one is indifferent, incidents of no concern, fragments of incoherent or unintelligible conversations, and so forth. This comparison certainly gives the best idea of what presents itself to the 'clairvoyant', voluntary or involuntary. The former has more excuse for mistaking the importance of his visions, in the sense that he must suffer some pain at learning that all his efforts, pursued perhaps for years, finally lead only to such a derisory result; but these things ought to appear entirely natural to the spontaneous 'clairvoyant', as in fact they are, and if it did not happen so often that someone persuades him that they are extraordinary, he would doubtless never dream of concerning himself more with what he encounters in the psychic domain than he does with its equivalent in the corporeal domain, nor seek marvelous or complex significations for what, in the immense majority of cases, wholly lacks them. There is indeed a reason for everything, even the least important and apparently most indifferent fact, but this is of so little import to us that we take no account of it and feel no need to investigate it, at least when it is a question of what is conventionally called 'ordinary life', that is to say the events of the corporeal world. If the same rule were observed with regard to the psychic world (which at root is no less 'ordinary' in itself, even if not in our perceptions of it), how many divagations would be spared us! It is true that this requires a degree of mental equilibrium with which, unhappily, 'clairvoyants', even spontaneous ones, are only rarely endowed, much less those who have undertaken the psychic 'training' spoken about above. However that may be, this total 'disinterestedness' with regard to phenomena is no less strictly necessary for anyone who, while possessing faculties of this kind, wishes nonetheless to undertake a spiritual realization. As for one who is not so naturally endowed, far from striving to obtain them he must, on the contrary, consider this deficiency to be a very appreciable advantage in view of this same realization, in the sense that he will thus have far fewer obstacles to avoid, a point to which we shall return shortly.

In the final analysis, the very word 'powers', when used in this way, has the great defect of evoking the idea of a superiority that these things in no way imply. If this term is at all acceptable, it is only as a synonym for the word 'faculties', which moreover has an almost identical meaning etymologically.[2] These are indeed possibilities of the being, but possibilities that are in no way 'transcendent' since they are entirely of the individual order, and even in that order are far from being the highest and most worthy of attention. As to conferring on them some initiatic value, even if only auxiliary or preparatory, this would be entirely contrary to the truth, and as this latter alone counts in our eyes, we must speak of things as they

---

2. The original meaning of the word 'faculty' is also that of the corresponding Sanskrit word *indriya*.

are without concerning ourselves with what might please or dis-please anyone. Those who possess psychic 'powers' would surely be greatly mistaken to judge us harshly, for they would thereby only show even more clearly how entirely right we are in pointing out their own incomprehension and lack of spirituality. How indeed could one qualify otherwise an insistence on individual prerogative, or rather its appearance, to the point of preferring it to knowledge and the truth?[3]

3. Let no one object to what has just been said by maintaining that spontaneous 'powers' could be the result of some initiation received 'astrally' if not in 'previous existences'. It must be understood that when we speak of initiation, we intend only serious things and never fantasies of doubtful taste.

22

THE REJECTION
OF 'POWERS'

HAVING shown how little interest the so-called psychic 'powers'
present, and the absence of any connection between their development and a spiritual or initiatic realization, before leaving the subject we ought to emphasize further the fact that in regard to this
realization they are not only indifferent and useless, but even truly
harmful in most cases. They are in fact a 'distraction' in the rigorously etymological sense of the word. The one who lets himself be
absorbed by the many activities of the corporeal world will never
'center' his consciousness on higher realities, nor consequently
develop within himself the corresponding possibilities; this will be
all the more true for one who goes astray and 'disperses' himself in
the incomparably more vast and varied multiplicity of the psychic
world, with its indefinite modalities; and apart from exceptional
circumstances it is very likely that he will never succeed in freeing
himself from such phenomena, especially if he also harbors illusions concerning the value of these things which at least activities in
the corporeal world do not entail.

This is why anyone who firmly intends to follow an initiatic path
not only must never seek to acquire or to develop these all too
famous 'powers', but on the contrary must reject them pitilessly as
obstacles that will divert him from the single goal toward which he
strives, even when they come spontaneously and wholly accidentally. It is not that one must necessarily see them as 'temptations' or
as 'diabolical tricks' in the literal sense, as some too readily believe;
but something of the sort nevertheless does exist in that the world
of individual manifestation, as much in the psychic order as in the

corporeal order—if not even more so—seems as it were to try by every means to detain anyone who seeks to escape it. There is here something like a reaction of opposing forces, which, as with many other kinds of difficulty, can be due simply to a kind of unconscious hostility of the environment. Of course, since a man cannot isolate himself from this environment so as to become entirely independent of it as long as he has not arrived at the goal, or at least at a stage marked by liberation from the conditions of the individual human state, nothing prevents these manifestations from being at the same time the very natural though purely accidental results of his interior work, of which the outward repercussions sometimes take the most unexpected forms, going far beyond anything that can be imagined by those who have not themselves had occasion to experience them.

On the other hand, those who possess certain abnormal psychic powers are thereby, as we have already said, naturally at a certain disadvantage with regard to their spiritual development. Not only is it indispensable that they entirely dissociate themselves from them and hold them of no importance, but it may even be necessary to reduce the exercise of these powers to a minimum or even to suppress them altogether. Indeed, if it is recommended that the use of the corporeal senses be reduced to a minimum during periods of more or less prolonged effort in order to avoid distraction, the same thing is equally true of the psychic faculties; and furthermore, whereas man could not live if he completely and indefinitely ceased to exercise his senses, this is obviously not so in the other case and no serious inconvenience will result from this 'inhibition'. On the contrary, the being can only profit with regard to its organic and mental equilibrium, and thereafter be in a better condition to undertake the development of its higher possibilities without the risk of being hampered by a more or less pathological and abnormal state.

Those who produce extraordinary 'phenomena' are usually rather inferior beings intellectually and spiritually, or else have even gone wholly astray due to the special 'training' they have undergone. It is easy to understand that anyone who has spent part of his life engaged exclusively in producing 'phenomena' becomes incapable

of anything else and that possibilities of another order are henceforth irremediably closed to him. This is what generally happens to
those who give in to the attraction of the psychic domain. Even if
they have previously undertaken a work of initiatic realization, they
come to a halt on this path and go no further, and in fact are quite
fortunate if they remain where they are and are not drawn little by
little in the direction that, as we have explained elsewhere, is strictly
the reverse of spirituality and which can only lead finally to the 'dis-
integration' of the conscious being.[1] But even leaving aside this
extreme case, assuredly the mere cessation of all spiritual development is already in itself a consequence serious enough that it should
give pause to devotees of such 'powers', if they are not already
wholly blinded by the illusions of the 'intermediary world'.

One might perhaps object that there are authentically initiatic
organizations that train certain individuals in the development of
these 'powers'; but the truth is that the individuals involved lack initiatic qualifications and, on the contrary, have a special aptitude in
the psychic order, so that this is really all that can be done with
them; in such conditions, moreover, the development of psychic
powers is guided and controlled so as to keep the disadvantages and
dangers to a minimum. These beings even really benefit from the
link thus established with a traditional organization, which in its
turn can use them for ends of which they themselves are not conscious, not because they are willfully concealed from them, but
solely because, given the limitations of their possibilities, they are
wholly incapable of understanding them.

It goes without saying that the dangers we have just spoken of do
not exist for one who has arrived at a certain degree of initiatic realization; and it could even be said that such a one implicitly possesses
all such 'powers' without having to develop them particularly in any
way, by the very fact that he controls the forces of the psychic world
'from above'; but generally such an initiate will not exercise powers
of this kind because they have no more interest for him. In an analogous way, one who has understood the inmost essence of certain
traditional sciences takes no interest whatsoever in their application

---

1. See *Reign of Quantity*, chap. 35.

and never makes any use of them; pure knowledge suffices him, and is truly the only thing that matters, for all else is but mere contingency. Besides, all manifestations of such things are necessarily a 'descent' as it were, even if only an apparent one that cannot really affect the being itself. It must not be forgotten that the non-manifest is superior to the manifest and that consequently the fact of remaining in this 'non-manifestation' will be, so to speak, the most adequate expression of the state that the being has inwardly realized. This is what some people state symbolically by saying that 'the night is preferable to the day', and this is also represented by the image of the turtle withdrawing into its shell. If it later happens that such a being should manifest certain 'powers', this will only be, as we have already indicated above, in altogether exceptional cases and for particular reasons that the outer world necessarily cannot appreciate, reasons that of course differ entirely from those of ordinary producers of 'phenomena'. Besides these cases, such a being's only mode of action will be what the Far-Eastern tradition designates as 'non-acting activity', which, precisely by its character of non-manifestation, is the very fullness of activity.

Let us recall in this connection the perfect insignificance of phenomena in themselves, since it can happen that similar phenomena proceed from entirely different causes which may not even be of the same order. Thus it is easily understood that if the being that possesses a high degree of spirituality should occasionally produce some phenomenon, it will not do so in the same way as one that has acquired this power by means of some psychic 'training' and will act according to completely different modalities; the comparison of 'theurgy' with 'magic', which lies beyond our scope here, would occasion the same remark. This truth also ought to be recognized without difficulty by those belonging to the exoteric order, for if numerous cases of 'levitation' or 'bilocation' can be found in the lives of the saints, just as many can certainly be found in the lives of sorcerers. The appearances (that is to say, precisely, 'phenomena' in the strict and etymological sense of the word) are exactly the same in both cases, but no one would conclude from this that the causes are also the same. Even from the merely theological point of view two facts can be similar in every respect, but one may be considered a miracle while the other is not, and to distinguish them it would be necessary to resort to a different order of proofs, independent of the facts themselves. From another point of view, we could say that a fact will be a miracle if it is due to the action of a spiritual influence and that it will not be a miracle if it is due to the action of a psychic influence. This is illustrated very clearly by the contest between Moses and the Pharaoh's magicians, which also represents the contest between the forces of initiation and counter-initiation, at least in a certain measure and on the common ground where such a contest is possible. The counter-initiation can of course only exert its action in the psychic domain, as we have explained elsewhere, for everything of the spiritual domain is by its very nature absolutely forbidden to it.[2]

Enough has been said on this subject, and if we have dwelt on it so much, perhaps even too much in some people's eyes, it is because we have only too often seen the need for doing so. No matter how disagreeable the task may be at times, it is necessary to warn those with whom we are here concerned about the errors they court at each moment on their way, errors that are far from harmless. To conclude in a few words, we will say that initiation could never have the goal of acquiring 'powers' that, as does the very world in which they are exercised, belong in the final analysis to the domain of the 'great illusion'. Far from tying himself to them ever more strongly by new bonds, the one on the path of spiritual development must on the contrary loose himself from them entirely; and this freedom can only be obtained by pure knowledge on condition, of course, that this not remain merely theoretical but on the contrary become fully effective, for it is in this alone that the very realization of the being in all its degrees consists.

2. Ibid., chaps. 38 and 39.

23

SACRAMENTS
AND INITIATIC RITES

WE SAID EARLIER THAT religious rites and initiatic rites are of essentially different orders and that they cannot have the same goal, this being a necessary result of the distinction between the exoteric and esoteric domains to which they respectively belong. If confusions arise between them in some minds, they are due above all to a misunderstanding of this distinction, and perhaps in part to similarities that in spite of everything exist between these rites, at least in their outward forms, which can deceive those who observe things only 'from outside'. Nonetheless, the distinction is perfectly clear once it is a question of strictly religious rites, which are exoteric by definition and consequently brook no doubt; however, it must be said that doubts may arise in other cases, as in a tradition where there is no division between an exoterism and an esoterism, constituting as it were two separate aspects of the tradition, but only between different degrees of knowledge, where the transition from one to another can be almost imperceptible, as with the Hindu tradition in particular. This gradual transition will naturally show itself in the corresponding rites, so that in certain respects some of them may have a somewhat mixed or intermediate character.

It is precisely in the Hindu tradition that one finds rites concerning which one can legitimately ask whether or not they are initiatic; we mean the *upanayana*, that is, the rite by which an individual is effectively joined to one of the three higher castes, to which, before this rite is accomplished, he belongs only in what can be called an altogether potential fashion. This case in fact merits close examination, and for this it will be necessary in the first place to understand exactly what is intended by the word *samskāra*, usually translated as 'sacrament'. This translation seems to us far from satisfactory, for according to a tendency too common among Westerners it affirms an identity between things that, if comparable in certain respects, are nonetheless very different in fact. It is true that it is not the etymological meaning itself of the word 'sacrament' that occasions this objection, for in both cases it is evidently a question of something 'sacred'; moreover this meaning is much too broad to permit us to draw from it an idea that is at all precise, and if we were to leave things here, any rite at all could indifferently be called a 'sacrament'. But in fact this word has become inseparable from its specifically religious and narrowly-defined usage in the Christian tradition, where it designates something the exact equivalent of which is not found elsewhere. In order to avoid any ambiguity it is thus much better to accept this usage and to reserve the name 'sacrament' to a certain category of religious rites peculiar to the Christian traditional form; it is then the idea of 'sacrament' that is included in that of *samskāra* as a particular case, and not the reverse. In other words, one can say that the Christian sacraments are *samskāras*, but not that the Hindu *samskāras* are sacraments, for according to the most elementary logic the name of a genus belongs to each of the species it includes, but the name of one of these species cannot validly be applied either to another species or to the entire genus.

A *samskāra* is essentially a rite of 'admission' to a traditional community; and as one can immediately see, this definition is entirely independent of the particular form, religious or otherwise, assumed by the tradition under consideration. In Christianity this function is fulfilled by the sacraments, as it is elsewhere by *samskāras* of different kinds. We must nevertheless say that the word 'admission', which we have just used, lacks some precision and even exactness, and this for two reasons. First, if one limits oneself strictly to its proper meaning, it seems to designate the actual attachment to the tradition, in which case it should apply only to a single rite, that by which this attachment is effectively accomplished, whereas in reality there are in one and the same tradition a number of *samskāras*, from which it follows that the 'admission' in question includes many degrees or modalities, which generally correspond to the principal phases of an individual's life; on the other hand, this same word 'admission' can convey the idea of a relationship that remains in a sense outward, as if it were simply a matter of joining a 'group' or a 'society', whereas what is involved is of an entirely different order and implies an assimilation that could be called 'organic', for it involves a true 'transmutation' (*abhisambhava*) of the subtle elements of the individuality. For *samskāra*, A. K. Coomaraswamy has proposed the word 'integration', which seems to us preferable to 'admission' from both points of view, for it exactly translates the idea of assimilation; besides, it is easy to understand that an 'integration' can be more or less deep and complete and that, consequently, it could be accomplished by degrees, which accounts for the multiplicity of *samskāras* within one and the same tradition.

It should be noted that a 'transmutation' such as that just spoken of takes place not only in the *samskāras* but also in initiatic rites (*dīkshā*);[1] this is one of the characteristics that both share and which allows them to be compared in certain respects, whatever their essential differences may be. In both cases there is the transmission or communication of a spiritual influence, and it is this influence, 'infused' so to speak by the rite, that produces in the individual the 'transmutation' in question. But it goes without saying that the effects can be limited to this or that domain, depending on the particular goal of the rite being considered; and it is precisely by their goal, and so also by the domain or order of possibilities in which they operate, that initiatic rites differ profoundly from all others.

On the other hand, the most apparent outward difference, and thus the one that ought to be most easily recognized, even by those

---

1. In Sanskrit, the word *dīkshā* properly means 'initiation', although it sometimes has to be translated rather as 'consecration' (regarding these two ideas, refer to what we said above about the different meanings of the Greek word *mueo*). Thus in certain cases, for example when a person offers a sacrifice, the 'consecration' designated by the word *dīkshā* has a temporary effect, valid only during the sacrifice itself, and must be renewed if the same person later offers another sacrifice, even if it is of the same sort as the first. It is therefore impossible to see in this 'consecration' an initiation in the true sense of the word, for as we have already said, every initiation is necessarily something permanent that is acquired once and for all and can never be lost under any circumstances.

observing 'from the outside', is that the *samskāras* are common to all the individuals belonging to a tradition, that is to say, in the final analysis, to all those belonging to a given 'milieu', something that gives these rites what can properly be called a 'social' aspect, whereas initiatic rites on the contrary require certain particular qualifications and are reserved for a more or less restricted elite. From this one can see the error of ethnologists and sociologists who unthinkingly apply the term 'initiation' (the true meaning and real implications of which they evidently have no grasp) to rites that all the members of a tribe or people have access to at any moment of their existence, and in particular when it is a matter of so-called primitive societies. In reality, these rites have no initiatic character at all but are true *samskāras*. Naturally, the same societies can also have authentically initiatic rites, even if these are degenerate to some degree (and perhaps they are so less often than one might be tempted to suppose); but, here as everywhere, these are accessible only to certain individuals to the exclusion of others, and this, even without examining things more deeply, ought to suffice to make any confusion impossible.

We now come to the special case we mentioned at the outset, that of the Hindu rite of *upanayana*, which is essentially the investiture with the brahmanic thread (*pavitra* or *upavitā*) and normally gives access to the study of sacred scriptures. Is this an initiation? It appears that the question could be resolved by the sole fact that this rite is a *samskāra* and not a *dīkshā*, for this implies that it is not considered to be initiatic from the point of view of the Hindu tradition, which obviously must be given authority here; but again one can ask why this is so despite certain appearances to the contrary. We have already indicated that this rite is reserved for the members of the three primary castes, but this restriction is inherent to the very constitution of traditional Hindu society, and so it does not suffice to allow one to speak of initiation, any more, for example, than the fact that certain rites are reserved for men to the exclusion of women—or inversely—lets one attribute to them an initiatic character (to convince oneself of this one need only refer to the case of Christian ordination, which even requires other more particular qualifications, yet belongs no less incontestably to the exoteric order). Besides the one qualification we have just noted (designated by the term *ārya*), no other is required for *upanayana*; this rite is therefore common to all the members of the three primary castes without exception, and it is even more an obligation than a right; now this obligatory character, which is directly linked to what we have called the 'social' aspect of the *samskāras*, could not exist for an initiatic rite. A social milieu, however deeply traditional it may be, cannot impose on any of its members, whatever their qualifications, the obligation to enter an initiatic organization. This is something that by its very nature cannot depend on any outward constraint, not even the mere 'moral' constraint customarily termed 'public opinion', which, moreover, can obviously adopt no other legitimate attitude than to ignore purely and simply all that relates to initiation since this is an order of reality that by definition is closed to the collectivity as such. As regards *upanayana*, it can be said that caste is only virtual or even potential as long as this rite has not been accomplished (the only qualification required being the natural aptitude to belong to that caste), so that this rite is necessary in order for the individual to occupy a place and a given function in the social organization; for if his function must before all else conform to his own nature, it is still necessary for this nature to be 'realized' in order for it to be validly fulfilled and not remain merely an undeveloped aptitude. It is thus perfectly understandable and normal that the non-accomplishment of this rite within the prescribed period entails an exclusion from the community, or more exactly still, that it implies in itself this exclusion.

There is however yet another particularly important point to consider, for it is perhaps this above all that can lead to confusion. The *upanayana* confers the quality of *dvija* or 'twice born'; it is thus explicitly called a 'second birth', an expression that also applies in a very precise way to initiation. It is true that Christian baptism, although very different from *upanayana* in every other respect, is also a 'second birth', and it is only too evident that this rite has nothing in common with an initiation. But how can the same 'technical' term apply at once to the *samskāras* (including the sacraments) and to initiation? The truth is that the 'second birth' in itself and in its general meaning is strictly a psychic regeneration (note well that it is to the psychic domain that this directly refers, and not to the spiritual, for this would then be a 'third birth'); but this regeneration can have effects that are solely psychic, that is, limited to a more or less special order of individual possibilities, or it can be the point of departure for a 'realization' of a higher order. It is only in this last case that it will have a properly initiatic scope, whereas in the first it will belong to the most 'outward' side of the different traditional forms, namely to that in which all participate without distinction.[2]

The allusion we just made to baptism raises another question that is not without interest. Apart from its character as a 'second birth', baptism also resembles certain initiatic rites by its very form; one can also note that this form belongs to the rites of purification by the elements (a subject we shall return to later), a very general category of rites that can obviously be applied in very different domains. But perhaps there is something more to consider here. Indeed, there is nothing astonishing in the fact that exoteric rites are modeled after esoteric or initiatic rites; if the degrees of outward teaching in a traditional society can be closely modeled on those of initiation, as we shall explain later, then with all the more reason a similar 'exteriorization' can take place in a higher though still exoteric order, that is to say with religious rites.[3] In all of this the hierarchy of normal relationships is strictly respected, for according to these relationships, applications of a lower or more outward order must proceed from those of a more principial character. Thus, if we consider such things as the 'second birth' or purification by the elements, to limit ourselves only to these examples, it is their initiatic signification that

2. The limitation of the effects of regeneration accomplished in exoteric mode explains why it cannot in any way take the place of initiation or allow it to be dispensed with, although both have in common the character of a 'second birth', understood in its most general sense.

3. It should be noted that from this point of view religious ordination represents an 'exteriorization' of sacerdotal initiation, and that the consecration of kings is an 'exteriorization' of royal initiation, both being determined by the conditions in which the corresponding functions ceased to be reserved to initiates, as they were previously.

is really primary, and their other applications must be derived more or less directly from this, for in any traditional form there can be nothing more principial than initiation and its proper domain, and it is in this 'interior' aspect that the true spirit of every tradition resides.

24

PRAYER AND INCANTATION

WE HAVE JUST SEEN that there are cases where the distinction between the exoteric and esoteric domains does not seem to be absolute, as a result of the particular way in which certain traditional forms are constituted, and this leads to a sort of continuity between them. There are other cases, on the contrary, where this distinction is perfectly clear, and this is particularly the case where exoterism has a specifically religious form. In order to give a precise and well-defined example of this latter we will consider the difference between prayer in the exoteric order and what in the esoteric order we will call 'incantation', using this word for lack of a clearer one in Western languages, and waiting until later to define it exactly. With regard to prayer, we must first of all note that although in current language the word is usually understood in a very vague way, to the point where it is sometimes taken as a synonym for 'orison' in all its generality, we think it appropriate to keep or to assign to it the much more special and restricted meaning that comes from its etymology, for the word 'prayer' properly and exclusively signifies 'petition'[1] and cannot without abuse be used to designate anything else. It must therefore not be forgotten that it is in this sense alone that we will understand it in the course of the following considerations.

In order to indicate how prayer can be understood, let us first of all consider some collectivity, be it religious or merely 'social' in the outward or even wholly profane sense in which this word is usually

---

1. The French word is *prière*. This distinction is perhaps less obvious in modern English than in Guénon's French, but even today the little-used 'orison' does not have the sense of 'petition' that the word 'prayer' often has. ED.

taken in our time.[2] Each member of this collectivity is bound to it to some degree, which is determined by the extent of its sphere of action, and in turn the member must logically participate to the same degree in certain benefits. In some instances these benefits are wholly material (as is the case with present-day nations, for example, or the many kinds of associations based on no more than a simple solidarity of interest, which associations needless to say are generally wholly profane), but in others they relate to extra-corporeal modalities of the individual, that is, to what can generally be called the psychic domain (such as consolations or other favors of a sentimental order, and sometimes even of a higher order); or again, to what, though material, is achieved by apparently immaterial means, or, to be more precise, by the intervention of elements that do not belong to the corporeal order but nonetheless act directly on it (obtaining a healing by prayer is a particularly clear example). In all of this we are speaking only of individual modalities, for these benefits can never transcend the individual domain, which is the only one attainable by any collectivity that is not an initiatic organization (for as we explained earlier, the latter are the only organizations to have the express goal of transcending this domain), and which occupies itself with contingencies and special applications of some practical interest from one point of view or another, though of course not only in the grossly 'utilitarian' sense to which purely profane organizations limit themselves and of which the field of action does not extend beyond the corporeal domain.

Each collectivity can thus be regarded as possessing, in addition to means of action that are purely material in the ordinary sense of the word, that is, belonging solely to the corporeal order, a subtle force made up in a way of the contributions of all its members past and present, and which consequently is all the more powerful and able to produce greater effects as the collectivity is older and composed of a greater number of members.[3] It is evident, moreover,

---

2. Of course, to acknowledge the existence in fact of purely profane social organizations, that is to say organizations lacking any element of a traditional character, in no way implies a recognition of their legitimacy.

3. This can be true even of profane organizations, though it is evident that they can only use this force unconsciously and for exclusively corporeal results.

that this 'quantitative' consideration essentially indicates that it is a question of the individual domain, beyond which this force can in no way intervene. Each of the members can at need use a part of this force to his own benefit, and for this it suffices that he put his individuality in harmony with the collectivity of which he forms a part, which he can do by conforming to the rules established by the latter for the purpose of addressing the different circumstances that may arise. Thus, if the individual formulates a petition, it is essentially—at least most immediately—to what can be called the spirit of the collectivity that he addresses it, consciously or not (although the word 'spirit' is certainly inappropriate here since it is really only a psychic entity that is in question). However, it is appropriate to add that every case is not always limited to this alone, for with collectivities of a regular and authentic traditional form, particularly with religious collectivities where the observation of the rules just mentioned consists in the accomplishment of certain rites, there is also the intervention of a truly 'non-human' element, that is, of what we have called a spiritual influence, which must be regarded as 'de-scending' into the individual domain and acting there by means of the collective force that it uses as a support.[4]

Sometimes the force we are speaking of, or more exactly the synthesis of the spiritual influence and the collective force in which it so to speak 'incorporates' itself, can focus on a corporeal 'support' such as a given place or object, which then plays the role of a 'condenser'[5] and produces perceptible manifestations, such as those reported in the Hebrew Bible of the Ark of the Covenant and the Temple of Solomon. Places of pilgrimage and the tombs of saints or other persons venerated by the adherents of a given traditional form can also be cited as examples to some degree or another. Here lies the principal cause of the 'miracles' occurring in the different religions, for these are facts of which the existence cannot be denied and which

---

4. It can be noted that in Christian doctrine the role of the spiritual influence corresponds to the action of 'grace', and that of the collective force to the 'communion of saints'.

5. In such a case there is something comparable to a complete living being, with a 'body' that is the 'support' in question, a 'soul' that is the collective force, and a 'spirit' that is naturally the spiritual influence acting outwardly by means of the other two elements.

are by no means limited to one religion. Moreover, it goes without saying that, despite common opinion, these facts must not be considered contrary to natural laws any more than, from another point of view, the 'supra-rational' can be taken for the 'irrational'. In reality—let us say it again—spiritual influences also have their laws, which, although of another order than those of natural forces, psychic as well as corporeal, are not without certain analogies to them; thus it is possible to determine the circumstances favorable to their action which can then be called forth and directed, given the necessary knowledge, by those who preside over them by reason of the functions with which they have been invested in a traditional organization. It must be noted that the 'miracles' in question here, in themselves and independently of their cause which alone has a 'transcendent' character, are purely physical phenomena, perceptible as such by one or more of the five external senses; such phenomena moreover are the only ones that can be witnessed without further distinction by the generality of ordinary 'believers', whose understanding does not go beyond the limits of the corporeal modality of the individuality.

The benefits to be obtained by prayer and by practicing the rites of a social or religious collectivity (rites that are common to all its members without exception and thus of a purely exoteric order, and obviously having no initiatic character as long as they are not considered in respect of their ability to serve as the support for a spiritual 'realization') are essentially relative and contingent, but they are nonetheless by no means negligible for the individual who, as such, is himself relative and contingent; the individual would therefore be wrong to deprive himself voluntarily of such benefits if he belongs to an organization that can provide them. Thus, as long as it is necessary to take into account the nature of the human being as he is in fact, that is to say in the order of reality to which he belongs, it is in no way blameworthy for one who is more than a mere 'believer' (making between 'belief' and 'knowledge' a distinction corresponding essentially to that between exoterism and esoterism) to comply with the outward prescriptions of a religion or a traditional legislation for the sake of some personal interest, precisely because it is an individual interest and thus outside any strictly doctrinal consideration, provided that he attributes to what he thus seeks only the proper importance and legitimate place, and provided as well that the collectivity does not impose on this compliance conditions that, although commonly admissible, would constitute a real *de facto* impossibility in this particular case. With these sole reservations, prayer, whether addressed to a collective entity or, through its inter-mediation, to the spiritual influence that it transmits, is perfectly allowable even with regard to the most rigorous orthodoxy in the domain of pure doctrine.[6]

By the comparison they allow, these considerations will make it easier to understand what we will now say about 'incantation'. It is essential to note that what we designate by this name has absolutely nothing to do with the magical practices to which the name is some-times given;[7] besides, we have already said enough about magic so that no confusion should be possible and no further comment nec-essary. In contrast to prayer, the incantation we spoke of is not a petition and does not even presuppose the existence of anything outward, which every petition necessarily supposes, because out-wardness cannot be understood except in relation to the individual, which here is precisely surpassed. It is an aspiration of the being toward the Universal in order to obtain what we might call in some-what 'theological' language a spiritual grace, that is, essentially an inward illumination that can naturally be more or less complete according to the case. Here the action of the spiritual influence must be seen in its pure state, if one can speak thus; instead of seeking to make it descend, as in prayer, the being tends on the contrary to rise toward it. The incantation thus defined as an entirely inward opera-tion in principle can nonetheless in many cases be expressed and 'supported' outwardly by words or gestures that constitute initiatic rites, such as the *mantra* in the Hindu tradition or the *dhikr* in the Islamic tradition, which must be thought of as producing rhythmic

6. 'Prayer' is of course not at all synonymous with 'adoration'; one can ask for benefits from someone without in any way 'divinizing' him.

7. In current usage, the word 'incantation' has undergone a degeneration simi-lar to that suffered by the word 'charm', which is also commonly used in the same sense, although the Latin *carmen*, from which it derives, originally designated poetry taken in its strictly 'sacred' sense. It is perhaps not without interest to note that the word *carmen* is very similar to the Sanskrit *karma*, understood in the sense of 'ritual action', as we have already said.

vibrations that reverberate throughout a more or less extensive domain in the indefinite series of the states of the being. Whether the result obtained be more or less complete, the final goal is always the realization in oneself of 'Universal Man' by the perfect communion of all these states in proper and harmonious hierarchy and in an integral expansion, both in 'amplitude' and 'exaltation', that is, both as to the horizontal expansion of the modalities of each state and the vertical superposition of the different states, according to the geometrical figuration that we have explained in detail elsewhere.[8]

This leads us to make another distinction in regard to the different degrees that can be attained depending on the extent of the result achieved in tending toward this goal. First, at the bottom and outside the hierarchy thus established, must be placed the host of the 'profane', that is, according to the meaning intended here, all those who, like simple religious believers, cannot obtain real results except through their corporeal individuality and within the limits of this portion or special modality of the individuality, because their effective consciousness goes no further or higher than the domain enclosed within these limits. Nonetheless, among these believers there are a small number who obtain something more (this is the case of certain mystics who can be considered in this sense more 'intellectual' than the others) and who, without leaving their individuality, but in 'prolongations' thereof, indirectly perceive realities of a higher order, not as they are in themselves, but expressed symbolically and clothed in psychic or mental forms. These are still phenomena (that is, etymologically, appearances, which are always relative and illusory insofar as they are formal), but they are suprasensible phenomena not ascertainable by everyone, and can lead those who perceive them to certitudes which, though always incomplete, fragmentary, and scattered, are nonetheless superior to the simple belief they replace. Moreover, this result is obtained passively, that is to say without the intervention of the will and merely by the ordinary means prescribed by the religions, particularly by prayer and the accomplishment of prescribed works, for all of this still remains in the domain of exoterism.

8. See *The Symbolism of the Cross*.

At a much higher degree, one already sharply distinct from the foregoing, are those who have extended their consciousness to the extreme limits of the integral individuality and have come to perceive the superior states of their being directly without, however, participating in them effectively. We are here in the initiatic domain, but this initiation, though real and effective with regard to the extension of the individuality in its extra-corporeal modalities, is still only theoretical and virtual with regard to the higher states since it does not actually achieve possession of them. It produces certitudes incomparably more complete, more developed, and more coherent than in the preceding case, for it no longer belongs to the phenomenal domain, but the one who acquires them can nonetheless be compared to a man who does not know the light except by the rays that reach him (in the preceding case, by contrast, he knows it only by its reflections or by the shadows projected on the field of his restricted individual consciousness, as do the prisoners in Plato's allegory of the cave), whereas in order to know the light perfectly in its intimate and essential reality it is necessary to reascend to and identify oneself with its very source.[9] This last case corresponds to the fullness of real and effective initiation, that is, to the conscious and voluntary taking possession of the totality of the states of the being according to both senses indicated; this is the complete and final result of incantation, which, as can be seen, is very different from all that mystics can attain by prayer, for it is nothing other than the very perfection of fully realized metaphysical knowledge. The *Yogis* of the Hindu tradition or the *Sufis* of the Islamic tradition, if these words be taken in their strict and true meaning, are those who have arrived at this supreme degree and who thus have realized in their being the total possibility of 'Universal Man'.

---

9. This is what the Islamic tradition designates as *ḥaqq al-yaqīn*, whereas the preceding degree, which corresponds to 'sight' without identification, is called *'ayn al-yaqīn*; and the first, that which simple believers can attain with the help of traditional exoteric teaching, is *'ilm al-yaqīn*.

25

INITIATIC TRIALS

WE SHALL NOW consider what are called initiatic 'trials', which fundamentally are only a particular case of initiatic rites though important enough to merit separate treatment, all the more so in that they are the occasion for many errors. The very word 'trials', which is used in many senses, is perhaps partly responsible for these ambiguities, unless some of its current meanings already derive from earlier confusions, which is equally possible. Indeed, it is not at all clear why every troublesome event is commonly called a 'trial', or why it is said of someone who suffers that he is 'tried'; it is difficult to see anything here but a mere abuse of language, the origin of which, moreover, it may not be without interest to investigate. However this may be, the common idea of the 'trials of life' does exist even if it does not correspond to anything very clearly defined, and it is this above all that has given rise to false assimilations concerning initiatic trials, to the point where some have come to see in these nothing but a symbolic image of the former, which by a strange reversal of things would lead one to suppose that it is the facts of outward human life that have an effective value and truly count from the initiatic point of view itself. It would certainly be too simple if this were the case, and all men would thus doubtless be candidates for initiation; it would suffice that each had gone through some difficult circumstance, which happens more or less to everyone, in order to achieve initiation, and one would find it difficult to say by whom and in the name of what it would be conferred. We think we have already said enough about the true nature of initiation that we need not dwell on the absurdity of such notions as these, for the truth is that 'ordinary life' as it is understood today has absolutely nothing to do with the

initiatic order since it corresponds to an entirely profane understanding of life; and if on the contrary one were to envisage human
life according to a traditional and normal understanding, one could
say that it is this that can be taken as a symbol, and not the reverse.

It is worth pausing for a moment at this last point. The symbol
must always be of an order inferior to what is symbolized (which, let
us note in passing, suffices to dismiss all the 'naturalist' interpretations the modernists may imagine); the realities of the corporeal
domain, being of the lowest and most narrowly-delimited order,
thus cannot be symbolized by anything at all; and they have moreover no need of being symbolized since they are directly and immediately comprehensible to everyone. On the other hand, because of
the correspondence that exists between all orders of reality, every
event or phenomenon, however insignificant it may be, can always
be taken as a symbol of a higher reality of which it is as it were a sensible expression by the very fact that it derives from it as a consequence derives from its principle; and in this respect, however
lacking in value and interest it may be in itself, the event or phenomenon can have a profound significance for one who is able to
see beyond immediate appearances. Here we have a transposition
the result of which will obviously have nothing in common with
'ordinary life' or even with outward life howsoever considered, since
this latter has merely supplied the support that allows a being
endowed with special aptitudes to escape from its limitations. And
this support, let us emphasize, can be anything whatsoever, since
everything here depends on the nature of the being that uses it.
Consequently, and this brings us back to the common idea of 'trials',
it is not impossible that in certain particular cases suffering should
be the occasion or support for a development of latent possibilities
exactly as anything else could be in other cases; it is the occasion, we
say, and nothing else, and this does not permit one to attribute to
suffering in itself any special or privileged virtue, despite all the
usual pronouncements on the subject. Let us also note that the
entirely contingent and accidental role of suffering, even thus
reduced to its proper proportions, is certainly more restricted in the
initiatic order than in certain other much more exterior 'realiza-
tions'; it is especially among the mystics that it has become in a way

habitual and seems to have acquired an importance capable of fostering illusions (and first of all among these mystics themselves), which is no doubt explained at least in part by considerations of a specifically religious nature.[1] It must also be added that profane psychology has certainly helped in good measure to spread over all of this the most confused and erroneous ideas; but in any case, whether it be a matter of mere psychology or of mysticism, all these things have absolutely nothing in common with initiation.

Having settled this, we must still explain a fact that could give rise to an objection. Although, as we were just saying, difficult or painful circumstances are certainly common to the lives of all men, it frequently happens that those who follow an initiatic way find them unusually multiplied. This fact is due simply to a sort of unconscious hostility in the environment, to which we have already had occasion to refer; it seems that the world, by which we mean the totality of beings and things that constitute the domain of individual existence, tries by all means to hold back one who is on the verge of escaping it; such reactions are perfectly normal and understandable and, unpleasant as they may be, there is certainly no cause to be astonished at them. This is therefore strictly a question of obstacles raised by adverse forces, and not, as people sometimes wrongly imagine, of 'trials' willed and imposed by the powers that preside over initiation. It is necessary to have done once and for all with such fables, which are surely much closer to occultist dreams than to initiatic realities.

What are called initiatic trials are something altogether different, and a single observation should suffice to cut short every ambiguity. These trials are essentially rites, which the so-called 'trials of life' never are, and they could not exist without this ritual character or be replaced by anything that does not possess this same character. By this it can immediately be seen that the most generally emphasized aspects of these trials are really wholly secondary; if they were intended to show whether a candidate for initiation possessed the

---

1. It might also be asked whether this exaltation of suffering is indeed inherent in the special form of the Christian tradition, or whether it is not rather 'superimposed' as it were by the natural tendencies of the Western temperament.

requisite qualifications, as the most 'simplistic' notion would have it, it would have to be admitted that they are very ineffectual, and it could be understood why those who so look at things are tempted to regard them as without value. But normally one who is permitted to undergo these trials already ought to have been recognized as 'well and duly qualified' by other more adequate means; and thus there must be something completely different involved here. It can therefore be said that these trials are a teaching given under a symbolic form and meant to be meditated upon later; this is very true, but as much could be said of any other rite, for, as we said earlier, all rites have an equally symbolic character and thus a meaning that each individual must fathom according to the measure of his own capacity. The essential purpose of a rite, as we explained at the beginning, is the efficacy inherent to it; it goes without saying that this efficacy is closely related to the symbolic meaning of its form, but it is entirely independent of the actual understanding of those who participate in it. One must therefore first place oneself at the point of view of the direct efficacy of the rite; the rest, whatever its importance, can only come second, and all that we have said till now is sufficiently explicit on this point so that we can dispense with dwelling on it further.

To be more precise, we will say that trials are rites preliminary or preparatory to the initiation itself; they form its necessary preamble, so that the initiation itself is like their conclusion or their immediate result. It should be noted that trials often take the form of symbolic 'voyages', a point we note only in passing for we cannot enlarge here on the symbolism of the voyage in general; we will only say that in this regard they appear as a 'search' (or better, as a 'quest', as was said in the Middle Ages) leading the being from the 'darkness' of the profane world to the initiatic 'light'. But this form, which can be understood on its own, is still only accessory, however appropriate it may be for what is under discussion. At root, trials are essentially rites of purification, and it is this that provides the true explanation of the very word 'trials', which here has a clearly 'alchemical' meaning and not the common meaning that has given rise to the misunderstandings we have pointed out. Now, in order to understand the fundamental principle of the rite, it is important to note that purification is effected by the 'elements' in the cosmological meaning of this word, and the reason for this can be stated in a few words. To say 'element' is to say simple, and to say simple is to say incorruptible. Thus ritual purification will always have as its material 'support' bodies that symbolize the elements and that are named after them (for it must be understood that the elements themselves are not the so-called 'simple' bodies, which is indeed a contradiction, but rather that from which all bodies are formed), or at least one of these bodies. And this applies equally in the traditional exoteric order, particularly in religious rites where this mode of purification is used not only for humans but also for other living things, for inanimate objects, and for places or buildings. If water seems to play a preponderant role here with regard to other bodies representative of the elements, it must nonetheless be said that its role is not exclusive; this preponderance can perhaps be explained by noting that in all traditions water is also more particularly the symbol of 'universal substance'. However this may be, there is hardly need to say that the rites in question (lustrations, ablutions, and others, including the Christian rite of baptism, which we have already said comes into this category) as well as fasts and the proscription of certain foods, which are equally ritualistic in character, have absolutely nothing to do with hygienic prescriptions or bodily cleanliness, according to the silly idea of certain modernists who, out of prejudice, wish to reduce everything to a purely human explanation and seem to take pleasure in always choosing the crudest interpretation imaginable. Indeed, ultimately the so-called 'psychological' explanations are equally worthless, even if they have a subtler veneer; for they all similarly neglect the only thing that really counts, that is, that the effective action of the rites is not a 'belief' or a theory, but a positive fact.

It can now be understood why, when these trials take the form of successive 'voyages', these latter are related respectively to the different elements; and it only remains for us now to indicate in what sense the word 'purification' itself must be understood from the initiatic point of view. What is involved is to bring the being back to a state of undifferentiated simplicity comparable, as we have said, to that of *materia prima* (understood here in a relative sense of course) so that it be enabled to receive the vibration of the initiatic *Fiat Lux*.

The spiritual influence the transmission of which will give him this first 'illumination' must not meet in him any obstacle due to disharmonious 'preformations' arising from the profane world;[2] and this is why he must first be reduced to this state of *materia prima*, which, if one would carefully reflect on it for a moment, clearly shows that the initiatic process and the Hermetic 'Great Work' are really one and the same thing: the conquest of the divine Light that is the unique essence of all spirituality.

2. In this respect, then, purification is also what in kabbalistic language is called a 'dissolution of shells'. In connection with this we have also pointed out elsewhere the symbolic meaning of the 'stripping of metals' (*Reign of Quantity*, chap. 22).

26

INITIATIC DEATH

ANOTHER QUESTION, which seems as little understood by those of our contemporaries who claim to treat of such things as that of initiatic trials, is that of 'initiatic death'. Thus we have often come across expressions like 'fictive death', which bears witness to a complete incomprehension of realities of this order. Those who express themselves in this way obviously see only the outwardness of the rite and have no idea of the effects it must produce on those who are truly qualified; otherwise they would realize that on the contrary this 'death', far from being 'fictive', is in a sense even more real than death understood in the ordinary meaning of the word, for it is obvious that the profane person who dies is not thereby initiated, and the distinction between the profane order (including in this not only what lacks a traditional character but also all exoterism) and the initiatic order is truly the only one that goes beyond the contingencies inherent in the particular states of the being, and consequently the only one that has a profound and permanent value from the universal point of view. In this regard it will suffice to recall that all traditions stress the essential difference between the posthumous states of the profane and of the initiated; if the consequences of death, taken in its usual meaning, are thus conditioned by this distinction, it is because the change that gives access to the initiatic order corresponds to a higher degree of reality.

Of course the word 'death' must here be taken in its most general sense, according to which we may say that every change of state whatsoever is at once a death and a birth, depending on whether it is considered from one side or from the other: death with respect to the antecedent state, birth with respect to the consequent state. Initiation is generally described as a 'second birth', which indeed it is;

but this 'second birth' necessarily implies a death to the profane world and follows so to speak as an immediate sequel to it, since these are strictly speaking only the two faces of one and the same change of state. As for the symbolism of the rite, it will naturally be based on the analogy which holds good for all changes of state; by reason of this analogy, death and birth in the ordinary sense themselves symbolize initiatic death and birth, these borrowed images being transposed by the rite into another order of reality. It is appropriate to note in particular here that every change of state must be considered to be accomplished in darkness, which explains the relevance of the symbolism of the color black to our subject:[1] the candidate for initiation must pass through total darkness before reaching the 'true light'. It is in this phase of darkness that what is called the 'descent into hell', takes place, of which we have spoken more fully elsewhere;[2] it is, one could say, a kind of 'recapitulation' of the antecedent states by which the possibilities relating to the profane state are definitively exhausted in order that the being may thenceforth freely develop the possibilities of a superior order that he bears within himself and the realization of which belongs properly to the initiatic domain.

On the other hand, since similar considerations apply to every change of state, and the later and successive degrees of initiation also correspond naturally to changes of state, it can be said that for accession to each of these latter degrees there will be a death and a birth, although the 'break', if one may put it so, will be less sharp and of a less fundamental importance than for the first initiation, that is to say for the passage from the profane order to the initiatic order. Moreover, it goes without saying that the changes undergone by the being in the course of its development are really indefinite in number; the initiatic degrees ritually conferred, whatever the traditional form may be, can thus correspond only to a sort of general classification of the principal stages to be traversed, and each of these can itself epitomize a multitude of secondary and intermediate

---

1. This explanation applies equally to the phases of the Hermetic 'Great Work', which, as we have already said, correspond strictly to those of initiation.
2. See *The Esoterism of Dante*.

stages. But in this process there is a point that is particularly important, where the symbolism of death must reappear in the most explicit way, and to this we now turn.

The 'second birth', understood as corresponding to the first initiation, is, as we have said, what can be properly called a psychic regeneration; and it is indeed in the psychic order, that is to say in the order where the subtle elements of the human being are found, that the first phases of initiatic development must take place. But these phases do not constitute a goal in themselves, for they are still only preparatory to the realization of possibilities of a higher order, by which is meant the spiritual order in the true sense. The point in the initiatic process to which we allude is therefore that marking the passage from the psychic order to the spiritual order; and this passage can be seen more particularly as constituting a 'second death' and a 'third birth'.[3] It is appropriate to add that this 'third birth' will be represented rather as a 'resurrection' than as an ordinary birth because it is no longer a question of a 'beginning' in the same sense as on the occasion of the first initiation; the possibilities already developed and acquired once and for all will be found again after this passage, but 'transformed' in a way analogous to that in which the 'body of glory' or the 'resurrected body' represent the 'transformation' of human possibilities beyond the restrictive conditions that define the mode of existence of the individuality as such.

Brought back thus to the essentials, the question is rather simple; what complicates it, as almost always happens, are the confusions introduced by mixing in considerations that really relate to something else altogether. This is what happens especially regarding the 'second death', to which many, because they cannot make certain essential distinctions among the diverse cases where this expression can be employed, attach a meaning that is particularly inopportune. According to what we have just said, the 'second death' is nothing other than the 'psychic death'; for the ordinary man this can be envisaged as occurring sooner or later after the bodily death, apart from any initiatic process; but then this 'second death' will not give access to the spiritual domain, and the being, leaving the human

---

3. In Masonic symbolism this corresponds to initiation to the grade of Master.

state, will merely pass to another individual state of manifestation. This is a dire eventuality for the profane who have every interest in remaining in what we have called the 'prolongations' of the human state, which, moreover, in all traditions is the principal reason for funeral rites. But it is otherwise for the initiate, since he realizes the possibilities of the human state only to pass beyond them to a higher state, which moreover he must do without awaiting the dissolution of his corporeal appearance.

In order not to omit any possibility, let us add that there is another, unfavorable aspect to the 'second death' which relates properly to the 'counter-initiation'. This latter, in effect, imitates true initiation in its phases, but its results are as it were the reverse of initiation and obviously can in no case lead to the spiritual domain since, on the contrary, it only leads the being further and further away from it. When the individual following this path comes to the 'psychic death', he finds himself in a situation not exactly like that of the merely profane person but much worse because of the development he has given to the most inferior possibilities of the subtle order. But we will not dwell on this any further and will be content to refer to the allusions we have already made to it on other occasions,[4] for in truth this is a case that can hold no interest except from a very special point of view, and, in any case, has absolutely nothing to do with true initiation. The fate of 'black magicians', as they are commonly called, is their own concern, and it would be useless to say the least to supply fodder for the more or less fantastic ramblings which this subject only too often provokes. Our only concern must be to denounce their misdeeds when circumstances require and to oppose them in the measure that this is possible; and in an age like our own these misdeeds are notably more widespread than those who have had no occasion to note them directly can imagine.

4. See *Reign of Quantity*, chaps. 35 and 38.

27

PROFANE AND
INITIATIC NAMES

WHILE SPEAKING EARLIER of the different kinds of more or less outward secrets that may exist in certain organizations, whether initiatic or not, we mentioned one bearing on the names of their members, which at first glance may seem no more than a precautionary measure meant to ward off dangers from adversaries and requiring no more profound explanation. Indeed, this is surely so in many cases, and it is at least the case with those secret organizations that are purely profane; but when it is a question of initiatic organizations there may well be something else, and this secret, as indeed everything else, may take on a truly symbolic character. It is all the more interesting to dwell briefly on this point in that curiosity about names is one of the most usual manifestations of modern 'individualism', which, when it comes to apply itself to things of the initiatic domain, bears still further witness to a grave misunderstanding of realities of this order and to an annoying tendency to want to reduce them to the level of profane contingencies. The 'historicism' of our contemporaries is not satisfied unless it gives proper names to everything, that is to say unless it attributes everything to specific human individualities following the most restricted conception possible, that which is current in profane life and which takes into account the corporeal modality alone. However, the fact that the origins of initiatic organizations can never be traced back to such individualities already ought to be matter for reflection in this regard; and when it is a question of the origins of the most profound organizations, even their members cannot be identified, not because they conceal themselves, which, however carefully it may be done, could not always be effective, but because strictly speaking they are not 'personages' at all in the sense intended by historians, so that whoever might think he is able to name them would by this very fact inevitably be in error.[1] Before entering into a more ample explanation of this, let us say that something analogous is found, *mutatis mutandis*, at all degrees of the initiatic ladder, even the most elementary, so that if an initiatic organization is really what it ought to be, the designation of any of its members by a profane name, even if 'materially' exact, will always be tainted with falsity, as would be the confusion between an actor and the character he plays, if one insisted on applying to him this character's name in all the circumstances of his life.

We have already emphasized the notion of initiation as a 'second birth'; it is precisely as an immediate logical consequence of this idea that in many organizations the initiate receives a new name different from his profane name; and this is no mere formality, for this new name must correspond to an equally different modality of his being, that of which the realization is made possible by the spiritual influence transmitted by the initiation. Moreover, it is to be noted that even from the exoteric point of view the same practice exists for analogous reasons in certain religious orders. We then have two distinct modalities of the same being, one manifesting itself in the profane order and the other within the initiatic organization;[2] and normally each modality ought to have its own name, that belonging to one being unsuitable for the other since these modalities are indeed situated in two different orders. We can go further: to each degree of effective initiation there corresponds yet another modality of the being, which therefore ought to receive a new name for each of these degrees; and even if that name is not given in fact, one might say it exists nonetheless as the characteristic

---

1. In the West, the true Brothers of the Rose-Cross are an especially good example of this.

2. The first modality must be regarded as having only an illusory existence with respect to the second, not only by reason of the different degrees of reality to which they respectively refer, but also because, as we have explained above, the 'second birth' necessarily implies the 'death' of the profane individuality, which thus cannot exist except as a mere outward appearance.

expression of that modality, for a name is really nothing other than this. Now, just as these modalities are arranged hierarchically in the being, so is it with the names that represent them respectively. Thus, a name will be all the more true to the extent that it corresponds to a deeper modality, for by this very fact it will express something closer to the true essence of the being. Contrary to popular opinion, therefore, it is the profane name, attached as it is to the most outward modality and the most superficial manifestation, that is the least true of all; and this is especially the case in a civilization that has lost all traditional character, and where names convey scarcely anything of the nature of the being. As to what one might call the true name of the human being—the truest of all, the name that furthermore is properly a 'number' in the Pythagorean and kabbalistic sense of this word—it is the one that corresponds to the central modality of its individuality, that is, to its restoration in the 'primordial state', for that is what constitutes the integral expression of its individual essence.

It follows from these considerations that an initiatic name need not be known in the profane world since it represents a modality of the being that cannot manifest itself therein, so that any knowledge of it would as it were fall into the void, finding nothing to which it could really be applied. And inversely, the profane name represents a modality that the being must cast off when it enters into the initiatic domain, and which thenceforth is nothing but a mere role to be played outwardly; this name can therefore no longer be valid in the initiatic domain, where what it expresses is as it were non-existent. Moreover, it goes without saying that these profound reasons for the distinction and for the separation, so to speak, of the initiatic name from the profane name insofar as these designate truly different entities, may not be consciously recognized everywhere that such a change of names is in fact practiced; it may happen that, because of the degeneration of certain initiatic organizations, and notwithstanding that it was originally something quite different, attempts are made to explain it by wholly outward motives, simply as a measure of prudence, for example, which, when all is said and done, is worth about as much as interpretations of ritual and symbolism along moral or political lines. On the other hand, if it is a matter of profane organizations only, these same exterior motives are indeed really valid, and nothing more can be involved, at least unless in certain cases there is also, as we have already said with regard to rites, the desire to imitate the practices of initiatic organizations, though naturally without this corresponding to the least reality. All of which illustrates once more that similar appearances may in fact hide the most unlike things.

Now, all that we have said to this point about the multiplicity of names representing as many modalities of the being, relates solely to the extensions of the human individuality taken in its integral realization, that is, initiatically, and to the domain of the 'lesser mysteries', as we shall explain more precisely later. When the being pro-ceeds to the 'greater mysteries', that is to say to the realization of supra-individual states, it thereby passes beyond name and form since, as Hindu doctrine teaches, these (*nāma* and *rūpa*) respectively express the essence and the substance of the individuality. Such a being truly no longer has a name, since that is a limitation from which it is henceforth liberated; in case of need it can take any name in order to manifest itself in the individual domain, but this name will not affect it in any way, since it is as 'accidental' to it as is a mere garment which is taken off or changed at will. This is the explanation of what was said above. In organizations of this order, the members have no name, and, furthermore, no longer do the organizations themselves; in these conditions, what is left that could pique profane curiosity? Even if certain names are discovered, they will have only an altogether conventional value; and this can even occur in organizations lower than these, where, for example, 'collective signatures' are used to represent either the organizations in their entirety or functions considered independently of the individualities fulfilling them. All of this, we repeat, results from the very nature of the initiatic order, where individual considerations count for nothing, and is never merely to divert inquiries, even though this might in fact be their consequence; but then, how could the profane understand anything besides the intentions they themselves might have?

From this also comes the difficulty, or even impossibility in many cases, of identifying the authors of works with an initiatic character.[3] Either they are entirely anonymous or, which amounts to the same thing, they have only a symbolic mark or conventional name as signature; moreover, there is no reason why their authors should have played any apparent role in the profane world. When, on the contrary, such works bear the name of an historic individual, things are not necessarily any more straightforward, for this does not necessarily reveal who or what is involved. The individual may very well have been only a spokesman or even a disguise, and in such a case his putative work would imply knowledge that he never really had; or he may have been only an initiate of a lower degree or even a merely profane person who was chosen for some contingent reason,[4] in which case it is obviously not the author who is important but solely the organization that inspired him.

Moreover, even in the profane order it is astonishing to see the importance attributed in our day to the author and all that concerns him, whether closely or remotely; does the value of the work then depend in some way on these things? On the other hand, it is easy to see that a concern to attach one's name to some work is found less in a civilization to the degree that it is more strictly linked to traditional principles, of which 'individualism' in all its forms is truly the very negation. It can be understood without difficulty that this is all of a piece, and we do not care to dwell on it further, all the more so as we have already explained these matters elsewhere; but it was not useless to note once again the role of the anti-traditional mentality, so characteristic of the modern age, as the principal cause for the

3. This can also be applied very generally in all traditional civilizations because of the fact that the initiatic character is attached to the crafts themselves, so that every work of art (or what is so called by the moderns), of whatever kind, participates therein in a certain measure. On this question of the superior and traditional meaning of anonymity, see *Reign of Quantity*, chap. 9.

4. For example, it seems that this was at least partly so for the romance of the Holy Grail; and all the discussions about the 'personality' of Shakespeare also relate finally to a question of this sort, although in fact those who take part in these discussions have never been able to put the question on its proper ground, so that they have hardly done more than muddle it up almost inextricably.

incomprehension of initiatic realities and of the tendency to reduce all things to profane points of view. It is this mentality that under such names as 'humanism' and 'rationalism' has for several centuries been at work reducing everything to the proportions of the ordinary human individuality, that is, to the restricted part of the individuality known to the profane, and to deny anything that transcends this narrowly limited domain, particularly all that relates to initiation of any degree whatsoever. It is hardly necessary to observe that the considerations we have just expressed are essentially based on the metaphysical doctrine of the multiple states of the being, of which they are a direct application.[5] How could this doctrine be understood by those who claim to make of individual man, and even of his corporeal modality alone, a complete and enclosed whole, a being sufficient unto itself, instead of seeing in it only what it really is, the contingent and transitory manifestation of a being in a very particular domain among the indefinite multiplicity of all those that, in their totality, constitute universal Existence, and to which, for this same being, correspond as many different modalities and states of which it can become conscious precisely by following the way opened to it by initiation?

5. For the complete explanation of this see our study *The Multiple States of the Being*.

28

THE SYMBOLISM
OF THE THEATER

WE HAVE JUST COMPARED confusing a being with its outward and profane manifestation to wishing to identify an actor with the role he is playing. In order to clarify the exactness of this comparison, some general considerations on the symbolism of the theater will not be out of place, although they do not pertain exclusively to the initiatic domain proper. This symbolism may of course be linked to the original character of the arts and crafts, all of which used to possess an initiatic value by virtue of their attachment to superior principles, from which they were derived as contingent applications; they only became profane, as we have often explained, because of the spiritual degeneration of humanity in the course of the descending movement of its historical cycle.

One can say in a general way that the theater is a symbol of manifestation, the illusory character of which it expresses as perfectly as possible;[1] and this symbolism can be envisaged either from the point of view of the actor or from that of the theater itself. The actor is a symbol of the 'Self' or the personality manifesting itself through an indefinite series of states and modalities which can be considered as so many different roles; and one should note as an exact expression of this symbolism the importance in antiquity of the use of the mask.[2] Under the mask, the actor in fact remains himself in all of

---

1. We do not say unreal, for it is clear that illusion must be considered only as a lesser reality.

2. It is worth noting that the mask was called *persona* in Latin; the personality is, literally, what is concealed behind the mask of individuality.

his roles, just as the personality remains 'unaffected' by all of its manifestations; the suppression of the mask, on the contrary, forces the actor to change his own physiognomy, and thus seems to alter his essential identity in some way. In every case, however, the actor remains fundamentally other than he appears to be, just as the personality is other than its multiple manifested states which are only the outward and changing appearances that it adopts in order to realize according to the various modes befitting their nature the indefinite possibilities that it contains within itself in the permanent actuality of non-manifestation.

From the other point of view we can say that the theater is an image of the world; both are 'representations', for the world itself, existing only as a consequence and an expression of the Principle, upon which it essentially depends in all its aspects, can be seen to symbolize the principial order in its own way; and this symbolic character confers upon it a higher value than that which it possesses in itself, since it is through its symbolism that it participates in a higher degree of reality.[3] In Arabic, the theater is designated by the word *tamthīl*, which like all words stemming from the root *mathl* denotes resemblance, comparison, image, or figure; and certain Islamic theologians use the expression *'ālam tamthīl*, which could be translated as 'imaginal world' or 'world of representation', to designate everything that is described symbolically in the sacred scriptures and should therefore not be taken in a literal sense. It is worth noting that some use this expression particularly of angels and demons, who indeed 'represent' the superior and inferior states of the being, and who can only be described symbolically in terms borrowed from the sensible world; and by a coincidence that is at the very least striking, there is the considerable role played precisely by these angels and devils in the religious theater of the medieval West.

Indeed, the theater is not necessarily limited to representing the human world, that is to say a single state of manifestation, for it may

---

3. It is this way of considering the world, whether in connection with the Principle or in itself alone, that fundamentally differentiates the point of view of the traditional sciences from that of the profane sciences.

also represent at the same time the higher and lower worlds. In the 'mystery plays' of the Middle Ages the stage was for this reason divided into several tiers corresponding to different worlds and generally arranged according to the ternary division: heaven, earth, and hell; and the action portrayed simultaneously on these various tiers really represented the essential simultaneity of the states of the being. Their failure to understand this symbolism leads the moderns to consider as 'naïveté', not to say a blunder, what precisely had the most profound significance; and what is astonishing is the rapid spread of this incomprehension, so striking among the writers of the seventeenth century. This radical break between the mentality of the Middle Ages and that of modern times is certainly not one of the least enigmas of history.

Since we have just spoken of 'mystery plays', we do not believe it profitless to point to the singularity of this designation, which has a double sense. In all etymological strictness one should write 'mistery', for this word is derived from the Latin *ministerium*, meaning 'office' or 'function', which clearly indicates to what extent theatrical representations of this sort were originally considered to form an integral part of the celebration of religious holidays.[4] But it is strange that this name should have been contracted and abridged so as to become a homonym of 'mystery', and finally to be confused with this other word, which has a Greek origin and an altogether different derivation; is it only by allusion to the 'mysteries' of religion, staged in the plays so designated, that this assimilation can have come about? This may no doubt be plausible, but if on the other hand one considers that analogous symbolic representations occurred in the 'mysteries' of antiquity, as in Greece and probably also in Egypt,[5] it is tempting to see here something going back much further in time, a sign of the continuity of an esoteric and initiatic tradition that has been outwardly affirmed at more or less

---

4. On the other hand, it is from *ministerium* that the word *métier* [craft] is likewise derived, as we have pointed out elsewhere (*Reign of Quantity*, chap. 8).

5. Furthermore, the ritual 'enactment' of the initiatic 'legends' of which we have spoken can be directly related to these symbolic representations.

distant intervals of time by similar manifestations, and adapted as required by the different circumstances of time and place.[6] Besides, we have frequently had occasion to point out the importance of phonetic assimilations between words that are philologically distinct as a modality of symbolic language; indeed, there is nothing arbitrary in this, whatever most of our contemporaries may think, this method being related more or less directly to the modes of interpretation based on the Hindu *nirukta*; but the secrets of the intimate constitution of language are so completely lost today that it is scarcely possible to allude to them without being suspected of indulging in 'false etymologies', or even in crude 'plays on words', and even Plato, who had recourse at times to this type of interpretation, as we noted incidentally in reference to 'myths', receives no mercy at the hands of the pseudo-scientific 'criticism' of those whose minds are limited by modern prejudices.

In order to conclude these few remarks, let us mention still another point of view in the symbolism of the theater, that of the playwright. The various characters, which are his own mental productions, may be considered to represent secondary modifications and prolongations of himself as it were, in almost the same way as the subtle forms produced in the dream state.[7] The same consideration could be applied to every product of the imagination, of whatever type; but in the particular case of the theater there is a special factor: the production is realized in a perceptible manner that gives it the very image of life, as happens also in dreams. In this respect, therefore, the author fulfills a truly 'demiurgic' function, since he produces a world drawn entirely from himself; and for that reason he may be considered as the very symbol of Being producing universal manifestation. In this case, as in that of dreams, the essential unity of the producer of 'illusory forms' is not affected by this multiplicity of accidental manifestations, any more than the unity of

6. Such an 'exteriorization' in religious mode in the Middle Ages may have been the result of such an adaptation, and thus does not constitute evidence against the esoteric character of that tradition itself.

7. Cf. *The Multiple States of the Being*, chap. 6.

Being is affected by the multiplicity of manifestation. Thus, from whatever point of view it is considered, the most profound reason for the theater, unknown though this may be to those who make of it something purely profane, is that by its very nature it is one of the most perfect symbols of universal manifestation.

29

'OPERATIVE'
AND 'SPECULATIVE'

WHEN TREATING the question of initiatic qualifications, allusion was made to a certain very widespread misunderstanding concerning the meaning of the word 'operative', and also, consequently, concerning that of 'speculative', which in a way is its opposite; and as we said then, it seems to us that there is reason to dwell more particularly on this subject in that there is a strict connection between this error and a general misunderstanding about what initiation really is. The question arises historically, so to speak, more particularly in connection with Masonry because it is here that the terms under discussion are most commonly used; but it is not difficult to understand that fundamentally it has a much more general scope and involves something that, according to different modalities, can apply to all initiatic forms, which is what constitutes all its importance from our point of view.

The starting-point of the error lies here. Because the form of Masonic initiation is linked to a craft, which is far from exceptional, as we have noted, and because its symbols and rites, in a word its particular methods in all their 'specificity', rest essentially on the craft of building, people have come to confuse 'operative' with 'corporative', stopping thus at the most outward and superficial aspect of things, as is natural for anyone who has no idea or even suspicion of initiatic 'realization'. The most widespread opinion can therefore be formulated as follows. 'Operative' Masons were exclusively craftsmen; little by little they 'accepted' as honorary members as it were people unacquainted with the art of building;[1] but finally this

---

1. In fact, however, these people had to have at least some indirect connection with this art, if only as 'protectors' (or *patrons* in the English sense of the word). It

second element came to predominate, so that 'operative' Masonry was transformed into a 'speculative' Masonry having only a fictitious or 'ideal' connection with the craft. This 'speculative' Masonry dates, as we know, from the beginning of the eighteenth century; but some, noting the presence of non-worker members in the former 'operative' Masonry, believe that they can conclude from this that these latter were already 'speculative' Masons. In each case it appears to be the almost unanimous opinion that the change that gave rise to 'speculative' Masonry marks a superiority with respect to that from which it derives, as if it represented a kind of 'progress' in the 'intellectual' sense and corresponded to a conception of a more elevated level; and they do not hesitate in this regard to oppose 'speculations' of 'thought' to the occupations of the craft, as if it were this that is in question, whereas it is instead a matter of things relating, not to profane activities, but to the initiatic domain.

There was formerly no other distinction in Masonry than that between 'free' Masons, men of the craft so called because of the exemptions granted by the sovereigns to their guilds (and no doubt also, and perhaps even especially, because the condition of free birth was one of the qualifications for admission to initiation),[2] and 'accepted' Masons, who were not professionals, and among whom ecclesiastics, who were initiated into special Lodges[3] in order to fulfill the function of 'chaplains' in ordinary Lodges, had a separate place. But both were equally, though in different capacities, mem-bers of one and the same organization of 'operative' Masonry; and how could it have been otherwise when no Lodge could function normally without a 'chaplain', and thus without at least

---

was in an analogous fashion that printers (whose ritual was formed principally by the Faust 'legend') later 'accepted' all those who had some connection with the art of the book, that is, not only booksellers but also the authors.

2. One cannot, without diverting words entirely from their legitimate meaning, give any other interpretation to the expression *free-born*, which is applied to the candidate for initiation and surely has nothing to do with freedom from some sort of so-called 'prejudice'!

3. In ancient 'operative' Masonry, these Lodges were called *Lodges of Jakin* and the 'chaplain' himself was called *Brother Jakin*.

one 'accepted' Mason among its members?[4] 'Speculative' Masonry, moreover, was formed precisely among these 'accepted' Masons and by their action;[5] and this can be explained simply enough by the fact that, not being directly attached to the craft and thus lacking a solid basis for the initiatic work in question, they could more easily or more completely than the others lose sight of a part of what constitutes initiation—we could even say the most important part since it is this that properly concerns 'realization'.[6] It must further be added that because of their social situation and their outward relationships they were perhaps more open to certain influences of the profane world, political, philosophical, or otherwise, all working in the same direction and 'distracting' them, in the proper meaning of the word, from the initiatic work, even if these influences did not go so far as to lead them into unfortunate confusions between the two domains, as was later to happen only too often.

Having started with historical considerations for the convenience of our account, we here touch on the very root of the question: the passage from 'operative' to 'speculative', far from representing 'progress' (as the moderns, who do not understand its significance, would like to think), is in fact quite the opposite from the initiatic point of view. It does not necessarily imply a deviation properly speaking, but it implies at least a degeneration in the sense of a diminution; and as we have just said, this diminution consists in the neglect and forgetfulness of all that realization is—for it is this that

4. Actually, we ought to say that it was obliged to have two, the other being a physician.

5. These Masons moreover did not receive all the 'operative' grades, and this explains the existence at the beginning of 'modern' Masonry of certain lacunae that had subsequently to be filled, which could not be done except through the intervention of the survivors from 'ancient' Masonry who were much more numerous in the eighteenth century than historians generally believe.

6. We pointed out this difference previously in connection with the present state of the Compagnonnage and Masonry, members of the former readily calling the Masons 'their speculative Brothers'; and while this expression implies the recognition of a common origin, it also sometimes contains a certain nuance of disdain, which is indeed not entirely unjustified, as one can understand from what we have explained here.

is truly 'operative'—leaving nothing more than a purely theoretical view of initiation. It must not be forgotten that 'speculation' and 'theory' are indeed synonyms, the word 'theory' of course not being taken here in its original meaning of 'contemplation' but solely in the sense it always has in current language, which the word 'speculation' no doubt expresses more clearly, since its very derivation implies the idea of something that is only a 'reflection', like an image seen in a mirror,[7] that is to say an indirect knowledge as opposed to the effective knowledge that is the immediate consequence of 'realization', or rather which is one with it. On the other hand, the word 'operative' must not be taken as an exact equivalent of 'practical', for this latter term always refers to 'action' (which conforms strictly to its etymology) and thus could not be employed here without equivocation or impropriety;[8] in reality, it is a question of that 'accomplishment' of the being that is initiatic 'realization', with all the different means that can be used in view of this end; and it is not without interest to note that a word of the same origin, *oeuvre*, is also used precisely in this sense in alchemical terminology.

It is thus easy to see what remains in the case of an initiation that has become merely 'speculative'. The initiatic transmission indeed still exists, since the traditional 'chain' has not been broken, but instead of the possibility of an effective initiation as long as some individual defect creates no obstacle, there remains no more than a virtual initiation that by the very nature of things is condemned to remain so, since the 'speculative' limitation properly signifies that this stage cannot be surpassed, as all that goes further belongs by very definition to the 'operative' order. This of course is not to say that the rites have no effect in such a case, for they always remain the vehicle of a spiritual influence even if those who accomplish them are no longer conscious of this; but this effect is so to speak 'deferred' with respect to its development 'in act' and is like a seed that lacks the conditions necessary to germinate, these conditions

---

7. The word *speculum* in Latin means 'mirror'.

8. Here we have all the difference that exists between the respective meanings of the Greek words *praxis* and *poesis*.

residing in the 'operative' work by which alone the initiation can be made effective.

In this connection we must again emphasize that such a degeneration of an initiatic organization changes nothing with regard to its essential nature, and that the continuity of the transmission itself suffices to render a restoration always possible should more favorable circumstances arise, this restoration then necessarily being seen as a return to the 'operative' state. But it is evident that the more an organization is thus diminished, the greater the possibility of at least a partial deviation, which naturally can occur in many different directions; and these deviations, while only of an accidental character, render any restoration increasingly difficult in fact, although, despite everything, it still remains possible in principle. However that may be, an initiatic organization possessing an authentic and legitimate filiation, whatever may be the more or less degenerate state in which it presently finds itself, could assuredly never be confused with any pseudo-initiatic organization whatsoever, which is nothing at all, or with the counter-initiation, which indeed is something, though something absolutely negative running directly counter to the purpose of all true initiation.[9]

On the other hand, the inferiority of the 'speculative' point of view as we have just described it illustrates yet again, almost to excess, that 'thought' cultivated for itself can never be the purpose of an initiatic organization as such, for an initiatic organization is not a place to 'philosophize' or to participate in 'academic' discussions, any more than to engage in any other kind of profane occupation.[10]

---

9. We have on many occasions pointed out that such precisions are not at all superfluous; thus we must formally protest against any interpretation that tends, either by an intentional or an unintentional confusion, to apply to any initiatic organization what, in our writings, really relates either to pseudo-initiation or to the counter-initiation.

10. We have never understood just what is meant by the expression 'societies for thought', contrived by certain people to designate a category of groups that seems rather ill-defined; but what is certain is that even if something exists to which this label might apply, it could never have the least connection with any initiatic organization whatsoever.

When philosophical 'speculation' is introduced into an initiatic organization, there is already a true deviation; whereas if 'speculation' about the initiatic domain be limited to itself rather than being a mere preparation for the 'operative' work, as it normally should be, there exists only the diminution of which we spoke earlier. Here we have another important distinction, though we think it sufficiently clear that further emphasis should not be necessary; it can be said in summary that a deviation exists, more or less serious as the case may be, whenever there is a confusion between the initiatic and the profane points of view. This must not be forgotten whenever one wishes to evaluate the degree of degeneration to which an initiatic organization may have succumbed; but aside from any deviation, the terms 'operative' and 'speculative' can always be applied in a very exact way to any initiatic form whatsoever by referring them respectively to effective initiation and to virtual initiation.

30

EFFECTIVE AND
VIRTUAL INITIATION

ALTHOUGH THE DISTINCTION BETWEEN effective initiation and
virtual initiation may already be sufficiently understood from the
preceding considerations, it seems important enough that we ought
to try to clarify it a bit more. We will note first of all that among the
conditions for initiation that we stated earlier, attachment to a regular traditional[1] organization (presupposing, naturally, the necessary
qualification) suffices for virtual initiation, whereas the interior
work that comes afterward properly pertains to effective initiation,
which in the final analysis is, in all its degrees, the development 'in
act' of the possibilities to which virtual initiation gives access. Virtual initiation is therefore initiation understood in the strictest
sense of the word, that is, as an 'entering' or a 'beginning'; this of
course is by no means to say that it can be regarded as something
sufficient unto itself, but only that it is the necessary starting-point
for all the rest. Having started on a path, one has still to follow it
and, if one can, even follow it to its end. This can be summed up in
a few words: entering on the path is virtual initiation; following the
path is effective initiation; but unfortunately many in fact remain on
the threshold, not always because they are incapable of going further but also, especially in the present conditions of the Western
world, because of the degeneration of certain organizations which,
having become solely 'speculative' as we have just explained, cannot
on this account help them in any way with the 'operative' work,
even in the most elementary stages, and furnish nothing that could

1. I.e., a regular traditional initiatic organization. ED.

lead them to suspect the existence of any sort of 'realization'. Nevertheless, even in these organizations there is still talk of the initiatic 'work', or at least of something that is considered to be such; but one can then legitimately ask the question: in what sense and in what measure does this still correspond to any reality?

To answer this question we will recall that initiation is essentially a transmission, adding that this can be understood in two different senses: on the one hand, transmission of a spiritual influence, and on the other transmission of a traditional teaching. It is the transmission of the spiritual influence that must be considered first, not only because it must logically precede any teaching, which is quite evident once one has understood the need for a traditional affiliation, but also and above all because it is this that essentially constitutes initiation in the strict sense, so much so that if it is only a question of virtual initiation, everything could stop here, without there being a need to add any teaching subsequently. Indeed, initiatic teaching, the particular character of which we will specify later, cannot be anything other than an outward aid brought to the inner work of realization in order to support and guide it as much as possible. This indeed is its unique purpose and it is in this alone that the outward and collective side of a true initiatic 'work' consists if this be truly understood in its legitimate and normal sense.

Now, what makes the question a bit more complex is that the two kinds of transmission we have just pointed out can never be wholly separated from each other even though they are in fact distinct by their very nature, something requiring still further explanation although we already dealt with this point implicitly when we spoke of the close connection between rite and symbol. Indeed, rites are essentially and above all the vehicle of spiritual influences, which cannot be transmitted in any way without them; but at the same time, by the very fact that all their constituent elements possess a symbolic character, they also necessarily embody a teaching, since, as we said, symbols are precisely the sole language really suitable for the expression of truths of the initiatic order. Inversely, symbols are essentially a means of teaching, and not only of outward teaching but of something more insofar as they serve above all as 'supports' for meditation, which is at the very least the beginning of inner work. But as the constituent elements of rites, and by reason of their 'non-human' character, these same symbols are also 'supports' for the spiritual influence itself. Moreover, if one reflects that the inner work would be ineffective without the action, or, if one prefers, without the collaboration of this spiritual influence, it will be understood that under certain conditions meditation on the symbols would itself take on the character of a true rite, a rite now conferring not only virtual initiation but permitting the attainment of a more or less advanced degree of effective initiation.

Rather than using symbols in this way, one can on the contrary limit oneself to 'speculating' about them without intending anything further, by which we certainly do not wish to say that it is illegitimate to explain symbols in the measure that this is possible, and to seek to develop by appropriate commentaries the different meanings they contain (on condition of avoiding all 'systematization', which is incompatible with the very essence of symbolism); but we do wish to say that this would always have to be regarded as a mere preparation for something else, and it is just this something else that by definition escapes the 'speculative' point of view as such. This latter point of view is limited to an outward study of symbols, which obviously cannot allow those who pursue it to pass from a virtual to an effective initiation; besides, they usually stop at the most superficial meanings since to penetrate further already requires a degree of comprehension that in reality presupposes something altogether different from mere 'erudition'. And one must even be considered fortunate not to go more or less completely astray in these 'peripheral' considerations, as, for example, in finding in these symbols the pretext for 'moralizing', or in drawing from them social or even political applications that would certainly have nothing initiatic or even traditional about them. In this last case the boundary has already been crossed at which the 'work' of certain organizations ceases entirely to be initiatic, even in a wholly 'speculative' way, and falls squarely into the profane point of view; this boundary naturally separates also simple degeneration from deviation, and it is only too easy to understand how 'speculation' taken as an end in itself unfortunately allows one to slip easily from the one to the other in an almost imperceptible way.

We are now able to conclude this question. Mere 'speculation', even when it remains at the initiatic point of view and does not deviate from it in one way or another, leads as it were to a dead end, for by its means one can in no way go beyond virtual initiation; and besides, virtual initiation would exist even without any 'speculation' at all, since it is the immediate consequence of the transmission of the spiritual influence. The effect of the rite by which this transmission is carried out is 'deferred', as we said above, and remains in a latent and 'shrouded' state so long as it has not passed from the 'speculative' to the 'operative', which is to say that theoretical considerations have no real value as properly initiatic work except as preparation for 'realization'; they are in fact a necessary preparation for it, but this is something that the 'speculative' point of view itself is incapable of recognizing and consequently of bringing to the consciousness of those who limit their horizon thereto.

31

INITIATIC TEACHING

WE MUST RETURN ONCE AGAIN to the characteristics proper to initiatic teaching, characteristics by which it differs profoundly from all profane teaching. What we wish to consider here can be called the exteriority of this teaching, that is, the means of expression by which it can in a certain measure and to a certain degree be transmitted as a preparation to the purely interior work by which the initiation, at first virtual, becomes more or less completely effective. Many, who do not realize what initiatic teaching really is, see in it no other feature worthy of note than the use of symbolism; moreover it is very true that symbolism does play an essential role in it, but one must still know why this is so. Now such people, seeing things only in a very superficial way and stopping short at appearances and outward forms, fail entirely to understand the purpose and even, one can say, the necessity of symbolism, which under these conditions they can only find strange and at best merely useless. Indeed, they suppose that the initiatic doctrine is in fact hardly more than a philosophy like all the others, doubtless a bit different in its method, but in any case nothing more, their mentality being so formed that they are incapable of conceiving anything else; but it is nevertheless quite certain that for the reasons we have given above philosophy has nothing to do with symbolism and is even in a certain way opposed to it. Even those who in spite of this misapprehension manage all the same—for whatever reasons, which usually have nothing initiatic about them—to find in the teaching of such a doctrine some value from one point of view or another, never make of it anything more than a sort of extension of profane teaching, a complement to ordinary education for the use of a relative elite.[1] But perhaps it is better to deny its value entirely, which amounts to ignoring it purely and simply, than to belittle it thus and, all too often, to present in its name and in its place certain more or less coordinated views about all sorts of things that are really not initiatic either in themselves or in the way they are treated, this being precisely that deviation of the 'speculative' work to which we have already alluded.

There is another way of envisaging initiatic teaching that is hardly less false than the former although it may seem completely contrary to it. This consists in trying to oppose it to profane teaching as if it were in a way situated on the same level by attributing to it as object of study a certain more or less vaguely defined special science that is always in contradiction and conflict with the other sciences, although it is always declared to be superior to them by hypothesis and without any clear reason being given. This viewpoint is particularly that of the occultists and other pseudo-initiates who, in reality, scorn profane teaching far less than they would like to believe, since they go so far as to make many more or less disguised borrowings from it; and what is more, this attitude of opposition can hardly be reconciled with their constant preoccupation with finding points of comparison between traditional doctrine, or what they believe to be such, and the modern sciences; and indeed, it is certainly true that opposition and similitude both presuppose that the things in question are of the same order. Here there is a double error: on the one hand, confusion of initiatic knowledge with the study of a more or less secondary traditional science (whether magic or something else of the kind) and, on the other, ignorance of what constitutes the essential difference between the point of view of the traditional sciences and that of the profane sciences; but after all that we have already said there is no need to dwell further on this.

Now, if initiatic teaching is neither a prolongation of profane teaching, as the first would have it, nor its antithesis, as the others maintain, if it is neither a system of philosophy nor a specialized

1. Of course those involved are equally incapable of conceiving of an elite in the only true sense of this word, one that also has a properly initiatic value, as we shall explain below.

science, this is because it is really something altogether different; but one must not seek to give it a definition in the strict sense, for this would inevitably deform it even more. The constant use of symbolism in the transmission of this teaching already suffices to hint at this once it is admitted, as is logical to do even without going to the heart of the matter, that there must be a mode of expression that is completely different from ordinary language in order to express ideas equally different from those expressed by ordinary language, ideas which cannot be completely translated into words and for which a less limited, more universal language is necessary, for the reason that they themselves are of a more universal order. It is necessary to add that if initiatic concepts are essentially different from profane concepts, this is because they proceed above all from another mentality than these,[2] from which they differ less by their object than by the point of view from which they consider that object; and this is inevitably so, given that this object cannot be 'specialized', which would amount to trying to impose on initiatic knowledge a limitation incompatible with its very nature. It is therefore easy to accept on one hand that everything that can be considered from the profane point of view can also be considered, though in a completely different way and with a different understanding, from the initiatic point of view (for as we have often said, there is really no profane domain to which certain things belong by their nature, but only a profane point of view, which is finally only an illegitimate and deviated way of looking at things),[3] whereas on the other hand there are things that totally escape every profane point of view[4] and that are exclusive to the initiatic domain alone.

2. In reality, the word 'mentality' is insufficient in this regard, as we will see below, but it must not be forgotten that only a stage preparatory to true initiatic knowledge is in question here, at which it is not yet possible to appeal to the transcendent intellect directly.

3. What we say here could be applied just as well to the traditional point of view in general as to the properly initiatic point of view; when it is simply a question of distinguishing them from the profane point of view, there is really no difference in this respect between the two.

4. And, we should add, totally escape the traditional exoteric point of view, which is essentially the legitimate and normal way of looking at what the profane point of view deforms, so that in a way both relate to the same domain, which in no way diminishes their profound difference; but beyond this domain, which can be

We have explained earlier that symbolism, which is like the sensible form of all initiatic teaching, is really a language more universal than the common languages, and this cannot be doubted for even an instant if one considers that every symbol is susceptible of multiple interpretations which, far from contradicting each other, are on the contrary complementary and equally true, although proceeding from different points of view; and if this is so, it is because the symbol is less the expression of a clearly defined and delimited idea (in the sense of the 'clear and distinct' ideas of Cartesian philosophy, which are supposed to be entirely expressible by words) than the synthetic and schematic representation of a whole ensemble of ideas and conceptions that each person can grasp according to his own intellectual aptitudes and in the measure that he is prepared to comprehend them. Whoever succeeds in penetrating to the deeper meaning of the symbol can thereby conceive incomparably more than what can be expressed directly; and thus it is the only means of transmitting, to the degree possible, all the inexpressible reality that makes up the proper domain of initiation, or rather, to speak more rigorously, of placing the seeds of conceptions of this order in the intellect of the initiate who must thereafter bring them from potency to act, and who must develop and cultivate them by his personal effort, for no one can do more than prepare him for this by tracing, with the appropriate formulas, the plan that he will afterward have to realize within himself in order to come to the effective possession of the initiation that he has received only virtually from the outside. It must not be forgotten, moreover, that if symbolic initiation, which is but the basis and support of effective initiation, is necessarily the only one that can be given from the outside, it can at least be preserved and transmitted even by those who understand neither its meaning nor its scope; it suffices that the symbols be maintained intact for them to remain able to awaken in anyone capable of it all of the conceptions of which they represent the synthesis. Let us again recall that it is here that the true initiatic secret

---

called exoteric since it concerns all men equally and without distinction, there is the esoteric and properly initiatic domain, of which those who remain in the exoteric order can only remain entirely ignorant.

lies, which is inviolable by its nature and which is itself its own protection against the curiosity of the profane, and of which the relative secret of certain outward signs is but a symbolic representation. As to this secret, each person will be able to penetrate it to a greater or lesser extent according to the range of his intellectual horizon, but even if he should penetrate it completely he can never effectively communicate to another what he himself will have understood; at most he will be able to help those who are capable of it to come to this same understanding.

This does not in any way prevent the sensible forms used for the transmission of the outward and symbolic initiation from having their own value as means of instruction, even apart from their essential role as support and vehicle of the spiritual influence. In this connection we may note (and this brings us back to the intimate connection between symbol and rite) that they render the fundamental symbols in gestures, taking this word in its widest sense as we have already done earlier, and that in this way they make the teaching presented to the initiate 'living' so to speak,[5] which is the most adequate and most generally applicable way to present it for his assimilation, for in the present conditions of existence all manifestations of the human individuality necessarily translate into diverse modalities of vital activity. But for all that, vitality must not be made into a sort of absolute principle, as many moderns wish to do; the expression of an idea in vital mode is, after all, only a symbol like the others, as also, for example, is its translation into spatial mode, which would constitute a geometric symbol or ideogram; but it is, one could say, a symbol that by its special character is capable of penetrating more immediately than any other into the very interior of the human individuality. In the final analysis, if every method of initiation in its different phases presents a correspondence, whether with the individual human life or even with the entirety of terrestrial life, it is because the development of vital manifestation itself, particular or general, 'microcosmic' or 'macrocosmic', is effected according to a plan analogous to that which the

---

5. Whence what we have called the 'enactment' of initiatic legends. One might also refer here to what we have said about the symbolism of the theater.

initiate must inwardly accomplish in order to realize in himself the complete development of all the potentialities of his being. Such plans correspond always and everywhere to one and the same synthetic conception, so that they are principially identical and, although different and indefinitely varied in their realization, all proceed from a single 'archetype', a universal plan laid out by the supreme Will designated symbolically as the 'Great Architect of the Universe'.

Thus each being tends, consciously or not, to realize in itself by the means appropriate to its particular nature what the Western initiatic forms, basing themselves on 'structural' symbolism, call the 'plan of the Great Architect of the Universe',[6] and thereby contributes, according to the function belonging to it in the cosmic totality, to the integral realization of this same plan, which is finally nothing other than a universalizing of its own personal realization. It is at the exact point in its development when a being really becomes conscious of this finality that effective initiation begins for it, which must lead it by degrees and in accordance with its personal path to this integral realization, a realization not achieved by the isolated development of certain special faculties but by the complete, harmonious, and hierarchic development of all the possibilities implied in the essence of that being. Moreover, since the end is necessarily the same for everything that shares the same principle, it is only the means employed to attain this end that are proper to each individual, considered within the limits of the special function determined for it by its individual nature, and which, whatever it may be, must be considered a necessary element of the total and universal order; and by the very nature of things this diversity of particular paths subsists so long as the domain of individual possibilities has not been effectively surpassed.

Initiatic instruction envisaged in its universality must therefore comprise, as so many indefinitely varied applications of one same

---

6. This symbolism is moreover far from being exclusively proper to Western forms; the *Vishvakarma* of the Hindu tradition in particular is exactly the same as the 'Great Architect of the Universe'.

transcendent principle, all the paths of realization that are proper, not only to each category of beings but also to each individual being considered separately; and thus including them all in itself, it sums up and synthesizes them in the absolute unity of the universal Way.[7] If, therefore, the principles of initiation are immutable, its modalities nonetheless can and must vary so as to adapt to the multiple and relative conditions of manifested existence, conditions of which the diversity requires mathematically as it were that there cannot be two identical things in the entire universe, as we have already explained on other occasions.[8] One can then say that it is impossible that, for two different individuals, there should be two initiations exactly alike, even from the outward and ritual point of view, and all the more so from the point of view of the inner work of the initiate. The unity and immutability of the principle in no way require a uniformity and immobility that in any case are unrealizable in fact and which, in reality, only represent an 'inverted' reflection of the former at the lowest degree of manifestation; and the truth is that the initiatic teaching, implying an adaptation to the indefinite diversity of individual natures, is thereby opposed to the uniformity that profane teaching on the contrary regards as its 'ideal'. The modifications in question are, of course, limited to the outward expression of initiatic knowledge and to its assimilation by this or that individuality, for in the measure that such an expression is possible it must perforce take relativities and contingencies into account, whereas what it expresses is independent of this in the universality of its principial essence, which includes all possibilities in the simultaneity of a unique synthesis.

Initiatic teaching, outward and transmissible by forms, in reality is and can only be—we have said this before and stress it again—a preparation of the individual for acquiring true initiatic knowledge by personal effort. Thus the way to be followed and the plan to be realized can be pointed out to him, and he can be encouraged to cultivate the mental and intellectual attitude necessary to acquire an

---

7. This universal Way is the *Tao* of the Far-Eastern tradition.
8. See in particular *Reign of Quantity*, chap. 7.

effective and not merely theoretical comprehension; he can also be helped and guided by a constant monitoring of his effort; but this is all, for no one else, were he even a 'Master' in the most complete meaning of the word,[9] can do the work for him. What the initiate must necessarily acquire for himself, because no one and nothing outside himself can communicate it to him, is effective possession of the initiatic secret properly speaking; to realize this possession in all its extent and with all that it implies requires that the teaching that serves in a way as foundation and support of his personal work be constituted in such a way that it open him to truly unlimited possibilities, and thus enable him to expand his conceptions indefinitely, both in breadth and depth, instead of enclosing them, as does every profane point of view, in the more or less narrow limits of some sort of systematic theory or verbal formula.

9. We mean by this what is called a *guru* in the Hindu tradition or a *shaykh* in the Islamic tradition, which have nothing in common with the fantastic ideas entertained thereupon in certain Western pseudo-initiatic circles.

32

THE LIMITS
OF THE MENTAL

WE HAVE JUST BEEN SPEAKING of the mentality necessary for
acquiring initiatic knowledge, a mentality that is altogether different from the profane mentality and to the formation of which the
observances of the rites and outward forms used in traditional
organizations greatly contributes, without detriment to their other,
deeper effects. But it must be understood that this is only a preliminary stage corresponding to a preparation that is still wholly theoretical, and is certainly not an effective initiation. Indeed, there is
good reason for stressing the insufficiency of the mental with
respect to all properly metaphysical and initiatic knowledge; we are
obliged to use the term 'mental' in preference to any other as an
equivalent to the Sanskrit *manas* because the two are linked by a
common root. By this term, then, we mean the totality of the faculties of knowledge that specifically characterize the human individual (which in many languages is itself designated by words derived
from the same root), of which reason is the foremost.

We have often enough drawn the distinction between reason, a
faculty of a purely individual order, and pure intellect, which on the
contrary is supra-individual, so that it would not be useful to return
to it here. We will only recall that metaphysical knowledge in the
true sense of this word, being of the universal order, would not be
possible if there were not in the being a faculty of the same order
and therefore transcendent with respect to the individual. This faculty is intellectual intuition in the strict sense. Indeed, since all
knowledge is essentially an identification, it is evident that the individual as such cannot attain to knowledge of what lies beyond the

individual domain, for this would be a contradiction; such a knowledge is possible only because the being that in a certain contingent state of manifestation is a human individual is at the same time also something else. It would be absurd to say that man, as man and by human means, can surpass himself, but the being that appears in this world as a man is really quite another thing by reason of the permanent and immutable principle that constitutes its deepest essence.[1] Any knowledge that can truly be called initiatic results from a communication consciously established with the higher states; and terms such as 'inspiration' and 'revelation' clearly refer to such a communication if they are understood in their true sense and no heed is given to their all too frequent abuse in the ordinary language of our time.[2]

Direct knowledge of the transcendent order, with the absolute certitude that it implies, is of course incommunicable and inexpressible in itself, for since any expression is necessarily formal by very definition, and consequently individual,[3] it is thereby inadequate to such knowledge and can only give as it were a reflection of it in the human order. This reflection may actually help certain beings attain this same knowledge by awakening in them higher faculties, but as we have already said it could never exempt them from personally accomplishing what no one else can do for them; it is only a 'support' for their inner work. In this regard, moreover, there is an important distinction to be made between symbols and ordinary language as means of expression. We explained earlier that because of their essentially synthetic character symbols are particularly apt for serving as a support for intellectual intuition, whereas language, which is essentially analytical, is strictly speaking only the

---

1. This is the fundamental distinction between the 'Self' and the 'ego', or between the personality and the individuality, which is at the very root of the metaphysical theory of the multiple states of the being.

2. These two words denote what is essentially the same thing considered from two slightly different points of view. What is 'inspiration' for the being who receives it becomes 'revelation' for the other beings to whom it is then transmitted, in the measure that this is possible, by being expressed outwardly in some way.

3. Let us recall that among the conditions of manifested existence, form is that which specifically characterizes any individual state as such.

instrument of discursive and rational thought. And we must add that by their 'non-human' aspect symbols bear in themselves an influence the action of which can directly awaken the intuitive faculty in those who meditate on them in the right way; but this relates solely to their ritual use so to speak as supports for meditation, and not to the verbal commentaries that can be made concerning their meaning, which in every case still represent only outward studies.[4] Since human language is strictly linked by its very constitution to the exercise of the rational faculty, it follows that all that is expressed or explained by means of such language necessarily takes on more or less explicitly the form of 'reasoning'; but it must be understood nonetheless that there can only be an apparent and outward similarity, one of form and not of substance, between ordinary reasoning, concerning the things of the individual domain to which it is specifically and directly applicable, and reasoning meant to reflect as much as possible something of the truths of the supra-individual order. This is why we have said that initiatic teaching can never take a 'systematic' form, but on the contrary must always remain open to limitless possibilities in order to preserve the prerogative of the inexpressible, which in reality is what is essential; and in this way language itself, when applied to initiatic truths, participates in a way in the character of symbols properly so called.[5] And yet, whoever has come to a theoretical knowledge of such truths by studying some discursive explanation still has no direct and real (or more exactly 'realized') knowledge, for which this discursive and theoretical knowledge can be no more than a mere preparation.

However indispensable this theoretical preparation may be in fact, it nonetheless possesses in itself only the value of a contingent and accidental means; as long as one remains at this stage there can

4. This is not of course to say that whoever explains symbols using ordinary language necessarily has only an outward knowledge of them, but only that this is all that he can communicate to others by such explanations.

5. This higher use of language is possible above all with sacred languages, which are sacred precisely because they are so constituted as to bear in themselves this properly symbolic character. It is naturally much more difficult with ordinary languages, especially when they are customarily employed only to express profane points of view, as is the case with modern languages.

be no question of an effective initiation, even of the most elementary degree. If there were nothing more than this, it would only be the analogue, in a higher order, of any 'speculation' concerning some other domain,[6] for such a merely theoretical knowledge comes only through the mind whereas effective knowledge comes through 'the spirit and the soul', that is to say through the whole being. This is why, outside of the initiatic point of view, mere mystics, who go no further than the limits of the individual domain, are, within their own order of the exoteric tradition, undeniably superior not only to philosophers but even to theologians; for the least fragment of effective knowledge is worth incomparably more than any mere mental reasoning.[7]

As long as knowledge is only mental it is a mere 'reflected' knowledge, like that of the shadows seen by the prisoners in Plato's allegory of the cave, and it is therefore indirect and entirely outward. To pass from the shadow to reality grasped directly in itself is truly to pass from the 'outward' to the 'inward' and also, from the more particular point of view that we adopt here, to pass from virtual to effective initiation. This passage implies the renunciation of the mental, that is, of the entire discursive faculty, which thenceforth becomes impotent since it cannot go beyond the limits imposed upon it by its very nature;[8] intellectual intuition alone lies beyond

---

6. Such a 'speculation' in the esoteric order could be compared, not to philosophy, which only refers to a wholly profane point of view, but rather to theology in the traditional exoteric and religious order.

7. We must specify that this superiority of mystics is to be understood exclusively with regard to their interior state, for in another respect it can happen, as we have already said above, that because of a lack of theoretical preparation they may be unable to express anything in an intelligible fashion; moreover, one must take into account the fact that, despite what they may have truly 'realized', they always risk going astray precisely because they cannot pass beyond the possibilities of the individual order.

8. This renunciation does not mean that the knowledge in question is in any way contrary or opposed to mental knowledge insofar as this is worthwhile and legitimate in its own relative order, that is to say in the individual domain; it cannot be said too often, in order to avoid any ambiguity, that the 'supra-rational' has nothing in common with the 'irrational'.

these limits because it does not belong to the order of individual faculties. Using traditional symbolism based on organic correspondences, one can say that the center of consciousness must be transferred from the 'brain' to the 'heart'.[9] For this transfer, any 'speculation' or 'dialectic' obviously can no longer be of use; and it is only from this point that it is truly possible to speak of effective initiation. The point where this latter begins thus lies well beyond the point where all that might be of some relative value in 'speculation' of any kind has its end; between the one and the other there is a veritable abyss that can only be crossed, as we have just said, by renunciation of the mental. Whoever clings to reasoning and does not free himself from it at the required moment remains a prisoner of form, which is the limitation by which the individual state is defined; he will then neither pass beyond form nor go further than the 'outward', which is to say that he will remain bound to the indefinite cycle of manifestation. The passage from the 'outward' to the 'inward' is also the passage from multiplicity to unity, or from circumference to center, to the single point whence the human being, restored to the prerogatives of the 'primordial state', can rise to the higher states[10] and, by the complete realization of his true essence, finally be effectively and actually what he is potentially from all eternity. He who knows himself in the 'truth' of the eternal and infinite 'Essence'[11] knows and possesses all things in himself and by himself, for he has come to the unconditioned state that leaves no possibility

9. There is hardly need to recall that the 'heart', taken symbolically to represent the center of the human individuality considered in its integrality, always corresponds, in all traditions, to the pure intellect, which has absolutely no connection with the 'sentimentality' attributed to it by the profane ideas of the moderns.

10. Cf. *The Esoterism of Dante*, chap. 8.

11. We take the word 'truth' here in the sense of the Arabic term *ḥaqiqah*, and the word 'Essence' in the sense of *adh-Dhāt*. It is to this that the following *ḥādith*, drawn from the Islamic tradition, refers: 'He who knows himself knows his Lord' (*Man arafa nafsahu faqad arafa Rabbahu*); and this knowledge is obtained by what is called the 'eye of the heart' (*'ayn al-qalb*), which is nothing other than intellectual intuition itself, as these words of Al-Ḥallāj affirm: 'I saw my Lord with the eye of my heart, and I said: "Who art Thou?" He said: "Thou."' (*Raaytu Rabbī bi-ayni qalbī, faqultu man anta, qāla anta.*)

outside of itself. And this state, with respect to which all the others, no matter how elevated, are really still only preliminary stages having no common measure with it,[12] this state which is the ultimate goal of all initiation, is precisely what must be understood by the 'Supreme Identity'.

12. This must not be understood only of the states that correspond to extensions of the individuality, but also of the still conditioned supra-individual states.

33

INITIATIC KNOWLEDGE
AND PROFANE 'CULTURE'

WE HAVE ALREADY POINTED OUT that one must be on guard against any confusion between doctrinal knowledge of the initiatic order, even when this is still only theoretical and merely preparatory to 'realization', and anything that belongs to purely outward instruction or profane scholarship, which in reality is without any connection with this knowledge. However, we must emphasize this point yet more strongly, for we have only too often seen the need to do so; it is necessary to put an end to the all too widespread prejudice that what is customarily called 'culture' in the profane and 'worldly' sense should have any value at all, even as a preparation for initiatic knowledge, when in fact it can have no connection at all with such knowledge.

In principle, there is in fact no question here of a connection of any kind, for at whatever level it is considered, profane education cannot be of any use to initiatic knowledge, and (with all due reservation for the intellectual degeneration that the adoption of the profane point of view itself implies) it is not even incompatible with it,[1] being simply indifferent in this respect as is a manual skill acquired in the exercise of some mechanical trade, or even the

---

1. In particular, it is quite clear that someone who has from childhood received profane and 'compulsory' instruction in school could not be held responsible for this, nor be regarded as 'disqualified' for initiation because of it; the whole question is to know what 'impression' will remain with him afterward, for it is upon this that his particular possibilities really depend.

'physical culture' so much in vogue today. Envisaged from our point of view all this fundamentally belongs to one and the same order, but the danger is to allow oneself to be deceived by the misleading appearance of an 'intellectuality' that has absolutely nothing to do with pure and true intellectuality; and the constant abuse of the word 'intellectual' by our contemporaries is enough to prove that this danger is only too real. Among other disadvantages, this can often result in a tendency to link or rather to mix things of totally different orders. In this connection, but without repeating what has been said regarding the intrusion of a type of utterly profane 'speculation' into certain Western initiatic organizations, we will simply call to mind the futility which we have often pointed out of all attempts to establish some link or resemblance between modern science and traditional knowledge,[2] some having even gone so far in this direction as to claim to find in modern science 'confirmations' of traditional knowledge, as if this latter, based on immutable principles, could derive the slightest benefit from an accidental and altogether outward resemblance to the hypothetical and ever-changing results of that uncertain and groping research that moderns are pleased to dignify with the name 'science'.

But it is not this side of the question that we must emphasize just now, nor even the danger that may exist, when the importance of this inferior (often even wholly illusory) knowledge is exaggerated, of devoting all one's activities to it to the detriment of a higher knowledge, the very possibility of which thus comes to be unappreciated or even wholly ignored. We know only too well that this is indeed the case with the immense majority of our contemporaries, for whom the question of a link with initiatic knowledge, or even with traditional knowledge in general, obviously no longer arises since they do not even suspect that such a knowledge exists. But even without going to such an extreme, profane education may very often constitute, in fact if not in principle, an obstacle to the acquisition of true knowledge (the exact opposite, that is, of an effective preparation), and this for various reasons that we must now explain in more detail.

2. Cf. especially *Reign of Quantity*, chaps. 18 and 32.

To begin with, profane education imposes certain mental habits of which it may be more or less difficult to rid oneself later; it is only too easy to see that the limitations and even deformities that are the usual result of a university education are often irremediable, and that in order to escape entirely from this unfortunate influence special aptitudes, which can only be exceptional, are necessary. We are speaking here in a very general way, and will not dwell on more particular drawbacks such as the narrowness of outlook that inevitably results from 'specialization', or the 'intellectual myopia' that usually accompanies 'scholarship' cultivated for its own sake; what is essential to note, however, is that whereas profane knowledge in itself is simply indifferent, the methods by which it is instilled are really the very negation of those that give access to initiatic knowledge.

And then it is necessary to take into account as a far from negligible obstacle that sort of self-conceit often caused by so-called scholarship, which among many people is all the more marked as this scholarship is the more elementary, inferior, and incomplete. Moreover, even without going beyond the contingencies of 'ordinary life', the misdeeds of primary education in this respect are easily recognized by all who are not blinded by certain preconceived ideas. Of two individuals who are ignorant, it is obvious that the one who recognizes that he knows nothing is much more favorably disposed toward acquiring knowledge than the one who believes that he knows something; the natural possibilities of the first are intact, one could say, while those of the second are as it were 'stifled' and can no longer develop freely. Besides, even admitting good will on the part of both individuals alike, the second would still always have to rid himself of the false ideas with which his mind is encumbered, while the first could at least dispense with this preliminary and negative task, which represents what Masonic initiation symbolically calls the 'stripping of metals'.

This easily explains a fact we have frequently noted concerning people described as 'cultured'. The ordinary meaning of this word is well-known; it does not even refer to an ever so insubstantial knowledge, no matter how limited and inferior its scope, but to a superficial smattering of all sorts of things, to an education that is above all 'literary' and in any case purely bookish and verbal, one that allows

its possessor to speak with assurance about everything, even including what he is most ignorant of, and is liable to deceive those who
are easily taken in by such brilliant veneers and who fail to see that
what lies behind them is nothing at all. On another level, this 'culture' generally produces effects rather similar to those we have just
now recalled on the subject of primary education; of course there
are exceptions, for it can happen that someone who has received
this kind of 'culture' may be endowed with natural dispositions
favorable enough to enable him to judge it at its just value and not
be duped by it; but we are not exaggerating when we say that, dis-
counting these exceptions, the great majority of 'cultured' people
must be numbered among those whose mental state is least suited
for receiving true knowledge. There is in them a kind of resistance
to true knowledge, often unconscious but sometimes also deliberate, yet even those who do not formally deny all that belongs to the
esoteric or initiatic order deliberately and *a priori* show at least a
complete lack of interest in this regard, and it even happens that
they make a show of their ignorance about these things, as if in their
own eyes it were one of those marks of superiority that their 'culture' is supposed to confer on them! Let no one think that we have
any intention of indulging in caricature; we simply describe exactly
what we have seen on many occasions, not only in the West but
even in the East, where in any case this type of 'cultured' man hap-
pily has little importance, having made his appearance only recently
and as the product of a certain kind of 'Westernized' education,
from which it results, let us note in passing, that this 'cultured' man
is necessarily at the same time a 'modernist'.[3] The conclusion to be
drawn from this is that people of this sort are simply the least 'initiable' of all the profane, and that it would be perfectly unreasonable
to take the least notice of their opinion, even if only to try to adapt
the presentation of certain ideas to it; and it is appropriate to add

---

3. On the connection between 'modernism' and the opposition to all esoterism,
see *Reign of Quantity*, chap. 11. [This book was first published in 1953. In the half
century since, this ideal of the 'cultured' man has come and gone, in the East as in
the West, to be replaced by a modernism of more barbaric propensities. ED.]

that concern for 'public opinion' in general is as 'anti-initiatic' an attitude as it is possible to have.

Here we must clarify yet another point that is closely connected with these considerations. This is that all exclusively 'bookish' knowledge has nothing in common with initiatic knowledge, even when envisaged at its purely theoretical stage. This might seem obvious after what we have just said, for all bookish study is undeniably a part of the most outward kind of education; if we dwell on this point, it is because one could be mistaken when this kind of study bears on books of which the content is initiatic. Anyone who reads such books after the manner of 'cultured' people, or who even studies them in a 'scholarly' manner and according to profane methods, will not for all that come any nearer to true knowledge, because he brings to them dispositions that do not enable him to penetrate their true meaning or in any way to assimilate them; the example of the orientalists, who generally display a total incomprehension in this regard, is a particularly striking illustration of this. Altogether different is the case of one who takes these same books as 'supports' for his interior work, which is the role for which they are essentially intended, and who knows how to see beyond the words and find in them an opportunity and a support for the development of his own possibilities; here one retains the properly symbolic usage of which language is susceptible and about which we have already spoken. This, it will be easily understood, has nothing in common with mere bookish study, even though it begins with books. The accumulation of verbal notions in the memory is not even the shadow of real knowledge; the only thing that counts is to penetrate to the 'spirit' clothed in the outward forms, which presupposes that the being bears within itself the corresponding possibilities, for all knowledge is essentially identification; and unless this qualification inheres in the very nature of the being, the highest expressions of initiatic knowledge, in the measure that it can be expressed, and the sacred scriptures of all the traditions themselves, will never be to it more than a 'dead letter' and *flatus vocis*.

34

ACADEMIC MENTALITY
AND PSEUDO-INITIATION

ONE OF THE CHARACTERISTIC MARKS of most modern pseudo-initiatic organizations is the way they employ certain terms of comparison drawn from 'ordinary life', which, in short, is to say from profane activity under one or another of its contemporary forms. It is not only a question of analogies that despite the annoying banality of the images used and the fact that they are as far removed as possible from any traditional symbolism could still be more or less useful within certain limits (we say 'more or less' because it must not be forgotten that, in the end, the profane point of view as such always contains within itself something illegitimate inasmuch as it is really a negation of the traditional point of view); but what is more serious still is that these things are taken in the most literal way, to the point that there is a kind of assimilation of so-called spiritual realities to forms of activity that, at least in present conditions, are strictly opposed to any spirituality. Thus, in certain occultist schools with which we were once acquainted, a recurrent theme was that of 'debts to pay', a theme that was pushed to the point of obsession; and in Theosophy and its various more or less direct derivatives one constantly heard the refrain of 'lessons to learn', everything being described in 'academic' terms—which brings us again to the confusion of initiatic knowledge with profane teaching. The entire universe is here conceived as nothing more than a vast school in which beings progress from one class to another in the measure that they have 'learned their lessons'; and this image of successive classes is furthermore intimately linked to the idea of 'reincarnation'. But this is not the point that interests us presently, for we propose to draw attention to the error inhering in these 'academic' metaphors and to the essentially profane mentality from which they proceed, independently of the relationship they may have in fact with this or that particular theory.

Profane instruction as it exists in the modern world, and on which all the figures of speech under discussion are modeled, is obviously one of those things that exhibit an anti-traditional character in the highest degree. One can even say that in a way it was devised only for this purpose, or at least that its primary and principal purpose lies in this characteristic, for it is evident that it is one of the most powerful instruments for achieving the destruction of the traditional spirit. It would be useless to dwell on these considerations again, but there is one other point that might seem less evident at first glance, which is that even if such a deviation had not occurred, 'academic' representations of this sort would still be erroneous once one intended to apply them to the initiatic order; for although it would not then be profane as it is today but, on the contrary, legitimate and even traditional in its own order, outward instruction is always, by its very nature and purpose, something entirely different from what relates to the initiatic domain. In any case, there would thus be a confusion between exoterism and esoterism, a confusion testifying not only to an ignorance of the true nature of esoterism but even to the loss of the traditional sense in general, which indeed is itself a manifestation of the profane mentality. But in order to understand this still better, we should clarify a bit more than we have up till this point certain profound differences that exist between outward instruction and initiation; and this will make more apparent a defect that already appears in certain authentic though degenerate traditional organizations, and which naturally is found all the more in the pseudo-initiatic organizations to which we have alluded, accentuated to the point of caricature.

In this regard it must first be said that in university instruction, or rather, university instruction as first instituted, there is something much less simple and even more enigmatic than is ordinarily believed, at least until one asks oneself a question that ought nonetheless to arise immediately for anyone capable of the least reflection. If there is an obvious truth, it is that one cannot confer or transfer to others something that one does not oneself possess;[1] how then could university degrees have been originally instituted unless through the intervention under one form or another of an authority of a superior order? There must therefore have been a veritable 'exteriorization',[2] which can also be considered as a 'descent' into that lower order to which all 'public' teaching necessarily belongs even if it be established on the most strictly traditional bases (which we will then gladly call 'scholastic' according to the usage of the Middle Ages, reserving for the word 'academic' its usual profane meaning); and it is by virtue of this 'descent' that this teaching could, within the limits of its own domain, effectively participate in the very spirit of the tradition. This fits well on the one hand with what is known of the general characteristics of the age to which the origin of the universities belongs, that is to say, the Middle Ages, and on the other hand more particularly with the little-noted fact that the distinction of the three university degrees is quite obviously modeled after the form of an initiatic hierarchy.[3] Let us also recall here that, as we have already said elsewhere,[4] while the sciences of the *trivium* and the *quadrivium* in their exoteric sense were the divisions of a university curriculum, they also corresponded, by an appropriate transposition, to the degrees of initiation.[5] But it goes without saying that if such a correspondence strictly respects the

1. We have seen a Masonic writer affirm that 'it was indeed necessary that the first initiate initiate himself,' and this with the intention of denying the 'non-human' origin of initiation. It would be difficult to push absurdity any further than this, as we have shown by explaining the true nature of initiation, but in any domain whatsoever it is hardly less absurd to suppose that someone should give himself what he does not have, and even more that he should pass it on. We have elsewhere already raised a similar question regarding the eminently suspect character of psychoanalytic transmission (*Reign of Quantity*, chap. 34).

2. We have already spoken of such an 'exteriorization' in another order in connection with the relationship between certain exoteric rites and initiatic rites.

3. The three degrees, bachelor, licentiate, and doctor, reproduce the ternary division frequently adopted by initiatic organizations, and which is found particularly in Masonry, with its three degrees: Apprentice, Fellow-Craft, and Master.

4. See *The Esoterism of Dante*, chap. 2.

5. One then has another division, now no longer ternary but septenary, which was used in particular by the medieval 'Fedeli d'Amore' and, in antiquity, in the

normal relationships between the different orders, it could never imply the transfer into the initiatic domain of such things as a system of classes and examinations such as those necessarily included in outward teaching. And it should hardly be necessary to add that since, in modern times, Western universities have turned entirely away from their original spirit and thus can no longer have the least connection with a higher principle able to legitimize them, the degrees they have preserved, instead of being a sort of outward image of initiatic degrees, are no more than a parody of them, just as a profane ceremony is the parody or counterfeit of a rite, and the profane sciences themselves, in more than one respect, are a parody of the traditional sciences. This last case, moreover, is altogether comparable to that of university degrees, which, even if there has been continuity in their preservation, are really only a 'residue' of what they were originally, just as the profane sciences are a 'residue' of the ancient traditional sciences, as we have explained on more than one occasion.

We have just alluded to examinations, and it is on this point that we now wish to dwell. As can be seen by their continual use in the most varied civilizations, these examinations have their place and purpose even in outward instruction, traditional instruction not excepted, where, almost by definition, they include no criterion of another order. But when, on the contrary, it is a matter of a purely inward domain such as that of initiation they become entirely vain and ineffectual and can normally play no more than an exclusively symbolic role, somewhat as the secret concerning certain ritual forms is only a symbol of the true initiatic secret; besides, they are perfectly useless in an initiatic organization as long as this is truly

---

Mithraic mysteries; in both cases the seven degrees or stages of initiation seem to have been related to the seven planetary heavens.

[Roman Mithraism should perhaps be considered a borderline spiritual tradition since it was compounded from previous traditions and so was to that extent syncretistic. On the other hand, there may have been a genuine initiatic tradition behind it, and the fact that participation in it was largely limited to one class of Roman society, that of the soldiery (which could be considered as very loosely analogous to the Kshatriya caste in the Hindu tradition), seems to support this view. Ed.]

all that it ought to be. However, it is necessary in fact to account for certain cases of degeneration where, because no one can any longer apply correct criteria (especially in consequence of a complete forgetfulness of the traditional sciences that alone can furnish them, as we have said in connection with initiatic qualifications), this is compensated for as much as possible by establishing, for the sake of passing from one degree to the next, examinations similar in form if not in content to university examinations, which, like the former, can only bear on things 'learned', just as, in the absence of any effective interior authority, one establishes administrative forms comparable to those of profane governments. Since these two things are really only two effects of the same cause, they appear quite closely connected, and are almost always found together in the same organizations; this not only in real organizations but also in the imaginary framework of pseudo-initiatic organizations. Thus the Theosophists, who are so fond of 'academic' formulations, also imagine what they call the 'occult government of the world' divided up into different 'departments' of which the attributes are all too obviously inspired by the ministries and bureaucracies of the profane world. This last remark leads us moreover to what might be the principal source of this sort of error: since the fabricators of pseudo-initiatic organizations have not even an outward knowledge of any authentically initiatic organization other than those fallen into this state of degeneration (and naturally so, since only these still exist in the West today), they think they can do no better than imitate them, and it is inevitable that they should imitate what is most outward, which is also what is most affected by the degeneration in question since this is where that degeneration is most clearly affirmed by things such as those we are considering. And, not content with introducing this imitation into the constitution of their own organizations, they have also, so to speak, projected it imaginatively onto an 'other world', that is, onto the image they have made for themselves of the spiritual world, or what they believe to be such. The result is that whereas as long as they have not undergone any deviation, initiatic organizations are constituted in the image of the true spiritual world, the caricature of this spiritual world is, inversely, made in the image of pseudo-initiatic organizations that, wishing to copy the appearance of certain initiatic organizations, have imitated only those aspects that have been deformed by borrowings from the profane world.

Whether it be a matter of more or less degenerate initiatic organizations or of pseudo-initiatic organizations, one can see that what is wrought by the introduction of profane forms is exactly the inverse of the 'descent' we had in mind when speaking of the origins of university institutions, and by which, in an age of traditional civilization, exoterism modeled itself in a certain way on esoterism, and the inferior on the superior. But the great difference between the two cases is that, with an initiation that is diminished or even deviated up to a point, the presence of these parasitic forms does not, despite everything, prevent the continued transmission of a spiritual influ-ence; whereas in pseudo-initiation there is nothing behind these same forms but the void pure and simple. What the promoters of the pseudo-initiation are evidently unaware of is that in bringing their 'academic' ideas, and other things of the sort, into their image of the universal order, they have simply marked it with their own profane mentality. What is most regrettable is that those to whom they present these fantasies are no more able than they to discern this mark, which, if they were able to fathom all that it signifies, would suffice to put them on guard against such undertakings, and even to turn them away from them forever.

35

INITIATION
AND 'PASSIVITY'

WE SAID ABOVE that nothing pertaining to initiatic knowledge can be the object of discussion and that discussion in general is, if one may put it thus, a profane undertaking par excellence. Some have claimed to infer from this that initiatic teaching must be received 'passively', and have even gone so far as to make this an argument against initiation itself. Here is yet another equivocation that it is particularly important to dispel. In order to be truly profitable, initiatic teaching naturally requires a 'receptive' mental attitude, but 'receptivity' is not at all a synonym for 'passivity'; on the contrary, this teaching requires of the one who receives it a continual effort of assimilation, which is essentially active, and even active to the highest degree that can be conceived. It is really profane teaching that can with some reason be reproached with passivity, since it has no other purpose than to furnish information that must be 'learned' instead of understood, that is, which the student need merely register and store in his memory without really assimilating it. By its wholly outward character and results, any personal and inward activity is obviously reduced to a minimum, if it is not completely lacking.

But at the root of this equivocation there is something still more serious. Indeed, we have often noted among those who claim to be enemies of esoterism a regrettable tendency to confuse it with its counterfeits, and consequently to include in similar attacks things that are in reality quite different, and indeed even totally opposed. This is of course another example of modern incomprehension, for ignorance of all that touches upon the esoteric and initiatic domain is so complete and widespread in our time that nothing can be astonishing in this regard, and in many cases this may excuse those who act in this way; moreover, one is sometimes tempted to wonder whether this is really a sufficient explanation for anyone who wants to go to the root of things. First of all, it goes without saying that this very incomprehension and ignorance are part of the scheme to destroy every traditional idea, the implementation of which has continued throughout the modern period, and that therefore they can only have been intentional and undertaken by the subversive influences working toward this destruction. But apart from this entirely general consideration, it seems that there is also something more in what we are alluding to, answering to a precise and clearly-defined plan. Indeed, when initiation is deliberately confused with pseudo-initiation, or even with the counter-initiation, and everything is jumbled together so inextricably that nothing can be recognized any longer, it is truly very difficult for anyone capable of the least reflection not to wonder who or what profits from all these confusions. It is of course not a question of good or bad faith that we wish to raise here, something that would in any case have only a very secondary importance, since the malevolence of false ideas so circulated would thus be neither increased nor decreased; and it is quite possible that the very prejudice some people exhibit is due solely to the fact that they are unconsciously obeying some suggestion. What is to be concluded from all this is not only that the enemies of the initiatic tradition make dupes among those they attract to organizations directly or indirectly 'controlled' by them, but that even the very people who believe themselves to be combatting them are in fact sometimes instruments just as useful for the ends they have in view, though in a different way. When the counter-initiation cannot entirely dissimulate its undertakings and purposes, it is doubly to its advantage to attribute them to true initiation, for by this they cause it undeniable harm and at the same time deflect the danger that threatens them by misleading those who might be on the trail of certain discoveries.

We have frequently been occupied with this subject,[1] more recently in particular with reference to a book published some time

---

1. In this connection there are in certain anti-Masonic campaigns quite extraordinary 'underhanded dealings'.

ago in England by a former member of certain organizations of dubious character, by which we mean those pseudo-initiatic organizations most clearly marked by the influence of the counter-initiation. Although the author left these organizations and even openly turned against them, he was still very much affected by the teaching he had received from them, which is quite apparent in his conception of initiation. This conception, in which precisely the notion of passivity predominates, is strange enough to warrant our close attention because it serves as the guiding idea of what was meant to be a history of initiatic organizations, or what are so called, from antiquity down to our own day, an eminently fanciful history in which everything is jumbled together as we just described, and which is supported by many irregular citations, most of which are taken from very dubious 'sources'. But since here we do not mean to undertake a review of this book, this is not what presently interests us, any more than what simply conforms to the 'accepted' ideas invariably found in all works of this kind. We prefer to limit ourselves to exposing the errors implied in the guiding idea itself, errors that the author clearly owes to his previous attachments, so that, ultimately, he simply helps to disseminate and sanction the views of those whose adversary he believes he has become, continuing to take for initiation what they have presented to him as such, but which is really only one very efficacious way of preparing agents or instruments for the counter-initiation—this being what is most 'instructive' from our point of view.

All this is naturally limited to a purely psychic domain, and for this reason can have no connection with true initiation, since this, on the contrary, is of an essentially spiritual order. Here it is largely a question of 'magic', and as we have already sufficiently explained, magical operations of whatever sort in no way constitute an initiatic process. On the other hand, we find in this book the singular belief that every initiation must be based on the awakening and ascent of the subtle force that the Hindus call *Kundalinī*, something that is in fact a method proper only to certain very particular forms of initiation. What is more, this is not the first time we have noticed, in what we are inclined to call anti-initiatic legends, a sort of obsession with *Kundalinī*, which is curious to say the least, and for which the reasons are generally not very clear. Here it is linked fairly closely with an interpretation of the symbolism of the serpent taken in an exclusively 'malefic' sense, for the author seems not to have the least idea of the double meaning of certain symbols, a very important subject that we have already treated elsewhere.[2] However this may be, *Kundalinī Yoga*, as practiced particularly in the Tantric initiation, is assuredly something altogether different from magic, although what is abusively considered under this name in the present instance may well be nothing more than that. Indeed, if it were only a case of pseudo-initiation, it would doubtless be even less than that, a 'psychological' illusion pure and simple. But if the counter-initiation intervenes in any degree, there can well be a real deviation and even a sort of 'inversion' leading to contact, not with a transcendent principle or with higher states of the being, but quite simply with the 'astral light', what we would prefer to call the world of 'wandering influences', that is to say, in the final analysis, with the nethermost part of the subtle domain. The author, who accepts the expression 'astral light', describes this outcome as 'illumination', thus making this term curiously equivocal; rather than referring to something of a purely intellectual order and to the acquisition of a higher knowledge as it should normally do if taken in a legitimate initiatic sense, it then relates only to phenomena of 'clairvoyance' or to other powers of the same kind, of little interest in themselves, and especially negative in this case besides, for it seems that ultimately they serve to render the one afflicted by them accessible to suggestions emanating from so-called unknown 'Masters' who, under the circumstances, could only be sinister 'black magicians'.

We readily admit the accuracy of such a description for certain auxiliary organizations of the counter-initiation, for these generally seek nothing more than to make of their members mere instruments to be used as it pleases; but we do wonder, for this point does not seem perfectly clear, just what is the precise role played by the so-called 'initiate' in the magical operations leading to this result, and it seems that fundamentally this can only be the entirely passive one of a 'subject', in the sense in which 'psychics' of every sort understand the word. What we categorically deny, however, is that this same result has anything at all in common with initiation,

---

2. *Reign of Quantity*, chap. 30.

which on the contrary excludes all passivity. We have already explained that this is one reason why initiation is incompatible with mysticism; with all the more reason, then, is it incompatible with something implying a passivity of an incomparably lower order than that of the mystics, one in short that, since the advent of spiritualism, belongs to what is popularly called 'mediumship'. Perhaps, let us say in passing, what is involved here is entirely comparable to the actual origin of 'mediumship', and of spiritism itself; and when 'clairvoyance' is obtained by psychic 'exercises', even if *Kundalinī* plays no role, the usual effect is to render the subject eminently 'suggestible', as is proven by the unvarying conformity, alluded to above, of his visions to the special theories of the school to which he belongs. It is therefore not difficult to see to what advantage this can be put by 'black magicians', that is, the conscious representatives of the counter-initiation, nor is it difficult to realize that all of this goes directly against the true aim of initiation, which is properly speaking to 'deliver' the being from all contingencies, and not to impose new bonds over and above those naturally conditioning the existence of the ordinary man. The initiate is not a 'subject'; indeed, he is exactly the contrary; every tendency to passivity can only be an obstacle to initiation, and where it predominates it constitutes an 'irremediable' disqualification. What is more, every initiatic organization that has retained a clear understanding of its true purpose regards all hypnotic and other practices implying the use of a 'subject' as unlawful and strictly forbidden; and we might add that an active attitude is even prescribed toward the transitory spiritual states that may be reached in the first steps of 'realization' in order to avoid any danger of 'auto-suggestion'.[3] Strictly speaking, from the initiatic point of view passivity is only conceivable and admissible exclusively in face of the supreme Principle.

We are well aware that it might be objected that certain initiatic paths include a more or less complete submission to a *guru*; but this objection is by no means valid, firstly because we are speaking of a submission to which the initiate freely consents, not a subjection

---

3. This is what a Shaykh explained once in these words: 'A man must dominate the *ḥāl* (a not yet stabilized spiritual state) and not the *ḥāl* the man. (*Lāzim al-insān yarkab al-ḥāl, wa laysa al-ḥāl yarkab al-insān.*)

imposed without his knowledge, and secondly because the *guru* is always someone known to the disciple, someone with whom he has a real and direct relationship, and not some unknown figure who manifests himself 'astrally', that is, all phantasmagoria apart, who conveys suggestions by a kind of 'telepathic' influence without the disciple knowing whence they come. Furthermore, this submission is no more than a simple 'pedagogic' method, one could say, of entirely transitory necessity; not only would a true spiritual teacher never abuse it, but he would use it only to enable his disciple to free himself from it as soon as possible, for if there is any unvarying affirmation to be made in such a case, it is that the true *guru* is purely inward, that he is no other than the being's very 'Self', which the outward *guru* does no more than represent for as long as the being remains unable to enter into conscious communication with this 'Self'. Initiation ought precisely to lead to the fully realized and effective consciousness of the 'Self', which can obviously be the case neither with children in the nursery nor with psychic automata. The initiatic 'chain' is not meant to bind the being, but on the contrary to furnish a support that allows it to raise itself indefinitely and to go beyond its limits as an individual and conditioned being. Even when there are contingent applications that can coexist secondarily with its essential goal, an initiatic organization has no use for blind and passive instruments, whose normal place could in any case only be in the profane world, since they lack all qualification. What must exist among all its members at all levels and in all functions is a conscious and voluntary collaboration that implies all the effective understanding of which each is capable; and no true hierarchy can be realized or maintained on any other basis than this.

36

INITIATION
AND 'SERVICE'

THERE IS PERHAPS NO MORE GENERAL or more striking characteristic of modern pseudo-initiatic organizations than the attribution of an esoteric and initiatic value to considerations that can really have an acceptable meaning only in a purely exoteric domain. Such confusion, which corresponds quite well to the use of those images drawn from 'ordinary life' of which we spoke earlier, is in any case inevitable on the part of profane individuals who, wanting to pass for something they are not, claim to speak on matters of which they are in fact ignorant and about which they naturally form an idea cut to the measure of their own understanding. No less naturally, the considerations of this kind that they most insist on will always conform to the predominant tendencies of the present age, which shape even their secondary variations. Here one might ask how submitting to the influence of the profane world in this manner can be reconciled with the slightest initiatic claim, but of course those concerned are not at all aware of the contradiction. One could easily cite organizations that initially gave the illusion of a kind of intellectuality, at least to those who did not go to the heart of the matter, but which later came to limit themselves more and more to the worst sentimental banalities; clearly, this display of sentimentality only corresponds to what one presently sees in the 'outside world'. In both, moreover, one finds exactly the same formulas, as empty as they are pompous, the effect of which results from those 'suggestions' we mentioned earlier, although those who employ them are certainly not always conscious of where all this leads; and their absurdity in the eyes of anyone capable of even a little reflection becomes even greater when they parody esoterism. Such absurdity is furthermore a true 'mark' of the influences that are really behind all of this, even if those who yield to them are very far from suspecting it; but rather than continue with these general remarks, we wish to consider here a particular case that we find especially significant and which is connected in a certain way with what we have just said about 'passivity'.

In the special phraseology of these organizations, the words 'service' and 'servant' recur with ever-increasing frequency; one finds them everywhere, no matter what the subject. It is like a kind of obsession, and one might legitimately ask to what kind of 'suggestion' are they due. We must no doubt make allowances here for the Western mania for 'humility' or, more precisely, for its outward display, for the reality may be quite different, as when the most violent and hateful quarrels are accompanied by grand words about 'universal brotherhood'. Furthermore, it is clear that this is only a 'secular' and 'democratic' humility, perfectly consonant with an 'ideal' that, instead of raising the lower as much as possible, reduces the higher to the level of the lower. One must clearly be imbued with this modern and essentially anti-hierarchical 'ideal' not to see what is so disagreeable in such expressions, even where the intentions behind them are completely praiseworthy; it would doubtless be necessary in this last regard to distinguish among the very different applications that could be made of these expressions, but what is important to us here is only the state of mind betrayed by the words employed.

If these general considerations are equally valid in all cases, they are nonetheless insufficient when pseudo-initiation more particularly is involved; this brings in an additional confusion due on the one hand to the preponderance given by moderns to action, and on the other to the social point of view, and this leads them to imagine that these points of view should apply even to a domain where in reality they have no place. By one of those strange reversals of every normal order so customary to our epoch, the most external activities come to be regarded as essential conditions of initiation and, sometimes, even its goal, for, incredible as it may be, some even go so far as to see in initiation nothing but a means for better 'service'; and a further aggravating circumstance should be noted: that these activities are conceived in the most profane manner, devoid of the traditional, though of course entirely exoteric, character they could at least assume if envisaged from a religious point of view. But it is certainly a long way from religion to the mere 'humanitarian' moralism that is the mark of pseudo-initiates of every category!

On the other hand, it is undeniable that all forms of sentimentality are disposed toward a certain 'passivity'; here we rejoin the question treated previously, and here also is very likely the principal reason for the 'suggestion' now under consideration and what, in any case, renders it particularly dangerous. Indeed, by repeating to someone that he must 'serve' something, even if only vague 'ideal' entities, he is eventually put into such a disposition that, when the occasion presents itself, he is ready to 'serve' all who claim to incarnate those entities or to represent them in a more positive way; and the orders that he will receive from them, whatever their character— even if of the worst extravagance—will thus find in him the obedience of a true 'servant'. We can readily understand how this is one of the best possible means for molding instruments that the counter-initiation can have at its disposal; it also has the advantage of being one of the least compromising, since the 'suggestion' in such cases can very well be exercised by ordinary dupes, that is, by other unconscious instruments, so that those in charge need never intervene directly.

Let no one object that where there is a question of 'service' there might be what the Hindu tradition would call a *bhaktic* way. Despite the sentimental element it possesses to a certain degree (although it never degenerates into 'sentimentalism'), it is something else altogether; and even if one wishes to render *bhakti* as 'devotion' in Western language, as is usually done—though this is at most a derived meaning, for the first and essential meaning of the word is 'participation', as A.K. Coomaraswamy has shown—'devotion' is not 'service', or it could only be 'divine service' and not 'service' to anyone or anything. As for 'service' to a *guru*, if one insists upon using this word, where such a thing exists it is only as a preparatory discipline, and concerns only those one might call 'aspirants' and not those who have already achieved an effective initiation; and here we are still very far from the lofty spiritual goal so curiously attributed to 'service' by the pseudo-initiates. Finally, to forestall all possible objections, let us note that, in regard to the bonds between members of an initiatic organization, one obviously cannot give the name of 'service' to the assistance rendered by the superior as such to the inferior, nor more generally to relationships where the double hierarchy of degrees and functions (to which we shall return) must always be strictly observed.

We will not dwell any longer on this subject, which, all told, is a rather disagreeable one; but we thought it necessary, in view of the many diverse and doubtful 'services' to which people today are invited from all quarters, to point out the danger they hide and to say as clearly as possible what it is. To conclude on a brief note, we will simply add this: the initiate need not be a 'servant', or, at least, must be a servant only to the Truth.[1]

---

1. In Arabic *al-Ḥaqq*, which is, one must not forget, one of the principal divine names.

37

THE GIFT
OF TONGUES

A QUESTION DIRECTLY LINKED TO INITIATIC teaching and its adaptations is that of what is called the 'gift of tongues', often mentioned as one of the 'privileges' of the true Brotherhood of the Rose-Cross, or, more exactly (for the word 'privileges' can too easily give rise to false interpretations), one of their characteristic signs, although one capable of a much more extended application than is made by particular traditional forms. In fact, it seems that no one has ever clearly explained how we should understand this from the strictly initiatic point of view, for many who have used the expression seem to have understood it almost solely in the most literal sense, which is insufficient even though this literal meaning can certainly be justified in some ways. Indeed, the possession of certain keys to language can furnish means quite distinct from the ordinary for understanding and speaking the most diverse languages; and in the order of the traditional sciences, there certainly does exist what one could call a sacred philology, which is entirely different from the profane philology that first came to light in the modern West. However, even while accepting this first interpretation and situating it in its proper place among the contingent applications of esoterism, there is a symbolic meaning of a higher order that is superimposed upon the first without in any way contradicting it, and which moreover agrees with the initiatic ideas common to all traditions of both East and West.

From this point of view, one can say that he who truly possesses the 'gift of tongues' speaks to each person his own language in the sense that he always expresses himself in a form appropriate to the ways of thinking of those he addresses. This is what is alluded to in a more outward way when it is said that the Brotherhood of the Rose-Cross had to adopt the dress and habits of the country in which they found themselves; and some have even added that they had to take a new name—as if to take on a new individuality—each time they changed countries. Thus a representative of this Brotherhood, by virtue of the spiritual degree he had reached, was no more bound to any definite form than to the special conditions of a particular place,[1] and this is why he was a 'Cosmopolitan' in the true sense of the word.[2] We meet the same teaching in Islamic esoterism: Muḥyi 'd-Dīn ibn al-'Arabī says that 'the true sage does not tie himself to any beliefs' because, having obtained the knowledge of their common principle, he is beyond all particular beliefs; yet precisely because of this he is able, according to the circumstances, to speak the language proper to each belief. Moreover, regardless of what the profane may think, there is no 'opportunism' or dissimulation here; on the contrary, this is the necessary consequence of a knowledge superior to all forms but which can only be communicated (to the extent that it is communicable) through forms, each of which, by the very fact that it is a special adaptation, cannot be suitable for all men indiscriminately. To understand this, we can compare it to the translation of one idea into different languages; the idea always remains the same, in itself independent of any expression, but each time it is expressed in another language it becomes accessible to men who otherwise could not have known it; and this comparison also conforms strictly to the very symbolism of the 'gift of tongues'.

He who has arrived at this point has, by a direct and profound knowledge (and not by a merely theoretical or verbal one), reached

---

1. Nor, we might add, to any particular epoch; but a proper understanding of this, which pertains to the attribute of 'longevity', requires more ample explanation than we can provide here, though we will later give some indications concerning this question of 'longevity'.

2. We know that the name 'Cosmopolitan' has served as a 'covert' signature for diverse personages who, if not themselves members of the Brotherhood of the Rose-Cross, seem at least to have served as spokesmen for them in the outward transmission of certain teachings, and who could, insofar as they fulfilled this particular function, thereby identify with them to a certain extent.

the self-same foundation of all traditional doctrines, and, by placing himself at the central point from which they all emanate, has found the one truth hidden under the diversity and multiplicity of outward forms. Indeed, the difference exists only in form and appearance, the essential foundation being always and everywhere the same, for there is only one truth, even though it has multiple aspects according to the more or less special points of view from which it is considered and because, as the Muslim initiates say, 'the doctrine of Oneness is one.'[3] But a variety of forms is necessary to fit the mental conditions of a particular country or epoch, or, if one prefers, to correspond to the various particular points of view determined by these conditions; and those who stop at the form see the differences above all, to the point of taking them for oppositions, whereas they disappear for those who go further. Such people can subsequently descend again into the form, but are no longer affected by it in any way, and without their profound knowledge of it being in any way modified; and, just as one draws the consequences from the principle, they can realize all the adaptations of the fundamental doctrine by proceeding from higher to lower, from inward to outward (and it is in this way that true 'synthesis' is completely the opposite of vulgar 'syncretism', as we have previously explained). Thus, to use the same symbolism, they are no longer restricted to any particular language and therefore they can speak them all, for they have learned the very principle from which all languages derive through adaptation; and what we here call languages are all traditional forms, religious or otherwise, which in effect are only adaptations of the great primordial and universal Tradition, that is, diverse garments of the unique truth. Those who have passed beyond all particular forms to arrive at universality and who thus 'know' what others can only 'believe', are necessarily 'orthodox' in regard to every regular tradition; and only they can claim to be fully and effectively 'catholic' in the strictly etymological sense of the word,[4] whereas the others can only be so virtually, by a kind of aspiration that has not yet realized

---

3. *At-tawḥīd wāhidun.*

4. The word 'catholic', taken thus in its original sense, frequently recurs in writings of more or less direct Rosicrucian inspiration.

its object, or by a movement that, though directed toward the center, has not really succeeded in reaching it.

Those who have passed beyond form are thereby freed from the limitations inherent in the individual condition of ordinary humanity; even those who have only reached the center of the human state, without yet having effectively realized the superior states, are at least freed from the limitations by which a man, fallen from that 'primordial state' into which they are now reintegrated, is tied to a particular individuality as well as to a determinate form, since all individualities and all forms of the human domain have their immediate principle at the very point where they now stand. That is why, as we said earlier, they are able to put on diverse individualities in order to adapt to every circumstance, these individualities being truly no more important to them than mere garments. By this we can understand what the change of name really signifies, which naturally relates to what we have previously explained about initiatic names. Moreover, wherever this practice is found it always represents a more or less profound change of state; in the monastic orders its purpose is fundamentally the same, for there too the profane individuality[5] must disappear to be replaced by a new being; and even when the symbolism is no longer entirely understood in its profound sense, it nonetheless retains a certain efficacy.

If one understands these few indications, it will also be evident why the Brotherhood of the Rose-Cross could never have constituted anything even remotely resembling a 'society' or an external organization of any sort; they were no doubt able to more or less directly but invisibly inspire outward organizations that are formed temporarily for a special and definite purpose, as initiates of a like degree still do in the East, especially in the Far East; but though these organizations might for this reason be called 'Rosicrucian', they were not linked to them in any way and, except perhaps in some altogether exceptional cases played no apparent role in them. What in the West has been called the Brotherhood of the Rose-Cross

---

5. Strictly speaking, one should instead say the 'profane modality' of the individuality, for it is evident that, in the exoteric order, the change cannot be deep enough to have a bearing on anything more than mere modalities.

from the fourteenth century onward, and which has received other names in other times and places (since this name has only a purely symbolic value and must itself adapt to circumstances), is not some association, but rather the collectivity of beings that have reached the same state superior to that of ordinary humanity, the same degree of effective initiation (of which we have just noted one essential aspect), and who also possess the same inward qualities which suffice for them to recognize one another without requiring any outward sign. That is why they have no meeting-place other than 'the Temple of the Holy Spirit, which is everywhere', so that the descriptions sometimes given of it can only be understood symbolically; and that is also why they necessarily remain unknown to the profane among whom they live and to whom they are outwardly similar although in reality entirely different, for their distinctive marks are purely inward and thus perceived only by those who have reached the same level of spiritual development, so that their influence, which derives rather from an 'action of presence' than from any outward activity, is exercised in ways that are utterly incomprehensible to the common man.

38

ROSE-CROSS
AND ROSICRUCIANS

Since we have been led to speak of the Brotherhood of the Rose-Cross, it will perhaps not be in vain to clarify some points about it, even though this subject relates to a particular case rather than to initiation in general, for the name 'Rose-Cross' is presently used in a vague and often improper fashion and applied indiscriminately to very different people, very few of whom have a legitimate claim to it. To avoid all these confusions, it would seem best to make a clear distinction between the Brotherhood of the Rose-Cross and the Rosicrucians, the latter term being susceptible of a far wider application than the first; and it is probable that most of the so-called Brothers of the Rose-Cross were really only Rosicrucians. To understand the utility and importance of this distinction, one must first remember that, as we have just said, the true Brotherhood of the Rose-Cross was never an organization with definite outward forms, and that even though from at least the beginning of the seventeenth century there were numerous associations that can be called Rosicrucian,[1] this does not mean that their members belonged to the Brotherhood of the Rose-Cross. Indeed, we can even be certain that they were not solely from the fact that they belonged to such associations; this may seem paradoxical and even

---

1. Leibnitz in particular belonged to an organization of this type. We have spoken elsewhere of the manifestly Rosicrucian inspiration of some of his ideas, but we have also shown that it is not possible to consider him as having received more than a merely virtual initiation, incomplete in itself even from the theoretical point of view (see *Metaphysical Principles of the Infinitesimal Calculus*).

contradictory at first glance, but can nonetheless be easily understood in view of the considerations stated previously.

The distinction we are noting is far from a mere question of terminology, and in reality relates to something much more profound, since, we have already explained, the term Rose-Cross properly speaking designates an effective initiatic degree, that is to say a certain spiritual state the possession of which clearly does not necessarily involve membership in a specific organization. This degree is what can be called the perfection of the human state, for by its two constituent elements, the very symbol of the Rose-Cross stands for the reintegration of the being into the center of this state and the full expansion of his individual possibilities from that center, thereby marking very accurately the restoration of the 'primordial state', or, which amounts to the same thing, the completion of initiation into the 'lesser mysteries'. On the other hand, from what we can call the 'historical' point of view, we must take into account the fact that the name 'Rose-Cross', which is expressly linked to the use of a certain symbolism, has been used only in certain definite circumstances of time and place, outside of which its use would be illegitimate; one could say that those possessing the degree in question appeared as Brothers of the Rose-Cross in these circumstances only, for contingent reasons, just as in other circumstances they could have appeared under other names and other aspects. This does not of course mean that the symbol itself to which this name refers may not be much more ancient than this use of it, and, just as for every genuinely traditional symbol, it would no doubt be altogether pointless to try to find a definite origin for it. We mean only that the name derived from the symbol was given to an initiatic degree beginning only in the fourteenth century, and furthermore that this nomenclature is limited to the Western world; the name therefore is applied only with reference to a certain traditional form, that of Christian esoterism, or more precisely still, Christian Hermeticism; we will return later to what precisely should be understood by the term 'Hermeticism'.

An indication of what we have just said is given by the very 'legend' of Christian Rosenkreutz, whose name, in any event, is purely symbolic and who very probably is not an historical personage, despite what some have said about him, but rather represents what one could call a 'collective entity'.[2] The general sense of the 'legend' of this supposed founder, and in particular the meaning of the travels attributed to him,[3] seems to be that, after the destruction of the Order of the Temple, the initiates of Christian esoterism reorganized themselves in accord with the initiates of Islamic esoterism in order to maintain as much as possible the link that had apparently been broken by this destruction. But this reorganization had to be concealed—made invisible, as it were—and without taking its support in an outwardly known institution, which, as such, could once again have been destroyed.[4] The true Brothers of the Rose-Cross were properly those who inspired this reorganization, or, if one wishes, they were those who possessed the above-mentioned initiatic degree considered especially insofar as they played this role, which continued until the moment when, because of other historical events, the traditional link in question was finally broken in the West in the course of the seventeenth century.[5] It is said that the Brotherhood then withdrew to the East, which signifies that henceforth in the West there was no longer any initiation permitting one to attain that degree effectively, and also that the action that had hitherto been exercised for maintaining the corresponding traditional teaching ceased to manifest itself here, at least in a regular and normal fashion.[6]

---

2. This 'legend' is of essentially the same type as the other initiatic 'legends' to which we have already referred.

3. Let us recall here the allusion made above to the initiatic symbolism of the journey. There are, moreover, especially with regard to Hermeticism, many other journeys, such as those of Nicolas Flamel, the meaning of which seem to be primarily symbolic.

[Nicholas Flamel (1330–1418) was a Parisian scrivener turned alchemist who left behind a series of engraved alchemical hieroglyphs that have been the subject of much discussion in subsequent alchemical literature. Ed.]

4. Hence the name 'College of the Unseen' sometimes given to the collectivity of the Brotherhood of the Rose-Cross.

5. The precise date of this rupture is marked in the visible history of Europe by the conclusion of the treaties of Westphalia, which put an end to what still existed of medieval 'Christendom' in order to substitute for it a purely 'political' organization in the modern and profane sense of the word.

6. It would be altogether useless to try to determine 'geographically' the place to which the Brotherhood of the Rose-Cross retreated; of all the assertions one comes

As for knowing who were true Brothers of the Rose-Cross, and saying with certainty whether this or that person was of their number, this appears altogether impossible by the very fact that it is essentially a question of a spiritual state, purely interior, which it would be very imprudent to judge by any outward signs. Furthermore, because of their role, these Brothers of the Rose-Cross could not as such leave any visible trace in profane history, so that even if their names were known, they would be of no significance to anyone. In this connection, we will refer the reader to our earlier remarks regarding name changes, which sufficiently explain what is really involved here. As for those people whose names are known, particularly as authors of writings of one kind or another, and who are commonly named among the members of this Brotherhood, it is most probable that they were often influenced or more or less directly inspired by the true Brothers of the Rose-Cross whom they served as spokesmen,[7] which we can express by saying that they were merely Rosicrucians regardless of whether they belonged to any of the groups to which we can give the same name. On the other hand, if it were discovered, exceptionally and as if by accident, that a true Brother of the Rose-Cross had played a role in external events, this would have been as it were despite his degree rather than because of it, in which case historians would not in the least suspect this degree, so much do the two things [that is, the spiritual state and the outward event] belong to different domains. All of this will hardly satisfy the curious, but they will have to be content with it, for many things escape the methods of profane history which, by their very nature, allow one to grasp only what might be called the 'exteriority' of events.

---

across on this subject, the most probable is that they withdrew to the 'Kingdom of Prester John', which is nothing else, as we have explained elsewhere (*The King of the World,* chap. 1), than a representation of the supreme spiritual center, where all the traditional forms that for one reason or another have ceased to manifest themselves outwardly are preserved in a latent state until the end of the present cycle.

7. It is very doubtful that any Brother of the Rose-Cross has himself ever written anything whatsoever, and even had one done so it could only have been strictly anonymously, his very status forbidding him thus to present himself as a mere individual speaking in his own name.

We must add yet another reason why the true Brothers of the Rose-Cross had to remain unknown: no member is ever allowed to claim that he is such, any more than in Islamic initiation an authentic *Sufi* claims that title. There is a similarity here that is particularly interesting, although the two names are really not equivalent, for what is implied in the name *Sufi* is of a higher order than what is indicated by the name Rose-Cross and refers to possibilities that surpass those of the human state, even considered in its perfection. Strictly speaking, this name should even be reserved for the being that has attained the realization of the 'Supreme Identity', that is, the ultimate goal of all initiation;[8] but it goes without saying that such a being possesses *a fortiori* the degree of the Rose-Cross and if necessary can accomplish the corresponding functions. Besides, the name *Sufi* often suffers the same abuse as the name Rose-Cross, to the point of sometimes being applied to those who have merely entered on the path leading to effective initiation and have not yet reached even its first degrees. In this regard one can note the similar unwarranted extension that is currently given to the word *Yogi* in the Hindu tradition, to the point that this word, which likewise properly designates one who has reached the supreme goal and which is thus the exact equivalent of *Sufi*, comes to be applied to those who are still at the preliminary stages, even the most outward. Not only in such a case, but even for the one who has arrived at the highest degrees without however having reached the final goal, the designation that properly applies is *mutaṣawwuf*; and because the *Sufi* himself is not marked by any outward distinction, this same designation is also the only one that he is able to take or accept, not because of such purely human considerations as prudence or humility, but because his spiritual state is truly an incommunicable secret.[9] This is a distinction analogous to the former, but in a more restricted order (because it does not surpass the limits of the human

---

8. It is not without interest to note that, by the value of the letters that compose it, the word *Sufi* is numerically equivalent to *al-hikmah al ilahiyyah*, that is, 'the divine wisdom'. The difference between the Brothers of the Rose-Cross and the *Sufis* corresponds exactly to that existing in Taoism between 'true man' and 'transcendent man'.

9. This is one of the meanings of the Arabic word *sirr* ('secret') in its particular use in the 'technical' vocabulary of esoterism.

state) that can be expressed by the terms 'Rose-Cross' and 'Rosicrucian', for the latter can designate every aspirant to the state of the Rose-Cross, whatever degree he may have effectively reached, even if he has only received a virtual initiation in the form to which this designation properly applies. On the other hand, one can draw from these remarks a kind of negative criterion, in the sense that if someone calls himself a Brother of the Rose-Cross or a *Sufi*, one knows from that very fact, and without need to look further into the matter, that in reality he is certainly nothing of the sort.

Another negative criterion results from the fact that the Brotherhood of the Rose-Cross never established ties with any outward organization; if someone is known to have been a member of such an organization, it can again be affirmed, at least as long as he was an active member, that he was not a true Brother of the Rose-Cross. We should in any case note that organizations of this type did not take the title of Rose-Cross until quite late, since as we said earlier it does not appear until the beginning of the seventeenth century, that is, shortly before the true Brotherhood of the Rose-Cross withdrew from the West; and there are many clear indications that the organizations which took that name had already deviated to some degree, or at least were very far from the original source. This is even more true of organizations that were later formed under the same name, most of which doubtless could not claim for themselves, however indirectly, any authentic and regular affiliation to the Brotherhood of the Rose-Cross;[10] this of course is not to mention the many contemporary pseudo-initiatic organizations that have nothing to do with the Rose-Cross except the name they have usurped, and that possess not a trace of traditional doctrine, having, through the entirely individual initiative of their founders, simply adopted a symbol that everyone interprets according to his own fancy, for lack of any knowledge of its true meaning, which escapes these so-called Rosicrucians as completely as it does any of the profane.

There remains one point to which we must return with more precision. We have said that when Rosicrucianism originated there

---

10. This was very probably the case in the eighteenth century for organizations such as those known by the name 'Golden Rose-Cross' [*Rose-Croix d'Or*].

must have been a collaboration between initiates of the esoteric traditions of Christianity and of Islam; this collaboration must also have continued subsequently, since it was precisely a matter of maintaining the link between the initiations of the East and West. We will go even further and say that the same people, whether from Christianity or from Islam, were able to be at once Brothers of the Rose-Cross and *Sufis* (or *mutaṣawwufīn* of the higher degrees), if they lived in both East and West (and the constant allusion to their travels, all symbolism aside, leads us to think that this must have been the case for many of them), for the spiritual state they had reached implies that they were beyond the differences that exist among outward forms, which differences do not affect the essential and fundamental unity of traditional doctrine. Of course it is no less appropriate to maintain that there exists between *taṣawwuf* and true Rosicrucianism a distinction as between two different forms of traditional teachings; and the true Rosicrucians, the more or less direct disciples of the Brothers of the Rose-Cross, are uniquely those who follow the special path of Christian Hermeticism. However, there cannot be any initiatic organization fully worthy of the name, one possessing an effective consciousness of its goal, which does not have at the summit of its hierarchy beings that have gone beyond the diversity of formal appearances. These beings will be able to appear as Rosicrucians, as *mutaṣawwufīn*, or even in other forms, according to circumstances; they are truly the living link between all the traditions because, by their consciousness of unity underlying all traditional forms, they effectively participate in the great primordial tradition from which all the others are derived by adaptation to time and place and which, like Truth itself, is one.

39

THE GREATER
AND LESSER MYSTERIES

WE HAVE ALREADY SPOKEN of the distinction between the 'greater mysteries' and the 'lesser mysteries', names borrowed from Greek antiquity but in reality susceptible of an altogether general application; we must now dwell a little longer on the subject in order to show how this distinction is to be understood. What must be understood above all else is that these are not different kinds of initiation, but stages or degrees of the same initiation when considered as a complete whole that must be pursued to its ultimate end; in principle, the 'lesser mysteries' are therefore only a preparation for the 'greater mysteries' since their terminus is only one stage on the initiatic path. We say 'in principle' for it is quite clear that each being can progress only to the point where its own possibilities come to an end; thus, some may be qualified only for the 'lesser mysteries', or even for a somewhat limited aspect of these; but this only means that they are not capable of following the initiatic path to its end and not that they are following a different path from that of those who are able to go further.

The 'lesser mysteries' comprise all that is related to the development of the possibilities of the human state envisaged in its entirety; they therefore end in what we have called the perfection of this state, namely in what is traditionally called the restoration of the 'primordial state'. The 'greater mysteries', on the other hand, concern the realization of the supra-human states: taking the being at the point where the 'lesser mysteries' have left it, that is, the center of the domain of human individuality, they lead it beyond this domain, through the supra-individual states that are still conditioned, to the unconditioned state that alone is the true goal of all initiation and that is called the 'final Deliverance' or the 'Supreme Identity'. To characterize these two phases, one can apply geometric symbolism[1] and speak of 'horizontal realization' and 'vertical realization' respectively, the first serving as a basis for the second. This basis is represented symbolically by the earth, which corresponds to the human domain, and the supra-human realization is then described as an ascent through the heavens, which correspond to the superior states of the being.[2] Moreover, it is easy to understand why the second necessarily presupposes the first: the center of the human state is the only point where direct communication with the superior states is possible, and this is accomplished along the vertical axis which intersects the human domain at this point; it is therefore necessary to have reached this center first in order to raise oneself thereafter along the axis to the supra-individual states; and this is why, to use the language of Dante, the 'Terrestrial Paradise' is a stage on the path leading to the 'Celestial Paradise'.[3]

We have elsewhere cited and explained a text in which Dante relates the 'Celestial Paradise' and the 'Terrestrial Paradise' to what are, from the traditional point of view, the respective roles of the spiritual authority and the temporal power, in other words, to the priestly and royal functions;[4] we will content ourselves with recalling briefly the important consequences that follow from this correspondence according to our present point of view. The 'greater mysteries' are indeed directly related to 'sacerdotal initiation', and

1. See our account of this in *The Symbolism of the Cross*.

2. We have explained this symbolism more fully in *The Esoterism of Dante*.

3. In Islamic tradition, the states to which the 'lesser mysteries' and the 'greater mysteries' correspond are respectively designated as 'primordial man' (*al-insān al-qadīm*) and 'universal man' (*al-insān al-kāmil*); these two terms therefore correspond to the 'true man' and the 'transcendent man' of Taoism, as we mentioned in a previous note (see chap. 38, n8).

4. See *Spiritual Authority and Temporal Power*, chap. 8. This is the text in which, at the end of his treatise *De Monarchia*, Dante defines the respective attributes of pope and emperor, who represent the plenitude of these two functions in 'Christendom'.

the 'lesser mysteries' to 'royal initiation';[5] if we use terms borrowed from the terminology of the Hindu system of castes, we can say that normally the first can be regarded as the proper domain of the Brahmins and the second that of the Kshatriyas.[6] It can be added that the first of these two domains is 'supernatural' or 'metaphysical', whereas the second is only 'natural' or 'physical', and this in fact effectively corresponds to the respective attributes of spiritual authority and temporal power; this also allows us to distinguish clearly between the orders of knowledge to which the 'greater mysteries' and 'lesser mysteries' refer and which they effect for that part of initiatic realization that concerns them: the 'lesser mysteries' essentially imply a knowledge of nature (envisaged, of course, from the traditional rather than the profane point of view, which latter is that of the modern sciences), while the 'greater mysteries' imply the knowledge that is beyond nature. Pure metaphysical knowledge therefore properly derives from the 'greater mysteries' and knowledge of the traditional sciences from the 'lesser mysteries'; and since the first is the principle from which all the traditional sciences necessarily derive, the 'lesser mysteries' depend entirely upon the 'greater mysteries' and there find their very principle, just as temporal power depends for its legitimacy upon spiritual authority, where it also finds its principle.

We have spoken only of the Brahmins and the Kshatriyas, but must not forget that the Vaishyas can also be qualified for initiation; in fact, we find everywhere, as if especially destined for them, initiatic forms that are based on the practice of the crafts; we will not re-examine these here since we have sufficiently explained their principle and purpose elsewhere,[7] and since we shall have to speak of them again on different occasions, for it is precisely to such forms that everything that still exists of initiatic organizations in the West

---

5. The priestly and royal functions include all the applications of which the principles are provided by the corresponding initiations, whence the use of such expressions as 'sacerdotal art' and 'royal art' to designate these applications.

6. On this point, see also *Spiritual Authority and Temporal Power*, chap. 2.

7. See *Reign of Quantity*, chap. 8.

is linked. For Vaishyas even more than for Kshatriyas, the most suitable initiatic domain is that of the 'lesser mysteries'; this community
of domain, so to speak, has moreover frequently led to contacts
between the forms of initiation destined for each,[8] and consequently to rather close relations among the organizations by which
these forms are respectively practiced.[9] It is evident that beyond the
human state the individual differences upon which the craft initiations are essentially based disappear entirely and can no longer play
any role; once the being has reached the 'primordial state', the differentiations that give rise to diverse 'specialized' functions no longer
exist, even though it is here that all these functions have their
source, or rather, for this very reason; and it is indeed a matter of
returning to this common source, by going to the very limit of the
'lesser mysteries', if one would possess in its plenitude all that is
implied by the exercise of any function.

If we look at the history of humanity as taught by traditional doctrines, in conformity with cyclical laws, we must say that at the
beginning man, by the very fact that he was in full possession of his
state of existence, naturally possessed the possibilities corresponding to all functions, prior to any distinction among them. The division of these functions occurred at a later stage that represents a
state already inferior to the 'primordial state', but one in which each
human being, even while having no more than certain determinate
possibilities, still possessed an effective consciousness of these possibilities. It was only in a period of greater obscuration that this consciousness came to be lost; and since that time, initiation has
become necessary to permit mankind to recover the earlier state
which is inherent to it, together with a consciousness of it. This
indeed is its primary goal, that which it has most immediately in

8. In the West, it is in chivalry that were found, in the Middle Ages, those forms
of initiation appropriate to the Kshatriyas, or what must be considered to be the
nearest equivalent.

9. This is what explains, confining ourselves here to one characteristic example,
how an expression like 'royal art' may have been used and preserved up to the
present day by an organization such as Masonry, which is linked by its origin to the
exercise of a craft.

view. Such a possibility implies a transmission reaching back by an uninterrupted 'chain' to the state to be restored, and thus, step by step, to the 'primordial state' itself; yet initiation does not stop here, and as the 'lesser mysteries' are only a preparation for the 'greater mysteries', that is, for the acquisition of the higher states of the being, it is finally necessary to go back even beyond the origins of humanity; and this is why the question of an 'historical' origin of initiation is entirely devoid of meaning. Moreover, it is the same with regard to the origin of the crafts, arts, and sciences, when these are considered traditionally and legitimately; all of them, spanning multiple though secondary differentiations and adaptations, derive equally from the 'primordial state' which contains them all in principle; and by this they are linked to the other orders of existence, beyond humanity itself, so that they can, each in its own level and according to its own measure, effectively work toward the realization of the 'plan of the Great Architect of the Universe'.

We must still add that since the 'greater mysteries' have for their domain pure metaphysical knowledge, which is essentially one and immutable by very reason of its principial character, it is only in the domain of the 'lesser mysteries' that deviations can occur; and this accounts for many things concerning certain incomplete initiatic organizations. In a general way, these deviations imply that the normal link with the 'greater mysteries' has been broken, so that the 'lesser mysteries' are taken as an end in themselves; under such conditions they cannot really reach their term but are as it were scattered in a development of more or less secondary possibilities, a development that, not being ordered to a higher end, therefore risks acquiring a 'disharmonic' character which, precisely, constitutes the deviation. From another point of view, it is also in the 'lesser mysteries', and here only, that the 'counter-initiation' is capable of setting itself against true initiation and of entering into battle with it;[10] the domain of the 'greater mysteries', which relates to the suprahuman states and to the purely spiritual order, is by its very nature beyond such opposition and therefore entirely closed to all that is

10. Cf. *Reign of Quantity*, chap. 38.

not true initiation as defined by traditional orthodoxy. The result of all this is that the possibility of deviation exists as long as the being has not been reintegrated into the 'primordial state', but it ceases to exist once the being has reached the center of the human individuality; and this is why it can be said that whoever has reached this point, namely the accomplishment of the 'lesser mysteries', is already virtually 'delivered',[11] although he is not delivered effectively until he has traveled the path of the 'greater mysteries' and finally realized the 'Supreme Identity'.

11. This is what in Buddhist terminology is called *anāgamī*, that is, 'the one who does not return' to a state of individual manifestation.

40

SACERDOTAL
AND ROYAL INITIATION

ALTHOUGH THE PRECEDING chapter suffices on the whole to characterize sacerdotal and royal initiation clearly enough, we believe we must dwell somewhat further on the question of the relationship between them because of certain erroneous conceptions we have encountered from diverse quarters which tend to present each of these initiations as forming a complete whole by itself, so that they appear to be two irreducible types of doctrine and not two different hierarchical degrees. The principal intention of those who propagate such a conception generally seems to be to oppose the Eastern traditions, considered to be of a sacerdotal or contemplative type, to the Western traditions, which are taken to be of the royal and warrior or active type; and even when they do not go so far as to proclaim the superiority of the latter over the former, they do at least put them on an equal footing. Let us add incidentally that when it is a question of the Western traditions, this is usually accompanied by rather fantastic views of their historical origins, as, for example, in the hypothesis of a primitive and unique 'Mediterranean tradition', which very probably never existed.

In reality, at their origins and prior to the division into castes, the two functions, sacerdotal and royal, did not exist in distinct and differentiated states; they were both contained in their common principle which is above castes, and from which they emerged only in a late phase of the cycle of terrestrial humanity.[1] It is evident

1. Cf. *Spiritual Authority and Temporal Power*, chap. 1.

moreover that from the time the castes came to be distinguished, every social organization has had to include them equally in one form or another, since they represent different functions that must necessarily coexist; one cannot after all conceive of a society composed solely of Brahmins, nor of another composed solely of Kshatriyas. The coexistence of these functions naturally implies their hierarchization in conformity with their own nature, and consequently that of the individuals comprising them; the Brahmin is superior to the Kshatriya by nature, not because he has more or less arbitrarily taken first place in society; he is superior because knowledge is superior to action, because the 'metaphysical' domain is superior to the 'physical' domain as the principle is superior to what derives from it; and from this no less naturally arises the distinction between the 'greater mysteries', which constitute the sacerdotal initiation proper, and the 'lesser mysteries', which constitute the royal initiation.

Thus to the extent that every tradition is regular and complete, it must simultaneously comprise in its esoteric aspect these two initiations, or more exactly, these two parts of initiation, namely the 'greater mysteries' and the 'lesser mysteries'; the second is in any case subordinate to the first, as their very names clearly indicate. This subordination could only have been denied by rebel Kshatriyas who strove to reverse the normal relationships and who, in certain cases, were able to set up a sort of irregular and incomplete tradition that was reduced to what corresponds to the domain of the 'lesser mysteries', the only one they knew and which they presented falsely as the total doctrine.[2] In such a case, only the royal initiation remains, degenerate and deviant moreover because it is no longer attached to the principle that made it lawful; as for the contrary case, where the sacerdotal initiation alone might exist, it is impossible to find an example of this anywhere, which suffices to substantiate our point: if there are truly two types of traditional and initiatic organization, it is because one is regular and normal and the other irregular and abnormal, one complete and the other incomplete

---

2. Cf. ibid., chap. 3.

(and, it must be added, necessarily incomplete on its higher side). Things could not be otherwise, and this is true in an absolutely general way, in the West as well as in the East.

As we have said on many occasions, contemplative tendencies are much more widespread in the East, at least in the present state of things, and active tendencies (or rather, 'busyness' in the most outward sense) is more common in the West; but this is after all only a question of proportion and not of exclusivity. If there were a traditional organization in the West (by which we mean an integral traditional organization that effectively possesses both the esoteric and exoteric aspects), it would normally include, as do those in the East, both the sacerdotal and the royal initiations, whatever particular forms they might assume to adapt themselves to the conditions of their environment; but the superiority of the first over the second would always be recognized, whatever the number of those respectively qualified to receive one or the other initiation, for number plays no role here and could in no way modify what is inherent to the very nature of things.[3]

What can deceive is the fact that in the West, although the royal initiation no more exists than does the sacerdotal,[4] one more readily finds vestiges of the first than of the second. This is especially due to the links that generally exist between royal initiation and the craft

---

3. To avoid any possible ambiguity, we must specify that, after what we have said about the respective correspondence of the two initiations with the 'greater mysteries' and the 'lesser mysteries', it would be altogether wrong to think that sacerdotal initiation does not include a passage through the 'lesser mysteries'; but the truth is that this passage can be accomplished much more rapidly in such a case because the Brahmins are by their nature more inclined to principial knowledge and thus need not linger over a detailed development of contingent possibilities, so that for them the 'lesser mysteries' can be reduced to a minimum, that is, to what is essential and aims immediately at reaching the 'primordial state'.

4. In all this it goes without saying that we intend these terms in their most general sense as designating the initiations appropriate, respectively, to the natures of Kshatriyas and Brahmins, since for what concerns the exercise of the corresponding functions in the social order, the anointing of kings and the ordination of priests only represent 'exteriorizations', as we have already said above; in other words, these functions belong exclusively to the exoteric order and do not imply any initiation whatsoever, even virtual.

initiations, as we said above, and for this reason such vestiges are to be met with in organizations derived from those craft initiations that still exist in the Western world.[5] But there is more. By a strange phenomenon, one sometimes observes the more or less fragmentary but still very recognizable re-appearance of something from these diminished and deviated traditions that were the product, in very different circumstances of time and place, of the revolt of the Kshatriyas; the principal mark of these things is always their 'naturalistic' character.[6] Without wishing to pursue the matter, we will only draw attention to the preponderance often accorded in such cases to a certain 'magical' point of view (by which we need not understand exclusively a quest for outward and more or less extraordinary effects, as in the case of pseudo-initiation), which results from the alteration of the traditional sciences when they are separated from their metaphysical principle.[7]

Moreover, the 'mingling of castes', that is to say in the final analysis the destruction of all true hierarchy that is characteristic of the final phase of the *Kali-Yuga*,[8] renders it more difficult, especially for those who do not go to the heart of things, to determine exactly the real nature of elements such as those to which we are alluding; and we have doubtless not yet arrived at the most extreme degree of this

---

5. Here one can recall especially the existence of grades of 'chivalry' among the higher grades that were superimposed on Masonry properly so called; whatever the more or less ancient historical origin of these degrees may be—a question that one could discuss indefinitely without ever arriving at any precise answer—the real principle of their existence can be explained only in the way we have just mentioned, which is all that matters from our present point of view.

6. Manifestations of this kind seem to have been most widespread during the time of the Renaissance, but they are very far from having ceased even in our day, although they generally have a very hidden character and are normally completely unknown, not only to the 'general public', but even to the majority of those who claim to specialize in the study of what are usually, and rather vaguely, called 'secret societies'.

7. It is necessary to add that these inferior and deviated initiations are naturally those that most readily provide an opening for the action of influences emanating from the counter-initiation; on this subject, let us recall what we have said elsewhere regarding the utilization of all that has the character of a 'residue' in the work of subversion. See *Reign of Quantity*, chaps. 26 and 27.

8. On this subject, see especially the *Vishnu-Purāna*.

confusion. Having started at a level higher than the distinction of the castes, the historical cycle, by a gradual descent the various stages of which we have traced elsewhere,[9] must end at a level lower than this same distinction, for as we said above there are obviously two opposed ways of being beyond caste: one can be above or below, that is, above the highest or below the lowest of them; and if the first case was normal for men at the beginning of the cycle, the second will have become so for the immense majority in its final phase; we now see such clear evidence of this that it would serve no purpose to dwell further on this point, since no one, unless he be completely blinded by certain prejudices, can deny that this tendency to a leveling from below is one of the most striking characteristics of the present.[10]

One could however raise this objection: if the end of one cycle must necessarily coincide with the beginning of another, how can the lowest point rejoin the highest point? We have already answered this question elsewhere.[11] A rectification will indeed have to take place, and this will only be possible precisely when the lowest point is reached; this relates to the secret of the 'reversal of the poles'. Moreover, this rectification will have to be prepared, even visibly, before the end of the present cycle; but this can only be done by one who, by uniting in himself the powers of Heaven and Earth, of East and West, will manifest outwardly, both in the domain of knowledge and in that of action, the twin sacerdotal and royal power that has been preserved across the ages in the integrity of its unique principle by the hidden keepers of the primordial tradition. But it would be vain to seek to learn at present just when and how such a manifestation will occur, and doubtless it will be very different from anything one could imagine; the 'mysteries of the Pole' (al-asrār-al-quṭbāniyah) are assuredly well guarded, and nothing will be known of them outwardly until the fixed time is accomplished.

---

9. Cf. *Spiritual Authority and Temporal Power*, chap. 7.

10. Cf. *Reign of Quantity*, chap. 7.

11. Ibid., chaps. 20 and 23.

41

SOME REFLECTIONS
ON HERMETICISM

WE HAVE SAID before that properly speaking the Brothers of the
Rose-Cross were beings that had effectively achieved the completion of the 'lesser mysteries', and that the Rosicrucian initiation
inspired by them was a particular form linked to Christian Hermeticism. Relating this to what we have just explained, one must
already be able to understand that Hermeticism belongs in a general
way to the domain of 'royal initiation'. However, it will be good to
bring more precision to this subject, as here again much confusion
has arisen, the word 'Hermeticism' itself being used by many of our
contemporaries in a very vague and uncertain way. We do not mean
only the occultists, for whom this is only too evident, for there are
others who, even while pursuing the question more seriously seem,
perhaps because of certain preconceived ideas, not to realize just
what is at issue.

First of all, it must be noted that the word 'Hermeticism' indicates that we are dealing with a tradition of Egyptian origin, afterward clothed in a Hellenized form (doubtless in the Alexandrian
epoch), and in the Middle Ages transmitted in this form both to the
Islamic and Christian worlds, and, let us add, to the second in great
part by the intermediary to the first,[1] as is proven by the numerous
Arabic or Arabized terms adopted by the European Hermeticists,

1. This relates to what we have said concerning the relationship that Rosicrucianism had at its origins with Islamic esoterism.

beginning with the word 'alchemy' itself (al-kimyā).[2] It would therefore be quite wrong to extend this designation to other traditional forms, just as it would be, for example, to consider the 'Kabbalah' to be anything other than Hebrew esoterism.[3] It is not, of course, that it has no equivalents elsewhere, for these do exist to the degree that the traditional science of alchemy[4] has its exact correspondence in doctrines found in India, Tibet, and China, although with methods of realization that are naturally quite different; but as soon as one says 'Hermeticism' one specifies a clearly determined form the provenance of which can only be Greco-Egyptian. Indeed, the doctrine thus designated is by this very fact related to *Hermes* insofar as the latter was considered by the Greeks to be identical with the Egyptian *Thoth*; moreover, this presents the doctrine as being derived essentially from a sacerdotal teaching, for *Thoth*, in his role as guardian and transmitter of tradition, is nothing other than the very representation of the ancient Egyptian priesthood, or rather, to be more precise, of the principle of 'supra-human' inspiration from which this priesthood held its authority and in whose name it formulated and communicated initiatic knowledge. One should not see in this the least contradiction with the fact that this doctrine belongs to the domain of the royal initiation, for it must be clearly understood that in every regular and complete tradition it is the priesthood that, by virtue of its essential teaching function, confers both initiations, directly or indirectly, and that this ensures the true legitimacy of the royal initiation itself by relating it to its higher

---

2. This word is Arabic in its form but not in its root, deriving in all likelihood from the name *Kémi* or 'black earth' given to ancient Egypt, which again indicates the origin in question.

3. The significance of the word *Kabbalah* is exactly the same as that of the word 'tradition'; but since this word is Hebraic, there is no reason when using a language other than Hebrew to apply it to traditional forms other than that to which it properly belongs, which would only raise confusions. Similarly, the word *taṣawwuf* in Arabic can be taken to designate everything of an esoteric and initiatic character, in any traditional form whatsoever; but when another language is used it is proper to reserve *taṣawwuf* for the Islamic form to which it pertains by virtue of its origin.

4. Let us note that one must not confuse, or simply identify, alchemy and Hermeticism; strictly speaking, the latter is a doctrine and the former is only one of its applications.

principle, in the same way that the temporal power can receive its legitimacy only from a consecration by the spiritual authority.[5]

This being said, the principal question that must be asked is whether what has been maintained under the name of 'Hermeticism' can be regarded as constituting a traditional doctrine complete in itself. The answer can only be that it cannot, for here we are dealing with knowledge that is not of a metaphysical order, but is only cosmological, understanding this word in both its 'macrocosmic' and 'microcosmic' applications, for it goes without saying that in every traditional conception there is always a close correspondence between these two points of view. It is therefore not admissible that Hermeticism, in the sense that this word acquired in the Alexandrian epoch and has retained ever since, represents the integrality of the Egyptian tradition even as a 're-adaptation', all the more so as this would be clearly contradictory to the essential role played in this tradition by the priesthood, as we have just recalled. Although the cosmological point of view seems to have been particularly developed there—insofar as it is still possible to know anything about it in detail, which will in any case be what is most apparent in the vestiges that still remain, whether they be texts or monuments—we must not forget that it can never be but a secondary and contingent point of view, an application of the principial doctrine to the knowledge of what can be called the 'intermediary world', that is, the domain of subtle manifestation where the extracorporeal prolongations of the human individuality are situated, that is, the very possibilities the development of which properly concerns the 'lesser mysteries'.[6]

It might be interesting, although doubtless rather difficult, to inquire how this part of the Egyptian tradition could find itself isolated in a certain way, preserve itself in an apparently independent fashion, and then incorporate itself into both Islamic esoterism and

---

5. Cf. *Spiritual Authority and Temporal Power*, chap. 2.

6. The cosmological point of view also includes, of course, knowledge of corporeal manifestation, but since it envisages this above all insofar as it relates to subtle manifestation as to its immediate principle, it differs entirely from the profane point of view of modern physics.

the Christian esoterism of the Middle Ages (which a complete doctrine could not have done), to the point of becoming a truly integral part of both and furnishing them with a complete symbolism that, through an appropriate transposition, was even able to serve as a vehicle for truths of a higher order.[7] We do not wish to enter now into these extremely complex historical considerations; whatever the answer to this particular question, we will recall that the cosmological sciences are those which, in traditional civilizations, have been especially the province of the Kshatriyas or their equivalents, while pure metaphysics, as we have already said, belonged to the Brahmins. That is why, as a result of the revolt of the Kshatriyas against the spiritual authority of the Brahmins, one sometimes sees incomplete traditional currents arise which are reduced to these sciences alone, separated from their transcendent principle, and even, as we said above, deviated in a 'naturalistic' direction by a negation of metaphysics and a failure to recognize either the subordinate character of 'physical' science[8] or—the two things are closely related, as our earlier explanations make sufficiently clear—the essentially sacerdotal origin of all initiatic instruction, even that which is more particularly destined for use by the Kshatriyas themselves. This is not to say of course that Hermeticism in itself constitutes such a deviation or that it implies any kind of illegitimacy, which would obviously have rendered its incorporation into orthodox traditional forms impossible; one should recognize, however, that by its very nature it can quite easily lend itself to deviations if favorable circumstances arise,[9] and this is generally where the danger lies for all of the traditional sciences when they are cultivated for their own sake,

7. Such a transposition is indeed always possible as long as the link with a higher and truly transcendent principle is not broken, and we have said that the Hermetic 'Great Work' itself can be regarded as a representation of the initiatic process in its entirety; but it is then no longer a question of Hermeticism in itself, but insofar as it can serve as the basis for something of another order, in a way similar to that in which traditional exoterism can be taken as the basis for an initiatic form.

8. It goes without saying that we take this word in its ancient and strictly etymological sense.

9. Such circumstances have arisen in the West, particularly in the period of the passage from the Middle Ages to modern times, and this explains the appearance and diffusion of certain deviations of this type during the Renaissance, as we pointed out above.

for then they are not seen in light of their relationship to the principial order. Alchemy, which we could define as being so to speak the 'technique' of Hermeticism, is indeed actually 'a royal art', if we understand by this a mode of initiation especially appropriate to the nature of the Kshatriyas;[10] but this in itself marks precisely its place in the totality of a regularly constituted tradition, and besides, we must not confuse the means of initiatic realization, whatever they may be, with its goal, which in the end is always pure knowledge.

On the other hand, we must reject entirely an assimilation sometimes made between Hermeticism and 'magic'. Even if the latter is taken in a rather different sense from that which is ordinarily intended, it is greatly to be feared that even this sense, which finally is an abuse of language, can only provoke unfortunate confusions. As we have fully explained, magic in its proper sense is nothing but one of the most inferior applications of traditional knowledge, and we do not see the slightest advantage in evoking the idea when it is really a question of things that, while still contingent, are nonetheless on a notably higher level. Moreover, here we may well have something more than a simple question of poorly applied terminology. In our age the word 'magic' exercises a strange fascination over some people, and, as we have already noted, the weight given to such a point of view, even if in intention only, is still linked to the distortion of the traditional sciences when separated from their metaphysical principle. This is undoubtedly the major stumbling-block that every attempt to reconstitute or restore such sciences is likely to face, unless one begins with what is truly the beginning in every respect, that is, with the principle itself, which is at the same time the goal toward which all the rest must normally be directed.

Another point there is good reason to emphasize is the purely 'inward' nature of true alchemy, which is properly of a psychic order when taken in its most immediate application, and of a spiritual order when transposed into its higher sense; in reality it is this that

10. We have said that 'royal art' is properly the application of the corresponding initiation; but alchemy has indeed in effect the character of an application of the doctrine, whereas the means of initiation, if one envisages them by placing oneself at a 'descending' point of view so to speak, are clearly an application of its very principle, while inversely, from the 'ascending' point of view, they are the 'support' that allows access to the latter.

constitutes the whole value from the initiatic point of view. Alchemy thus has absolutely nothing to do with the material operations of any 'chemistry' in the current sense of this word; almost all modern people are strangely mistaken about this, both those who wish to see themselves as defenders of alchemy and those who, on the contrary, are its detractors; and this misunderstanding is even less excusable among the first than among the second, who at any rate have never claimed to possess any sort of traditional knowledge. It is certainly easy to see in what terms the ancient Hermeticists speak of the 'puffers' and 'charcoal burners', in whom one must recognize the true precursors of present-day chemists, however unflattering this must be to these latter; and even in the eighteenth century an alchemist like Pernéty took every opportunity to underline the difference between 'Hermetic philosophy' and 'common chemistry'. Thus, as we have already said many times while demonstrating the 'residual' character of the profane sciences in relation to the traditional sciences (but these are things so foreign to the present-day mentality that one could hardly repeat them too often), what gave birth to modern chemistry is certainly not alchemy, to which it finally has no real connection, any more than the 'hyperchemistry' imagined by some contemporary occultists.[11] Indeed, this latter is only a deformation or a deviation resulting from the incomprehension of those people who, profane and devoid of any initiatic qualification and incapable of penetrating in any measure the true meaning of the symbols, thus took everything literally according to the most outward and popular meaning of the terms used, and believing therefore that nothing more than material operations were involved, threw themselves into an experimentation that was more or less disorganized, and in any case hardly worthy of interest.[12] In the Arab world, material alchemy has always been held in very low regard, and sometimes even identified with a kind of sorcery,

11. This 'hyperchemistry' relates to alchemy as so-called 'scientific' astrology relates to true traditional astrology (Cf. *Reign of Quantity,* chap. 10).

12. There still exist here and there pseudo-alchemists of this kind, and we have known some, in both East and West; but we can say with assurance that we have never met any who have obtained any results whatsoever that would be in keeping with the prodigious efforts spent in research that ended up absorbing their entire lives!

whereas 'interior' and spiritual alchemy, on the contrary, was held in great honor, often designated under the name of *al-kīmiyā as-sa'ādah* or 'alchemy of bliss'.[13]

This is not to say that we must therefore deny the possibility of metallic transmutations, which represent alchemy in the eyes of the common people; but we must reduce them to their proper importance, which is no greater than that of any other 'scientific' experiments, and not confuse things that are of entirely different orders. We do not even see, *a priori*, why it is impossible for such transmutations to be realized by the processes of merely profane chemistry (and basically the 'hyperchemistry' to which we referred earlier is nothing but an attempt of this kind).[14] There is however another aspect to the question. The being that has arrived at the realization of certain interior states can, by virtue of the analogical relation between 'macrocosm' and 'microcosm', produce outwardly corresponding effects; it is then perfectly admissible that one who has reached a certain degree in the practice of 'interior' alchemy may be capable of accomplishing metallic transmutations or other things of the same order, as a wholly accidental result involving none of the procedures of material pseudo-alchemy, but uniquely by a kind of outward projection of the energies he carries within himself. Moreover, there is yet another essential distinction to be made here. What is involved may be merely an action of a psychic order, that is, the putting into play of subtle influences belonging to the domain of human individuality, and then it would indeed again be a material alchemy, if one wishes, but now operating by means altogether different from those of pseudo-alchemy, which latter relate exclusively to the corporeal domain; or else, for a being that has reached a higher degree of realization, it can involve an outward action of true spiritual influences, like that produced in religious 'miracles', which we have mentioned previously. Between these two cases there is a difference comparable to that separating 'theurgy' from magic

---

13. There exists a treatise by Al-Ghazālī bearing just this title.

14. Let us recall in this connection that the practical results obtained by the profane sciences in no way either justify or legitimize the point of view of these sciences, any more than they prove the value of theories formulated by them, with which they really have only a purely 'occasional' connection.

(although, to repeat, here it is not properly a case of magic, and we mention this only by way of analogy), since that difference is in the final analysis that which exists between the spiritual and psychic orders. If the apparent effects are sometimes the same in both instances, the causes that produce them are nonetheless totally and profoundly different. We will add that those who really possess such powers[15] scrupulously refrain from making a display of them to impress the crowds, and that they generally do not even make use of them at all, at least outside of certain particular circumstances where their exercise is deemed legitimate because of other considerations.[16] Be that as it may, what we must never lose sight of, and what is at the very foundation of all truly initiatic teaching, is that any realization worthy of the name is of an essentially interior order, no matter what the external repercussions may be. Man can find the principles only in himself, and he can do so because he carries within himself a correspondence to everything that exists, for we must not forget that according to a formula of Islamic esoterism 'man is the symbol of universal Existence';[17] and if he succeeds in penetrating to the center of his own being, by this very fact he reaches total knowledge with all that this implies, which is to say that 'he who knows his Self knows his Lord,'[18] and he then knows all things in the supreme unity of the Principle itself, in which is contained 'eminently' the whole of reality.

15. Here we can rightly use this word 'powers', because it involves the consequences of an interior state acquired by the being.

16. In the Islamic tradition we find very clear examples of what we are talking about here. It is said that Seyidnā 'Alī had a perfect knowledge of alchemy in all its aspects, including those related to the production of outward effects, such as metallic transmutations, but that he always refused to make the slightest use of them. On the other hand, it is said that at the request of the Sultan of Egypt, who at the time had urgent need of it, Seyidi Abu'l-Ḥasan ash-Shādhilī, during his sojourn in Alexandria, transmuted into gold a large quantity of common metal; yet he did it without having recourse to any operation of material alchemy, or to any means of a psychic order, but solely by the effect of his barakah or spiritual influence.

17. Al-insānu ramz al-wujūd.

18. This is the ḥadīth that we previously cited: Man arafa nafsahu faqad arafa Rabbahu.

42

TRANSMUTATION
AND TRANSFORMATION

ANOTHER QUESTION also relating directly to Hermeticism is that of 'longevity', which has been considered one of the characteristics of the true Rosicrucians and which is spoken of in one form or another in all traditions. This 'longevity', the attainment of which is generally regarded as one of the goals of alchemy and as implicit in the very accomplishment of the 'Great Work',[1] has several significations that must be carefully distinguished from each other, for in reality they are situated on very different levels among the possibilities of the being. The meaning that immediately comes to mind, though it is by no means the most important, is obviously the prolongation of corporeal life; to understand this it is well to refer to the teaching that the length of human life has progressively diminished over the different phases of the cycle of terrestrial humanity, from its origin down to our present age.[2] If that part of the initiatic process relating to the 'lesser mysteries' is understood to cause man to retrace in a way the course of this cycle—as we have already suggested—so as to lead him stage by stage from his present state to the 'primordial state', it must thereby cause him at each stage to acquire all the possibilities of the corresponding state, including the possibility of a life longer than that of an ordinary man of the present day. Whether or not this possibility be effectively realized is another question, and it is in fact said that he who has truly become

---

1. The 'philosophers' stone' is also under different aspects the 'elixir of life' and the 'universal medicine'.

2. Cf. *Reign of Quantity*, chap. 23.

capable of thus prolonging his life generally does not do so unless he has very particular reasons for it, because it is really no longer of any interest to him (just as the transmutations of metals and other effects of this kind hold no interest for the person able to realize them, something related to the same order of possibilities); and indeed he will even find it to his advantage not to tarry at those stages, which are still only preliminary and far removed from the true goal, for the accomplishment of such secondary and contingent results, at whatever degree, can only distract him from the essential.

On the other hand—and this may further contribute to reducing the possibility in question to its due importance—in various traditions it is also said that the duration of corporeal life can in no case exceed a thousand years, it being of little importance moreover whether this number be taken literally or symbolically, for what must be grasped is that this duration is always limited, and that consequently the search for an alleged 'corporeal immortality' can only be perfectly illusory.[3] The reason for this limitation is basically easy enough to understand: every human life constitutes in itself a cycle analogous to that of humanity taken in its entirety, so that time 'shrinks' as it were for each being in the measure that it exhausts the possibilities of the corporeal state;[4] therefore, a moment must necessarily come when time will be contracted, so to speak, to a point, and then the being can literally no longer find in this world any duration in which it can live, so that there is no alternative but to pass on to another state subject to conditions different from those of corporeal existence, even if in reality that state is no more than one of the extra-corporeal modalities of the individual human domain.

3. We have known certain so-called esoteric schools that actually professed as their goal the achievement of corporeal immortality. It must be said that this is really only a case of pseudo-initiation, further complicated by elements of a rather suspect character.

4. Moreover, it is an everyday observation that as a man gets older the years seem to slip by more and more rapidly, which amounts to saying that their duration for him continually diminishes.

This leads us to consider the other meanings of 'longevity', which indeed refer to possibilities other than those of the corporeal state; but in order to understand exactly what is at issue it is first of all necessary to specify clearly the difference between 'transmutation' and 'transformation'. We always take the word 'transformation' in its strictly etymological sense, which is 'passage beyond form'; consequently, the being can be said to be 'transformed' only if it has effectively passed on to a supra-individual state (for every individual state, whatever it may be, is by that very fact formal), so that here it is a case of something of which the realization belongs essentially to the domain of the 'greater mysteries'. As for the body itself, its 'transformation' can be nothing other than its transposition into principial mode; in other words, what can be called the 'transformed' body is strictly speaking the corporeal possibility freed from the restrictive conditions to which it was subject in its existence in individual mode (which like all limitations has only a purely negative character), and necessarily finding itself again, at its own level and in the same way as all the other possibilities, in the total realization of the being.[5] It is evident that this is something that goes beyond any possible conception of 'longevity', for this by very definition implies a duration and consequently cannot, even at its greatest extent, go beyond 'perpetuity', or cyclical indefinity, whereas what is in question here, pertaining on the contrary to the principial order, belongs by that very fact to eternity, which is one of the essential attributes of that order. With 'transformation' one is therefore beyond all duration and no longer situated in duration of any kind, however indefinitely prolonged one might suppose it to be.

'Transmutation' on the other hand is properly speaking only a change of state within the formal domain that includes the totality

---

5. This is the higher meaning of 'resurrection' and of the 'glorious body', although these terms may sometimes also be used to designate something that is in fact situated only in the prolongations of the human state, but which corresponds there in a way to these principial realities and is a kind of reflection of them, especially for certain possibilities inherent in the 'primordial state', such as those we will consider a bit further on.

of individual states, or, more simply yet, a change of modality within the individual human domain, which moreover is in fact the only case worth considering.[6] With this 'transmutation' we thus return to the 'lesser mysteries', to which are related those extra-corporeal possibilities the realization of which can be comprised in the term 'longevity', taken now in a sense different from that first considered, which did not apply beyond the corporeal order. Here again are other distinctions to be made according to whether it is a ques-tion of just any extensions of the individual human state or of its perfection in the 'primordial state'. To begin with the less elevated possibilities, we will concede at the outset that it is conceivable that, in certain cases and by certain special procedures belonging specifically to Hermeticism or to what corresponds to it in the other traditions (for this is also known in the Hindu and Far-Eastern tradi-tions), the very elements that make up the body can be 'transmuted' and 'subtilized' so as to be transferred to an extra-corporeal modality, where the being can thenceforth exist in conditions that are less narrowly limited than those of the corporeal domain, particularly in respect of duration. In such a case the being may disappear at a given time without leaving behind any trace of its body; in certain circumstances it may also reappear temporarily in the corporeal world by reason of the 'interferences' that exist between this and other modalities of the human state. Many facts that the moderns are naturally quick to qualify as 'legends' but in which there is indeed some reality can be explained in this way.[7] Moreover, one must not see in such a case anything 'transcendent' in the true sense of the word, for this is still only a case of human possibilities of which the realization can be of interest only to a

---

6. There is indeed no interest in considering the passage to other individual states since the perfection of the human state itself allows a direct accession to the supra-individual states, as we explained earlier.

7. It appears that this is the case particularly for certain *Siddhas* of India who, judging by the descriptions given of their sojourn, really live on 'another earth', that is to say on one of the *dvipas* that successively make an outward appearance in the different *Manvantaras*, and who, during the periods when they pass into the 'non-sensible' state, exist in the extra-corporeal prolongations of the human domain.

being whom they enable to fulfill some special 'mission'; outside of this case it would only represent a 'digression' from the initiatic process and a more or less prolonged delay on the path that should normally lead to the restoration of the 'primordial state'.

It remains for us to speak specifically about the possibilities of this 'primordial state'. Since, as we said above, the being that has attained this state is already virtually 'delivered', it can be said that by this very fact it is also virtually 'transformed'; it is of course understood that this 'transformation' cannot be effective, since the being has not yet left the human state, having only integrally realized its perfection. But the possibilities that have been acquired at this point reflect and in a way 'prefigure' those of the truly 'transformed' being, since it is precisely at the center of the human state that the higher states themselves are directly reflected. The being that is established at this point occupies a position that is truly 'central' with respect to all the conditions of the human state, so that without having passed beyond them, it nonetheless dominates them in a certain way instead of being dominated by them, as is ordinarily the case; and this is true with regard to the temporal condition in particular as well as to the spatial condition.[8] From this position the being, if it so desires (and it is quite certain that, at the spiritual degree that it has attained, it will never do so without a profound reason), can transport itself to any place and to any moment in time.[9] As extraordinary as such a possibility may seem, it is nevertheless an immediate consequence of reintegration at the center of the human state; and if true Rosicrucians possess this state of human perfection, the 'longevity' attributed to them can be understood for what it really is, that is to say something even more than the word seems at first to imply, since it is the reflection in the human domain of principial

---

8. On the symbolism of the 'center of time' and the relations existing in this respect between the temporal and spatial points of view, see *The Esoterism of Dante*, chap. 8.

9. With regard to space, this possibility is what is called 'ubiquity'; it is the reflection of principial 'omnipresence', just as the corresponding possibility with regard to time is a reflection of eternity and of the absolute simultaneity that it essentially implies.

eternity itself. Moreover, this possibility may very well not manifest itself outwardly in any way during the ordinary course of events, though the being that has acquired it thenceforth possesses it permanently and unalterably, and nothing can take it away; it suffices for the being to retire from the outer world and enter again into itself, whenever necessary, in order once again to find at the center of its own being the true 'fountain of immortality'.

43

THE NOTION
OF AN ELITE

THERE IS A WORD we have used frequently on other occasions, the meaning of which we must now explain more precisely from the strictly initiatic point of view, something we did not do earlier, at least explicitly. This is the word 'elite', which we used to designate something that no longer exists in the present state of the Western world, something of which the constitution, or rather reconstitution, seems to us to be the first and essential condition for an intellectual rectification and a traditional restoration.[1] It must be said that this word is yet another of those that are strangely abused in our time, to the point where in their most current acceptation they no longer have anything in common with what they should normally signify. These deformations, as we have remarked in other connections, often take on the appearance of caricatures or parodies, and this is particularly so with words that, before any profane deviation set in, were in a way consecrated by traditional usage, which, as we shall see, was indeed the case with the word 'elite'.[2] Such words are related in a certain way, as 'technical' terms, to initiatic symbolism itself, and this symbolism does not cease to be what it truly is simply because the profane sometimes take a symbol they cannot understand, divert it from its meaning, and employ it in an

---

1. See *East and West* and *The Crisis of the Modern World*.
2. We pointed out above a deformation of this kind (and one that is particularly absurd) in the case of the word 'adept'; neither is the word 'initiation' itself sheltered from abuses of this sort, for it is sometimes used today to designate the rudimentary teaching of any profane 'knowledge' whatsoever, and one even sees it figuring in the titles of 'popular' works of the lowest level.

illegitimate way. Thus there is no valid reason why the abuse of a word should oblige us to avoid using it; besides, if it did, it is hard to see what terms would finally remain at our disposal, given all the disorder modern language displays.

When we began to use the word 'elite' as just described, the false conceptions to which it is commonly applied did not yet appear to be as widespread as we have noted since, and perhaps this was really so at the time, for these things continue to worsen noticeably and more and more rapidly; in fact, never has there been so much talk about the elite—on every occasion and from all quarters—as there has since it ceased to exist, and of course what is denoted by the word is no longer the elite in the true sense. But this is not all. There is now talk of 'elites', a term that claims to include all individuals who, by however little, surpass the 'average' in any order of activity whatsoever, be this the most inferior and furthest removed from any intellectuality.[3] Let us note in the first place that the plural here is truly nonsense; without even leaving the merely profane point of view it can already be said that this word is one of those that can have no plural because their meaning is as it were 'superlative', or again because they imply the idea of something that is by its very nature insusceptible of fragmentation and subdivision; but for us it is time to raise other more profound considerations.

For the sake of greater precision and to avoid any possible misunderstanding, we have sometimes used the expression 'intellectual elite'; but this is truly almost a pleonasm, for it is not even conceivable that the elite should be other than intellectual, or if one prefers, spiritual, these two words after all being equivalents in our eyes since we resolutely refuse to confound true intellectuality with 'rationality'. The reason for this is that the eminence that characterizes the elite by very definition can only be effected from 'on high', that is, in respect of the highest possibilities of the being; and this is easy to understand even after minimal reflection on the true meaning of the word, which quite directly stems from its etymology. Indeed, from the strictly traditional point of view, what gives this

---

3. In journalistic jargon there is even a 'sporting elite', which is indeed the lowest degree of degeneration to which one could subject this word!

word all its force is its derivation from 'elect'; and it is in fact this—
let us say it plainly—that led us to use it as we did in preference to
any other; but we must explain a bit further how it should be
understood.[4] It must not be thought that we stop at the religious
and exoteric sense, which is doubtless how the 'elect' are most often
spoken of, although even this could easily enough allow of an analogical transposition appropriate to what is actually in question; but
there is yet something else, which can be indicated by the well
known and often cited, but perhaps insufficiently understood, Gospel text: *Multi vocati, electi pauci* ['For many are called, but few are
chosen' (Matt. 22:14)].

In the final analysis, we could say that the elite as we understand
it represents the totality of those who possess the qualifications
required for initiation, and who naturally are always a minority
among men; all men are in a sense 'called' by reason of the 'central'
position the human being occupies among all the other beings
found in this same state of existence,[5] but few are 'chosen', and in
the conditions of the present age there are indeed surely fewer than
ever.[6] It could be objected that this elite always exists in fact, for
however few are qualified in the initiatic sense of this word, there are
nonetheless always some; besides, number counts for little here.[7]
This is true, but such people represent only a virtual elite, or, one
could say, the possibility of an elite; in order for this to be actually
constituted it is above all necessary that they become conscious of
their qualification. On the other hand, as we explained above, it
must be understood that initiatic qualifications, such as they can be

4. Naturally, we do not have to occupy ourselves here with the modern social
and profane notion of an 'election' proceeding from 'universal suffrage' and thus
effected from below and claiming to derive the higher from the lower, which is contrary to any conception of true hierarchy.

5. This is true not only for the corporeal world but also for the subtle modalities
that belong to the same individual domain of existence.

6. One could say that by reason of the cyclical movement of 'descent', there
must necessarily be ever fewer, and the traditional affirmation according to which
the present cycle will end once 'the number of the elect is complete' can be understood in this way.

7. It is evident that in all that relates to the elite, only 'quality' must be envisaged, not 'quantity'.

determined from the strictly 'technical' point of view, are not at all of an exclusively intellectual order but include other constituent elements of the human being as well; but this changes absolutely nothing with regard to what we said about the definition of the elite, since whatever these qualifications may be in themselves, they must always be considered in view of an essentially intellectual or spiritual realization, and since it is in this that their unique raison d'être ultimately resides.

Normally, all who are thus qualified ought by this very fact to have the possibility of obtaining initiation. If this is not so in practice it is solely because of the present state of the Western world; and in this regard the disappearance of an elite conscious of itself, and the absence, in any case, of initiatic organizations adequate to receive it, appear as two closely connected and in some way correlative facts, about which we need not ask which is a consequence of the other. But on the other hand it is evident that initiatic organizations capable of being fully and truly what they ought to be, and not merely more or less degenerated vestiges of what they once were, could only be reformed if they found members possessing not only the initial aptitude necessary as a preliminary condition, but also the effective dispositions determined by the consciousness of that aptitude, for it is above all up to these latter to 'aspire' to initiation, and it would be to reverse the normal relationships to think that this must come to them independently of that aspiration, since this aspiration is like a first manifestation of the essentially 'active' disposition required by everything of the truly initiatic order. This is why the reconstitution of an elite—we mean an elite conscious of its initiatic possibilities, although these may be only latent and undeveloped as long as a regular traditional affiliation has not been obtained—is the first condition on which all the rest depends, just as previously prepared materials are indispensable for the construction of a building, although these materials can obviously only fulfill their function once they have found their place in the building itself.

Supposing that initiation in the sense of an affiliation with a traditional 'chain' has really been obtained by those belonging to the elite, it still remains to consider how far each may go, that is, in the first place, with regard to the passage from virtual to effective initiation, and then with regard to attaining a more or less elevated degree according to the extent of the being's particular possibilities. Regarding the passage from one degree to another, there is reason then to consider what could be called an elite within the elite itself,[8] this being the sense in which some have spoken of the 'elite of the elite'.[9] In other words, one can envisage successive 'elections', each more and more restricted with regard to the number of individuals concerned, always effected 'from above' and following the same principle, and corresponding to the different degrees of the initiatic hierarchy.[10] The initiate can thus rise step by step until he reaches the supreme 'election', that belonging to the 'adept', that is to say the fulfillment of the ultimate goal of all initiation; and consequently the elect in the most complete sense of this word, whom we might call the 'perfect elect', will be he who finally achieves the realization of the 'Supreme Identity'.[11]

8. A sufficiently clear allusion to this still existed in eighteenth-century Masonry, where mention was made of a system of high grades 'in the interior' of an ordinary Lodge.

9. Of course there is no question here of different 'elites' but only of degrees within one and the same elite.

10. It is in this sense that the word 'elect' is found in the name of certain higher grades of various Masonic rites, for example, which is certainly not to say that a real understanding of its significance and of all that it implies has been preserved.

11. In the Islamic tradition, Al-Mustafā, 'the Elect', is one of the names of the Prophet; when this word is thus 'pre-eminently' employed, it refers to 'Universal Man'.

44

THE INITIATIC
HIERARCHY

WHAT WE HAVE JUST INDICATED regarding the initiatic hierarchy
still needs to be clarified in certain respects, for with this subject, as
with so many others, confusions too often arise, not only in the profane world, which, after all, should cause no surprise, but also
among those who for one reason or another normally ought to be
better informed about the matter. It also seems that the notion of
hierarchy, even outside of the initiatic domain, is particularly
obscure in our day, for it is among those ideas against which the
modern spirit is especially set, which, to tell the truth, is in perfect
conformity with its essentially anti-traditional character, of which
'egalitarianism' in all its forms is merely one aspect. But it is no less
strange and almost incredible to anyone not altogether incapable of
reflection to see this 'egalitarianism' frankly admitted and even
vociferously proclaimed by the members of initiatic organizations
which, however diminished or even deviated they may be from
many points of view, nonetheless necessarily preserve a certain hierarchical constitution without which they could not exist.[1] This is
obviously something paradoxical and even contradictory that cannot be explained except by the extreme disorder that presently
reigns everywhere; besides, without such disorder, profane ideas
could never have invaded as they have a domain strictly closed to
them by very definition and on which, under normal conditions,

1. This hierarchical form has in fact been altered by the introduction of certain
'parliamentary' forms borrowed from profane institutions, but despite everything
it exists nonetheless in organizations with superposed grades.

they can exercise absolutely no influence. We need not dwell further on this, for we would of course never dream of addressing ourselves to those who, because of prejudice, deny all hierarchy. But what we would like to say above all is that, when things have reached such a point, it is not astonishing that at times the idea of hierarchy should be more or less poorly understood even by those who still hold to it, and that they should sometimes be mistaken about the different applications of which it is susceptible.

All initiatic organizations are by nature hierarchical, so much so that this can be seen as one of their fundamental characteristics, although of course this characteristic is not exclusive to them since it also exists in 'outward' traditional organizations, by which we mean those belonging to the exoteric order; and it can even still exist in a certain sense (for there are naturally degrees in every deviation) in profane organizations insofar as they are constituted, in their own order, according to normal rules, at least in the measure that these rules are compatible with the profane point of view itself.[2] The initiatic hierarchy, however, is distinguished in a special way from all the others. It is formed essentially by degrees of 'knowledge', with all that is implied by this word taken in its true sense (which, when taken in its fullness, really means effective knowledge), for it is in this that the degrees of initiation themselves consist, and no other consideration should intervene. Some people have represented these degrees by a series of concentric enclosures that must be successively traversed, which is a very exact image, for here it is indeed a question of approaching closer and closer to a center until the last degree is finally reached. Others have compared the initiatic hierarchy to a pyramid the courses of which continually narrow as they rise from the base to the summit, here again ending at a unique point that plays the same role as the center does in the preceding figure. Whatever the symbolism adopted in this regard, it is precisely this hierarchy of degrees that we had in mind when speaking of the successive distinctions effected within the elite.

2. As an example of profane hierarchical organizations one can cite modern armies, which are perhaps the clearest example left in present conditions, for as to administrative hierarchies, these hardly merit the name at all any longer.

It must be clearly understood that these degrees may be indefinite in number, as are the states to which they correspond and which are essentially implied in their realization, for once knowledge is effective and no longer merely virtual, it is truly a question of different states, or at least of different modalities of one state, as long as the individual human possibilities have not yet been surpassed. Consequently, as we have already pointed out, the degrees within any initiatic organization never represent more than a sort of general classification that is, like all such classifications, necessarily schematic and limited to certain principal or clearly defined stages. According to the particular point of view adopted in establishing such a classification, the degrees so distinguished can naturally vary in number[3] without such differences being contradictory or incompatible, for this question bears on no doctrinal principle and merely relates to the special methods peculiar to each initiatic organization, be this within one and the same traditional form, or, and with all the more reason, in passing from one of these forms to another. Indeed, in all of this there is only one fundamental distinction to be made, that between the 'lesser mysteries' and the 'greater mysteries', that is to say, as we have already explained, between what relates respectively to the human state and to the higher states of the being. All the rest, in both domains, are only subdivisions that for contingent reasons can be developed to varying degrees.

On the other hand, one must also clearly understand that the allocation of the members of an initiatic organization among its different degrees is only 'symbolic' as it were with respect to the real hierarchy, because initiation at every degree can in many cases only be virtual, in which case naturally only degrees of theoretical knowledge would be in question, but that at least is what it should always be normally. If initiation were always effective, or had to become effective before the individual had access to a higher degree, the two hierarchies would entirely coincide; but even if this is perfectly conceivable in principle it must be recognized that it is hardly realizable in fact, and is even less likely in certain organizations that have

3. We mentioned above the divisions into three and seven degrees, and it is evident that, given the diversity of initiatic forms, there could be many others.

undergone a more or less marked degeneration and too easily admit, even to all degrees, members of whom most are unfortunately little qualified to receive more than a merely virtual initiation. However, these defects, though inevitable to some extent, do not in any way affect the notion of initiatic hierarchy itself, which remains entirely independent of all circumstances of this kind. Matters of fact, however regrettable, are powerless against a principle and can do nothing to affect it; and the distinction we have just noted naturally resolves the objection that could occur to some readers who, in whatever initiatic organizations with which they may be familiar, have observed even at the higher degrees, not to mention the summit of the apparent hierarchy, individuals who all too obviously lack any effective initiation.

Another important point is that an initiatic organization includes not only a hierarchy of degrees but also a hierarchy of functions, and that these are two entirely distinct things that must never be confused, for the function with which someone may be invested at a given level does not confer upon him a new degree and does not modify in any way the one he already possesses. The function has so to speak only an 'accidental' character with respect to the degree; the exercise of a given function may require the possession of this or that degree, but it is never bound necessarily to that degree, however elevated this may be; and what is more, the function may be only temporary and thus can come to an end for a variety of reasons, whereas the degree always constitutes a permanent acquisition, one that is obtained once and for all and which can never be lost by any means regardless of whether it is a question of an effective initiation or merely of a virtual initiation.

This—let us say it again—serves to clarify the true significance that must be attributed to certain secondary qualifications we mentioned earlier, for in addition to the qualifications required for initiation itself, there can also be other more particular qualifications that are required only to fulfill this or that function within the initiatic organization. The aptitude to receive initiation, even at the highest degree, does not necessarily imply the capacity to exercise any function, even the simplest; but in all cases the only truly essential thing is the initiation itself, with its degrees, for it is this that effectively influences the actual state of the being, whereas any function could never modify it or add anything at all to it.

The truly essential initiatic hierarchy is therefore the hierarchy of degrees, and furthermore it is this which in fact serves as the identifying mark of the constitution of initiatic organizations. Once it is clear that every initiation is properly a matter of knowledge, it becomes quite evident that the fact of being invested with a function has no importance in this respect, even with regard to merely theoretical knowledge, and with even more reason in regard to effective knowledge. A function may give one the faculty of transmitting the initiation to others for example, or again of directing certain works, but it cannot give one the power of attaining a higher state oneself. There can be no degree or spiritual state higher than that of the 'adept'; whether those who have reached this state in addition exercise certain functions, pedagogic or otherwise, or whether they exercise none at all, makes absolutely no difference in this respect; and what is true in this regard for the supreme degree holds equally for each of the lower degrees of the hierarchy.[4] Consequently, when the initiatic hierarchy is spoken of without further qualification, it must be understood that it is always the hierarchy of degrees that is in question; it is this and this alone, as we said above, that defines the successive 'elections', progressing gradually from a simple initiatic affiliation up to identification with the 'center', and not only, as at the completion of the 'lesser mysteries', with the center of the human individuality, but further, at the completion of the 'greater mysteries', with the very center of the whole being, that is to say the realization of the 'Supreme Identity'.

4. Let us recall that the 'adept' is properly he who has attained the fullness of effective initiation. Certain esoteric schools, however, make a distinction between those they call 'adepts minor' and those they call 'adepts major'; these expressions must then be understood, at least according to their original usage, to designate those who have come to perfection respectively in the 'lesser mysteries' and in the 'greater mysteries'.

45

TRADITIONAL
INFALLIBILITY

SINCE OUR SUBJECT has led us to speak about the hierarchy of initiatic functions, we ought also to consider another question more
particularly connected thereto, that of doctrinal infallibility. We can
do this, moreover, not only from the initiatic point of view, but also
from the traditional point of view in general, which includes the
exoteric as well as the esoteric orders. To understand what is
involved, the principle must first be granted that it is the doctrine,
and it alone, that is strictly speaking infallible, and not any individual human being as such; and if the doctrine is infallible, this is
because it is an expression of truth, which in itself is absolutely
independent of the individuals who receive and understand it. Ultimately, the guarantee of the doctrine lies in its 'non-human' character; and it can be said that every truth, of whatever order it may be,
when considered from the traditional point of view, participates in
this 'non-human' character, for it is truth only because it is linked to
higher principles and is derived from these as a more or less immediate consequence or as an application to a definite domain. Truth
is in no way made by man as the modern 'relativists' and 'subjectiv-
ists' would have it, but on the contrary it imposes itself on him, not
however 'from outside' in the manner of a 'physical' constraint, but
in reality 'from within', for man is obviously not obliged to 'recognize' it as truth unless he first has 'known' it, that is, unless it has
penetrated him and he has really assimilated it to himself.[1] It must
not be forgotten that all true knowledge is essentially, and in the

1. We say that man assimilates a truth to himself because this is the usual way of
speaking, but it could equally well be said inversely that he assimilates himself to
this truth. The importance of this remark will become clear in what follows.

exact measure that it is real, an identification of the knower and the known, an identification still imperfect and as if 'by reflection' in the case of merely theoretical knowledge, and a perfect identification in the case of effective knowledge.

It follows that any man will be infallible when he expresses a truth that he really knows, that is to say with which he is identified;[2] but it is not as a human individual that he will then be infallible, but insofar as he so to speak represents that truth by virtue of this identification. Strictly speaking, one ought not to say in such a case that he expresses the truth, but rather that the truth expresses itself through him. From this point of view infallibility does not appear to be anything extraordinary or exceptional, or as some sort of 'privilege', for in fact everyone possesses it to the degree that he is 'competent', that is, insofar as he 'knows' in the true sense of the word;[3] the difficulty, of course, is to determine the real limits of this competence in each particular case. It goes without saying that these limits will depend on the degree of knowledge that the being has attained, and that they will be the more extensive as this degree is the more elevated; and consequently it also goes without saying that infallibility in one order of knowledge does not imply infallibility in a higher or more profound order, and that, to apply this for example to the most general division that can be established among traditional doctrines, infallibility in the exoteric domain in no way implies infallibility in the esoteric and initiatic domain.

In what we have just said, we considered infallibility to be strictly tied to knowledge, that is, as inherent to the being that possesses this knowledge, or, more exactly, to the state it has thereby attained, and this not insofar as it is this or that particular being but insofar as, in this state, it really is identified with the corresponding truth.

---

2. The only reservation that might be made is that the expression or formulation of the truth may be inadequate, and even that it must always be so to a degree; but this in no way affects the principle itself.

3. Thus, to take the simplest example, even a child who has understood and assimilated an elementary mathematical truth will be infallible whenever he states this truth, but never when he only repeats things he has 'learned by heart' without having assimilated them.

One can say moreover that this is an infallibility that in a way concerns only the being to whom it belongs as an integral part of its interior state, and which may very well not be recognized by others if the being concerned has not been expressly invested with a particular function, and more precisely, with a function of doctrinal teaching. This infallibility will in practice avoid the errors of application that are always possible because of the difficulty we have just noted of determining 'from outside' the limits of that infallibility. But in every traditional organization there is also another kind of infallibility that is attached exclusively to the teaching function in whatever order this may be exercised, for this too applies simultaneously to both the exoteric and the esoteric domains, naturally considering each within its proper limits; it is especially in this respect that one can see particularly clearly that infallibility does not belong to individuals as such, for in the case before us now it is entirely independent of what the individual who exercises the function may be in himself.

Here it is necessary to refer to what we said earlier concerning the efficacy of rites. This efficacy essentially inheres in the rites themselves insofar as they are the means of action of a spiritual influence; the rite thus acts in every respect independently of the worth of the individual who accomplishes it, and even without the individual having an effective knowledge of this efficacy.[4] If the rite is reserved to a specialized function, it is only necessary that the individual should have received from the traditional organization to which he belongs the power to accomplish it validly; no other condition is required, and if this condition can in turn require certain particular qualifications, as we have seen, these do not refer to the possession of a certain degree of knowledge but are simply those that allow the spiritual influence to work through the individual as it were without his particular constitution hindering it. Such a one, then, truly becomes a 'carrier' or a 'transmitter' of the spiritual influence, and it is this alone that is important, for while under this influence of an essentially supra-individual order, and consequently insofar as he is

---

4. Let us recall that this is true of exoteric rites, as Catholic doctrine expressly recognizes, as well as for initiatic rites.

accomplishing the function with which he is invested, his individuality no longer counts and even disappears entirely. We have already emphasized the importance of the role of 'transmitter', particularly in regard to initiatic rites, for it is this same role that is exercised with respect to doctrine when the function of teaching is involved; and in fact between these two aspects, and consequently between the natures of the corresponding functions, there exists a very close relationship resulting directly from the character of the traditional doctrines themselves.

Indeed, as we have already explained in connection with symbolism, it is not possible to establish an absolutely clear distinction, still less a separation, between what pertains to rites and what pertains to doctrine, nor therefore between accomplishing the former and teaching the latter, for even if they actually constitute two different functions, they are nonetheless fundamentally of the same nature. The rite always bears within it a teaching, and the doctrine, by reason of its 'non-human' character (which, let us recall, is manifested especially by the symbolic form of its expression), also bears within itself the spiritual influence, so that they are really only complementary aspects of one and the same reality; and although we first spoke of this more particularly in connection with the initiatic domain, it can nonetheless be extended in a general way to everything of a traditional order. There is in principle no distinction to make in this regard; the only distinction that can in fact be made is that, in the initiatic domain, where the essential goal is pure knowledge, a teaching function of any degree ought normally to be conferred only on one who possesses an *effective* knowledge of what is to be taught (all the more in that what counts here is less the outwardness of the teaching than the result—inward—that the teacher must help produce in those who receive it), whereas in the exoteric order, the immediate goal of which is different, the one who exercises such a function can very well have a merely *theoretical* knowledge sufficient to explain the doctrine intelligibly. But in any case, this is not what is essential, at least for the infallibility attaching to the function itself.

From this point of view one can say that the fact of being regularly invested with certain functions confers, by itself alone and without any other conditions,[5] the ability to accomplish such and such rites; in the same way, the fact of being regularly invested with a teaching function entails by itself alone the possibility of validly accomplishing this function, and thereby necessarily confers infallibility within the limits of its exercise. The reason for this is fundamentally the same in both cases: on the one hand, the spiritual influence inheres in the very rites that vehicle it, and on the other, the same spiritual influence inheres equally in the doctrine by the very fact that it is essentially 'non-human'. Thus, in the final analysis it is always this spiritual influence that acts through individuals, whether in the accomplishment of rites or in the teaching of doctrine, and it is this influence that ensures that these individuals can effectively exercise the functions with which they have been charged, no matter what they may be in themselves.[6] In these conditions, of course, the authorized interpreter of doctrine, insofar as he exercises his proper function, can never speak in his own name but solely in the name of the tradition that he represents and that he so to speak 'incarnates', and which alone is really infallible. As long as this is the case, the individual no longer exists except in the capacity of a mere 'support' for the doctrinal formulation, and this support plays no more active a role here than does the paper on which a book is printed in regard to the ideas for which it serves as a vehicle. If in some other respect this individual should happen to speak in his own name, he would by that very fact no longer be exercising his function but merely expressing individual opinions, in which he is no more infallible than anyone else. In himself therefore he enjoys no special 'privilege', for once his individuality reappears and asserts itself, he immediately ceases to be the representative of the tradition and becomes no more than an ordinary man who, like any other, has worth in respect of the doctrine only in the measure of the knowledge he himself really possesses, and who cannot in any case claim to impose his authority on anyone.[7] Thus the infallibility

5. 'Regularly' necessarily implying possession of the requisite qualifications.

6. Catholic theology designates this action of the spiritual influence with regard to doctrinal teaching as the 'help of the Holy Spirit'.

7. All of this is in strict conformity with the Catholic idea of 'papal infallibility'. What may be surprising in this idea, and what in any case is peculiar to it, is only

belongs solely to the function and not at all to the individual, for outside the exercise of this function, or if the individual ceases to fill it for any reason, he retains nothing of this infallibility; and here we have an example of what we said above, that the function, in contrast to the degree of knowledge, adds absolutely nothing to what the being is in itself, and does not really modify its interior state.

We must further explain how doctrinal infallibility, as we have just defined it, is necessarily limited in the same way as is the function to which it is joined, and this in several ways. First, it can only apply within the tradition to which the function belongs and is nonexistent in respect of any other traditional form; in other words, no one can claim to judge one tradition in the name of another, for such a claim is necessarily false and illegitimate since one can only speak in the name of a tradition about what concerns that tradition itself, which is evident enough to anyone who has no preconceived idea on the matter. Next, if a function belongs to a certain determined order, it can only entail infallibility in what relates to that order, which may be more or less limited according to the case. Thus, without leaving the exoteric order, one could for example conceive of an infallibility that by reason of the particular character of the function to which it is attached concerns only this or that branch of the doctrine and not the doctrine as a whole; with all the more reason a function of an exoteric order, of whatever kind, would be unable to confer any infallibility, and consequently any authority, with regard to the esoteric order; and here again any contrary claim, which moreover would imply a reversal of normal hierarchical relationships, would be worth strictly nothing. It is absolutely necessary to observe these two distinctions at all times (on the one hand between the different traditional forms, and on the other between the esoteric and exoteric domains),[8] in order to prevent

---

that doctrinal infallibility is considered to be concentrated entirely in a function exercised exclusively by a single individual, whereas in other traditional forms it is generally recognized that all those who exercise a regular teaching function participate in this infallibility to an extent determined by the function itself.

8. Using geometrical symbolism, one could say that according the first of these two distinctions doctrinal infallibility is delimited horizontally since the traditional

any abuse or error in application in traditional infallibility, for beyond the legitimate limits belonging to each case there is no longer any infallibility because there is nothing to which it can be validly applied. If we have thought it necessary to dwell somewhat on this, it is because we know that too many people have the tendency to misunderstand these essential truths, either because their horizon is limited to one traditional form, or because, within this one form, they know only the exoteric point of view; all that one can ask, in order to reach an understanding with them, is that they know and be willing to acknowledge just how far their competence extends, so that they do not intrude upon another's territory, which would be especially regrettable for themselves, for by this they would only give proof of a truly irremediable incomprehension.

forms as such are situated on the same level, whereas according to the second it is delimited vertically since this involves hierarchically superposed domains.

46

TWO
INITIATIC DEVICES

THERE ARE TWO DEVICES in the higher grades of Scottish Masonry of which the meaning relates to several of our earlier considerations. One is *Post Tenebras Lux* [After Darkness, Light], and the other *Ordo ab Chao* [Order from Chaos]; and in truth their meanings are so closely connected as to be almost identical, although the second is perhaps susceptible of a wider application than is the first.[1] Both refer to initiatic 'illumination', the first directly and the second by way of consequence, since it is the original vibration of the *Fiat Lux* that sets in motion the beginning of the cosmogonic process by which 'chaos' will be so ordered as to become 'cosmos'.[2] In traditional symbolism, darkness always represents the state of undeveloped potentialities that constitutes 'chaos';[3] and, correlatively, light is related to the manifested world in which these potentialities will be actualized, namely the

---

1. If it is claimed that historically the device *Ordo ab Chao* originally expressed only the intention of putting into order the 'chaos' of the grades and the many 'systems' that saw the light during the second half of the eighteenth century, this does not constitute a valid objection against what we are saying here, for this is only a very special application that in no way prevents the existence of other, more important meanings.

2. Cf. *Reign of Quantity*, chap. 3.

3. There is also another and higher meaning to the symbolism of darkness, which relates to the state of principial non-manifestation; but here we have only to envisage the lower and properly cosmogonic meaning.

4. The Sanskrit word *loka*, 'world', derived from the root *lok*, which means 'to see', relates directly to light, as is shown by a comparison with the Latin *lux*. On the other hand, the connection of the word 'Lodge' with *loka*, possibly through the

'cosmos',[4] this actualization being determined or 'measured' at each instant of the process of manifestation by the extension of the 'solar rays', starting from the central point whence was uttered the initial *Fiat Lux*.

Light is thus truly 'after darkness', not only from the point of view of the 'macrocosm' but also from that of the 'microcosm', which is the point of view of initiation since in this respect darkness represents the profane world from which the newly elected member comes, or else his original profane state up to the exact moment when he is initiated by 'receiving the light'. Through initiation the individual being therefore passes 'from darkness to light' as does the world at its very origin (and the symbolism of 'birth' is equally applicable in both cases) through the act of the creating and ordering Word;[5] and thus initiation, in conformity with a general characteristic of traditional rites, is in truth an image of 'what was done from the beginning'.

'Cosmos' on the other hand, insofar as it is order or the ordered ensemble of possibilities, is not only drawn from 'chaos' as 'non-ordered', but is also produced from it as such (*ab Chao*), for in 'chaos' these same possibilities are contained in a potential and 'undifferentiated' state, thus making it the *materia prima* (in a relative sense, but more exactly, and with respect to the true *materia prima* or universal substance, the *materia secunda* of a particular world)[6] or the 'substantial' starting-point for the manifestation of this world, just as the *Fiat Lux* is, for its part, the 'essential' starting-point. In an analogous way the state of the being prior to initiation is the 'undifferentiated' substance of all that it can effectively become

intermediary of the Latin *locus* which is identical to it, is far from meaningless since the Lodge is considered a symbol of the world or the 'cosmos'. This is the 'illuminated and well-ordered place' opposed to the 'outer darkness' that corresponds to the profane world, where all is accomplished according to rite, that is, in conformity with 'order' (*rita*).

5. The double meaning of the word 'order' has a particular significance here, for the meaning of 'commandment' that also belongs to it is formally expressed by the Hebrew word *yomar*, which, in the first chapter of Genesis, is used to signify the working of the divine Word; we will return to this a little later.

6. Cf. *Reign of Quantity*, chap. 2.

thereafter,[7] for as we have already said, initiation cannot introduce possibilities that are not present in the being from the beginning (and this is the reason for the qualifications required as a precondition to initiation), any more than the cosmogonic *Fiat Lux* can add anything at all 'substantially' to the possibilities of the world for which it is uttered. But these possibilities are still only in the 'chaotic and dark' state,[8] and require 'illumination' to begin to be put in order and thereby pass from potency to act. It must be understood that this passage is not effected instantaneously but continues throughout the course of the initiatic work, just as from the 'macrocosmic' point of view it continues throughout the entire course of the cycle of manifestation of the world in question; the 'cosmos' or 'order' exist only virtually by the fact of the initial *Fiat Lux* (which in itself must always be regarded as having a strictly 'timeless' character, since it precedes the unfolding of the cycle of manifestation and thus cannot be situated within it), and in the same way initiation is only virtually accomplished by the communication of the spiritual influence for which the light is as it were a ritual 'support'.

The other considerations that can be deduced from the device *Ordo ab Chao* relate more to the role of initiatic organizations in regard to the outer world: since, as we have just said, the realization of 'order', insofar as it is equivalent to the very process of manifestation for the state of existence in a world such as ours, proceeds in a continuous fashion until all the possibilities implied in it are exhausted (and by which the extreme limit of this world's 'measure' is reached), all beings capable of becoming aware of this—each in its own place and according to its own possibilities— should cooperate effectively in this realization, which is also called the 'plan of the Great Architect of the Universe' in the general and outward order; at the same time, by the initiatic work properly so called, each also

---

7. This is the 'undressed stone' (*rough ashlar*) of Masonic symbolism.

8. Or 'formless and void', according to another translation that is almost equivalent to the *thohú va-bohú* of Genesis, and which Fabre d'Olivet translates as 'contingent power of being in a power of being,' expressing rather well the totality of particular possibilities contained, and, as it were, enveloped in a state of potentiality within the very potentiality of this world (or state of existence) envisaged in its integrality.

realizes within himself, inwardly and in particular, the plan that corresponds to this from the 'microcosmic' point of view. It is easy to understand that this can be applied in diverse and multiple ways in all domains; thus, in the social order in particular it could be a question of establishing a complete traditional organization under the inspiration of initiatic organizations which, as its esoteric part, would constitute something like the 'spirit' of the whole social organization,[9] the latter indeed representing, even in its exoteric aspect, a true 'order', as opposed to the 'chaos' of the purely profane state represented by the absence of such an organization.

We will also mention, though without dwelling on it unduly, another more particular signification that is more or less directly linked to what we have just discussed, for it refers essentially to the same domain. This signification relates to the use of exterior organizations, unconscious of this plan as such and apparently mutually opposed, for the realization of a common plan under a single 'invisible' direction which itself stands above all oppositions; we alluded to this previously when we noted that such an application is particularly evident in the Far-Eastern tradition. By the disordered action they produce, these oppositions constitute a kind of 'chaos' among themselves, at least apparently; but it is precisely a question of using this very 'chaos' (taken as in a way the 'matter' on which the 'spirit', represented by the highest and most 'interior' initiatic organizations, acts) in the realization of the general 'order', just as in the 'cosmos' as a whole all things that are apparently opposed are in the final analysis no less truly elements of the total order. For this to be so, that which presides over 'order' must fulfill the role of 'unmoved mover' with respect to the 'outer' world. This latter, which remains at the fixed point that is the center of the 'cosmic wheel', is thereby like the pivot around which that wheel turns, the norm by which its motion is regulated; it can play this role only because it does not itself participate in that motion, and it plays it without intervening

---

9. In connection with the device we now are speaking of, this is what is called in Scottish Masonry the 'reign of the Holy Empire', evidently in recollection of the constitution of ancient 'Christendom' considered as an application of the 'royal art' in a particular traditional form.

in this motion expressly, without mingling in any way, then, with that outward action which pertains entirely to the circumference of the wheel.[10] It is only contingent modifications, which change and pass, that are drawn along by the revolutions of this wheel; only that remains which, united to the Principle, stands unvarying at the center, immutable like the Principle itself; and the center, which nothing can affect in its undifferentiated unity, is the starting-point for the indefinite multiplicity of those modifications that constitute universal manifestation; and it is also their culminating point, for it is with respect to it that they are all finally ordered, just as the powers of each being are necessarily ordered in view of its final reintegration into principial immutability.

---

10. This is the very definition of the 'actionless activity' of the Taoist tradition, and it is also what we have previously called an 'action of presence'.

47

VERBUM, LUX, AND VITA

WE HAVE JUST ALLUDED to the action of the Word that produces
the 'illumination' which is at the origin of all manifestation, and
which is also found analogously at the beginning of the initiatic
process. Although the question may appear to be somewhat outside
our principal subject (although, because of the correspondence
between the 'macrocosmic' and 'microcosmic' points of view, this is
so only in appearance), this leads us to the close link that, from the
cosmogonic point of view, exists between sound and light, which is
very clearly expressed by the association and even identification
made at the beginning of the Gospel of Saint John between the
words *Verbum, Lux,* and *Vita.*[1] It is known that the Hindu tradition,
which considers 'luminosity' (*taijasa*) to be characteristic of the
subtle state (and we will soon see how this relates to the last of the
three terms we have just mentioned), affirms on the other hand that
the primordiality of sound (*shabda*) among the sensible qualities
corresponds to ether (*ākāsha*) among the elements. So stated, this
affirmation immediately refers to the corporeal world, but at the
same time it is also susceptible of transposition to other domains,[2]
for in reality it only translates the process of universal manifestation

---

1. It is not without interest to note in this connection that, in the Masonic organizations which have most completely preserved the ancient ritual forms, the Bible
placed on the altar must be opened precisely at the first page of the Gospel of Saint
John.

2. This obviously results from the fact that the theory on which the science of
mantras (*mantra-viḍyā*) is based distinguishes different modalities of sound: *parā*
or non-manifested, *pashyantī* and *vaikharī*, which is the spoken word. Only this last
refers strictly to sound as a sensible quality, belonging to the corporeal order.

with respect to the corporeal world, which, in the final analysis, is merely a particular case. If manifestation is considered in its totality, this same affirmation is that by which all things, whatever their state, are produced by the divine Word or divine Utterance, which is thus at the beginning or, better (for this is something essentially 'timeless'), at the principle of all manifestation,[3] which is explicitly stated at the beginning of the Hebrew Genesis where, as we have just said, the first word spoken at the starting-point of manifestation is the *Fiat Lux* by which the chaos of possibilities is illuminated and organized. This reveals precisely the direct relationship that exists in the principial order between what by analogy can be called sound and light, that is to say those realities of which sound and light in the ordinary meaning of these terms are the respective expressions in our world.

Here we should make an important remark. The verb *amar*, which is used in the biblical text and which is usually translated as 'to say', in reality has in both Hebrew and Arabic the principal meaning of 'to command' or 'to order'. The divine Word is the 'order' (*amr*) by which creation, that is to say the production of universal manifestation, either in its entirety or in some one of its modalities, is effected.[4] Likewise, according to Islamic tradition, the first creation is Light (*an-Nūr*), which is called *min amri' Llah*, that is, 'proceeding immediately from the divine order or command'; and this creation is situated so to speak in the 'world', that is to say the state or degree of existence which, for that reason, is called *'ālam al-amr* and forms the purely spiritual world properly speaking. Indeed, the intelligible Light is the essence (*dhāt*) of the 'Spirit' (*ar-Rūḥ*), which, when it is considered in its universal sense, is identified with the Light itself. This is why the expressions *an-Nūr al-Muḥammadī* [the Light or Reality of Muhammad] and *ar-Rūḥ al-Muḥammadiyah* [the Spirit of Muhammad] are equivalents, both

---

3. These are the very first words of the Gospel of Saint John: *In principio erat Verbum.*

4. We must recall here the connection that exists between the two different meanings of the word 'order' that we have already mentioned in an earlier note.

designating the principial and total form of 'Universal Man',[5] who is *Awwal khalqi' Llah*, 'the First of the Divine Creation'. This is the true 'Heart of the World' the expansion of which produces the manifestation of all beings and the contraction of which brings them back in the end to their Principle;[6] and thus it is both 'the first and the last' (*al-awwal wa 'l-ākher*) with respect to creation, just as Allah himself is 'the First and the Last' in the absolute sense.[7] 'Heart of hearts and Spirit of spirits' (*Qalb al-qulūbi wa Rūḥ al-arwāḥ*), it is in his bosom that the particular 'spirits', the angels (*al malā'ikah*) and the 'separated spirits' (*al-arwāḥ al-mujarradah*), are differentiated, which are thus formed of the primordial Light as their unique essence, with no admixture of elements representing the determining conditions of the lower degrees of existence.[8]

If we now pass on to the more particular considerations of our world, that is to say to the degree of existence to which the human state belongs (this state here considered in its entirety and not restricted to its corporeal modality alone), we must find in it, as 'center', a principle that corresponds to the 'Universal Heart', of which it is as it were only a specification with respect to this state. It is this principle that the Hindu doctrine designates as *Hiranyagarbha*; it is an aspect of *Brahmā*, that is, of the Word that produces manifestation,[9] and at the same time it is also 'Light', as is indicated

5. See *The Symbolism of the Cross*, chap. 6.

6. The symbolism of the double movement of the heart must be seen here as the equivalent of the two inverse and complementary phases of respiration, which are especially well known in the Hindu tradition. In both cases there is an alternating expansion and contraction which correspond to the two terms *coagula* and *solve* of Hermeticism, on the condition that it be carefully kept in mind that the two phases must be taken inversely according to whether they are considered in reference to the principle or in reference to manifestation, so that it is the principial expansion that determines the 'coagulation' of the manifested, and the principial contraction that determines its 'solution'.

7. This is also connected to the role of *Metatron* in the Hebrew Kabbalah. [See *The King of the World*, chap. 3. ED.]

8. It is easy to see that this can be identified with the domain of supra-individual manifestation.

9. It is 'producer' with respect to our world, but is at the same time 'produced' with respect to the Supreme Principle, which is why it is also called *Kārya-Brahmā*.

by the designation *Taijasa* given to the subtle state that forms its proper 'world', the possibilities of which it contains essentially within itself.[10] Here we find the third of the terms mentioned at the beginning. For the beings manifested in this domain, and in conformity with their particular conditions of existence, this cosmic Light appears as 'Life': *Et Vita erat Lux hominum* ['and that Life was the Light of men'], as the Gospel of Saint John says in exactly this sense. *Hiranyagarbha* is therefore in this respect like the 'vital principle' of this entire world, and this is why it is called *jīva-ghana*, all life being principially synthesized in it. The word *ghana* indicates that the 'global' form we spoke of above in connection with the primordial Light is also found here, so that 'Life' appears as an image or reflection of the 'Spirit' at a certain level of manifestation;[11] and this same form is also that of the 'World Egg' (*Brahmānda*) of which *Hiranyagarbha* is, as its name signifies, the vivifying 'seed'.[12]

In a certain state corresponding to the first subtle modality of the human order that properly constitutes the world of *Hiranyagarbha* (although of course without identification with this 'center' itself),[13] the being is aware of itself as a wave of the 'primordial Ocean',[14] without it being possible to say whether this wave is a sonorous vibration or a luminous wave. In reality, it is simultaneously the one and the other, indissolubly united in principle, and

10. See *Man and His Becoming according to the Vedānta*, chap. 14. This luminous nature is indicated in the very name Hiranyagarbha, for light is symbolized by gold (*hiranya*), which itself is 'mineral light' and corresponds among the metals to the sun among the planets; and we know that in the symbolism of all traditions the sun is also a figure of the 'Heart of the World'.

11. This remark can help to define the relationships between the 'spirit' (*ar-rūḥ*) and the 'soul' (*an-nafs*), the last being the 'vital principle' of each particular being.

12. Cf. *The Reign of Quantity and the Signs of the Times*, chap. 20.

13. The state in question is what Islamic esoterism calls a *ḥāl*, whereas the state corresponding to the identification with this center is properly a *maqām*.

14. In keeping with the general symbolism of the Waters, the 'Ocean' (in Sanskrit, *samudra*) represents the totality of possibilities contained within a certain state of existence. Within this totality each wave thus corresponds to the determination of a particular possibility.

beyond all differentiation, which arises only at a later stage in the development of manifestation. We speak analogously here, which goes without saying, for it is evident that in the subtle state there can be no question of sound or light in the ordinary sense, that is to say as sensible qualities, but only of those realities from which these respectively proceed; and on the other hand, vibration or undulation in their literal meanings necessarily imply the conditions of space and time proper to the domain of corporeal existence; but the analogy is nonetheless exact, and here it is the only possible mode of expression. The state in question is therefore directly related to the very principle of Life in the most universal sense in which this can be understood;[15] and an image of this is found in the primary manifestations of organic life itself, those that are strictly indispensable to its preservation, such as the pulsation of the heart and the alternate movements of respiration. And this is the true foundation of those multiple applications of the 'science of rhythm' the role of which is extremely important in most methods of initiatic realization. This science naturally includes the *mantra-vidyā*, which corresponds to its 'sonic' aspect;[16] on the other hand, since the 'luminous' aspect appears more particularly in the *nāḍīs* of the 'subtle form' (*sūkshma-sharīra*),[17] one can see without difficulty the relation of all this to the double nature, luminous (*jyotirmayī*) and sonorous (*shabdamayī* or *mantramayī*), that the Hindu tradition attributes to *Kundalinī*, the cosmic force that, insofar as it resides within the human being in particular, acts there as 'vital force'.[18]

---

15. In the Islamic tradition this refers especially to the aspect or attribute expressed by the divine name *al-Ḥayy*, ordinarily translated by 'the Living', but which can be rendered much more exactly as 'the Vivifying'.

16. It goes without saying that this does not apply exclusively to the *mantras* of the Hindu tradition but equally to what corresponds to them elsewhere, for example to the *dhikr* in the Islamic tradition. In a very general way it is a question of sonorous symbols that are ritually used as sensible 'supports' of 'incantation' taken in the sense we explained earlier.

17. See *Man and His Becoming according to the Vedānta*, chaps. 14 and 21.

18. Since *Kundalinī* is symbolically represented by a serpent coiled about itself in the form of a ring (*kundala*), one might recall here the relationship in traditional symbolism between the serpent and the 'World Egg' to which we just alluded in

Thus we always find the three terms, *Verbum, Lux,* and *Vita,* inseparable even at the origin of the human state; and on this point as on so many others, we can recognize the perfect accord of the different traditional doctrines, which in reality are only different expressions of the one Truth.

---

connection with *Hiranyagarbha*. Thus, among the ancient Egyptians, *Kneph* in the form of a serpent produces the 'World Egg' from his mouth (which implies an allusion to the essential role of the Word as producer of manifestation); and we will also mention the equivalent symbol of the 'serpent egg' of the Druids which was represented by the fossil sea urchin.

48

THE BIRTH
OF THE *AVATĀRA*

THE connection we have indicated between the symbolism of the heart and that of the 'World Egg' leads us, with regard to the 'second birth', to note another aspect than that which we considered earlier. This aspect is that of the birth of a spiritual principle at the center of the human individuality, which, as is well known, is represented precisely by the heart. Indeed, this principle always resides at the center of every being,[1] but in the case of the ordinary man it exists only latently whereas, when one speaks of 'birth', one means strictly the beginning of an effective development; and it is precisely this starting-point that is determined, or at least made possible, by initiation. In one sense, the spiritual influence that is transmitted by initiation is identified with the very principle in question; in another sense, and if account is taken of the pre-existence of this principle in the being, it could be said that initiation has the effect of 'quickening' (not in itself, of course, but with regard to the being in which it resides), that is to say of making 'actual' its presence which was at first only potential; and it is obvious that the symbolism of birth can apply equally in both cases.

Now it must be understood that in virtue of the constitutive analogy between 'macrocosm' and 'microcosm', what is contained in the 'World Egg' (and it is hardly necessary to underline the obvious connection of the egg with the birth of a being or the beginning of its development) is identical to what is also symbolically contained

---

1. See *Man and His Becoming according to the Vedānta*, chap. 3.

in the heart.[2] This is the spiritual 'seed' that in the macrocosmic order is, as we have already said, designated by the Hindu tradition as *Hiranyagarbha*; and this seed is the primordial *Avatāra*[3] with respect to the world at the center of which it lies. Now the birthplace of the *Avatāra*, as well as of that which corresponds to it in the 'microcosm', is precisely represented by the heart, also identified with the 'cavern', the initiatic symbolism of which would lend itself to explanations that we cannot possibly undertake here. This is very clearly indicated by texts such as this: 'Know that this *Agni*, which is the foundation of the eternal [principial] world, and by whom this may be attained, is hidden in the cave [of the heart].'[4] It might be objected that here, as in many other cases, the *Avatāra* is expressly called *Agni*, while on the other hand it is said that it is *Brahmā* who is enclosed in the 'World Egg', called for this reason *Brahmānda*, thence to be born as *Hiranyagarbha*. But apart from the fact that in reality the different names only designate different divine aspects or attributes which are always perforce connected with each other, and never separate 'entities', there is reason to recall more particularly that *Hiranyagharba* has the character of a luminous and thus igneous principle,[5] which truly identifies it with *Agni* himself.[6]

To proceed to the 'microcosmic' application, it suffices to recall the analogy between the *pinda*, the subtle embryo of the individual

2. Another symbol which, in this regard, has a similar relationship with the heart is the fruit, the center of which likewise contains the seed representing what is in question here. Kabbalistically, this seed is represented by the letter *iod*, which in the Hebrew alphabet is the principle of all the other letters.

3. It is not a question here of particular *Avatāras* who appear during different cyclic periods, but of what is in reality and from the beginning the very principle of all *Avatāras*, just as in the Islamic tradition *ar-Rūḥ al-muhammadiyah* is the principle of all prophetic manifestations, and this principle is at the very origin of creation. We will recall that the word *Avatāra* expresses the 'descent' of a principle into the domain of manifestation, and also that the word 'seed' is applied to the Messiah in many biblical texts.

4. *Katha Upanishad*, 1,14.

5. Fire (*Tējas*) contains the two complementary aspects of light and heat.

6. This reason is in addition to the central position of *Hiranygharba*, assimilating it symbolically to the sun.

being, and *Brahmānda* or the 'World Egg'.[7] This *pinda*, as permanent and indestructible 'seed' of the being, is moreover identified
with the 'kernel of immortality' which is called *luz* in the Hebrew
tradition.[8] It is true that in general the *luz* is not considered to be
situated in the heart, or at least this is only one of the different
'localizations' of which it is capable in its correlation with the corporeal organism, and that this is not the most usual; but the *luz* is
nonetheless to be found there as well, where it is in immediate relation with the 'second birth', just as it is found in all the other loca-
tions. Indeed, these 'localizations', which correspond to the Hindu
doctrine of the *chakras* or subtle centers of the human individual,
relate to as many of its conditions or to as many phases of its spiritual development, which are the very phases of effective initiation.
At the base of the spinal column is the state of 'sleep' where the *luz*
of the ordinary man is found; in the heart is the initial phase of 'germination', which is precisely the 'second birth'; at the frontal eye is
the perfection of the human state, that is to say the reintegration
into the 'primordial state'; and finally, at the crown of the head is
the passage to supra-individual states, which must lead finally to the
'Supreme Identity'.

We cannot dwell further on this without entering into considerations which, because they relate to the detailed examination of certain particular symbols, would be better left to other studies, for
here we have wished to restrict ourselves to a more general point of
view, and we have considered such symbols to the extent it was necessary only as examples or 'illustrations'. To end, it will therefore
suffice to note briefly that, insofar as it is a 'second birth', initiation
is fundamentally nothing other than the 'actualization' in the
human being of the very principle which, in universal manifestation, appears as the 'eternal *Avatāra*'.

---

7. *Yathā pinda tathā Brahmānda* (see *Man and His Becoming according to the Vedānta*, chaps. 5 and 13.)

8. See *The King of the World*, chap. 7. The assimilation of the 'second birth' with a 'germination' of the *luz* clearly recalls the Taoist description of the initiatic process as the 'endogeny of the immortal'.

INDEX

Lightning Source UK Ltd.
Milton Keynes UK
28 June 2010

156225UK00003B/67/A

9 780900 588327